The New Fr D1334884 e

The New Frontier of Religion and Science

Religious Experience, Neuroscience and the Transcendent

John Hick

First published 2006
Reissued with new Preface and Foreword 2010 by
PALGRAVE MACMILLAN

Palgrave Macmillan in the UK is an imprint of Macmillan Publishers Limited, registered in England, company number 785998, of Houndmills, Basingstoke, Hampshire RG21 6XS.

Palgrave Macmillan in the US is a division of St Martin's Press LLC, 175 Fifth Avenue, New York, NY 10010.

Palgrave Macmillan is the global academic imprint of the above companies and has companies and representatives throughout the world.

Palgrave® and Macmillan® are registered trademarks in the United States, the United Kingdom, Europe and other countries.

ISBN-13: 978-0-230-25280-6 paperback

This book is printed on paper suitable for recycling and made from fully managed and sustained forest sources. Logging, pulping and manufacturing processes are expected to conform to the environmental regulations of the country of origin.

A catalogue record for this book is available from the British Library.

Library of Congress Cataloging-in-Publication Data
Hick, John.
   The new frontier of religion and science : religious experience, neuroscience, and the transcendent / John Hick.
      p. cm.
   Includes bibliographical references (p.) and index.
   ISBN-13: 978-0-230-25280-6 (pbk)
   1. Psychology, Religious. 2. Religion and science. 3. Religion.
   4. Religions. 5. Experience (Religion) 6. Neurosciences.
   7. Transcendence (Philosophy) I. Title.
   BL53.H53 2007
   201'.65—dc22   2006051363

10   9   8   7   6   5   4   3   2   1
19 18 17 16 15 14 13 12 11 10

Printed and bound in Great Britain by
CPI Antony Rowe, Chippenham and Eastbourne

For my grandchildren
Jonathan, Emily, Rhiannon,
Alexander, Ellie, and Phoebe

Contents

Part II

Part III

Preface

The science/religion debate is active on several fronts. There is the strident argument, particularly in the USA, of Creationism or Intelligent Design versus Evolution – a debate which should have finished over a century ago! A more substantial current issue is whether the big bang of some thirteen billion years ago itself required a creator, and if so whether this must be the God of religion or might be an impersonal creative force. This connects with the claim that the universe's initial 'fine-tuned' state was so improbable as to require purposeful divine action to have brought about the stars, planets and life as we know it. This is countered by the multiverse theory, advocated today by a number of scientists, which reduces that improbability to near zero by seeing our universe as one of perhaps billions of universes, among which it is not at all improbable that there should be one, or indeed a number, that happen to have produced intelligent life. But the entire creation debate, although widely pursued, now seems to be repeating itself without any substantial progress.

Behind these issues, religion's fundamental debate is with materialism, or physicalism, which is incompatible with the existence of any ultimate transcendent reality such as the religions point to in their different ways. And today the frontier of this debate is in the human brain. The inescapable new question is whether the advance of the neurosciences have shown mind to be at most a mysterious temporary by-product of the functioning of the brain. If so, religious experience is not, in any of its forms, an authentic awareness of a reality transcending the material universe – for according to materialism there can be no such reality – but merely a reflection of physical events in the brain within the seamless causal continuity of the natural world.

The issue is vital because, as I shall try to show, the living heart of religion is to be found in religious experience, rather than in the religious institutions, with their creeds and hierarchical priesthoods. The latter are an inevitable development, but they have brought with them significant dangers as well as benefits. Religious experience also has its dangers, and criteria of authenticity are essential. But, given all this, the challenge of the modern neurosciences is to religious experience.

In discussing this, any unavoidable technical terms are explained, and the book throughout is intended to be fully accessible to the interested general reader. (When words in ancient languages are used in brackets after their English equivalent, I have omitted the diacritical marks – thus *nirvāṇa* is printed as *nirvana*).

I am grateful to numerous specialists in the neurosciences who have responded to requests for help. But above all I want to thank Dr Timothy Musgrove in Silicon Valley, California, whose philosophical training combined with expertise in the field of cognitive science have saved me from a number of errors. He has also provided new information and pointed out new arguments that have greatly strengthened several of the neuroscience chapters. I am much indebted to him.

John Hick

Preface to the 2010 Reissue

All three aspects of the subjects discussed in this book – religious experience, neuroscience, and religious pluralism – continue today to be debated, as they have been for many years.

The empirical study of religious experience has now been expanded from Europe and North America to the Far East, with a programme of ground-level research in China. And those doing this research would like in the future to extend it much further, into Russia, South America, Turkey, and other countries. But it is also necessary to revise the earlier results of research which showed that about one third of people in Britain and the United States report some form of 'peak' experience. For these results came mainly from responses to newspaper advertisements. But we have to remember that not everyone reads a newspaper, and of those who do, not everyone looks at the advertisements, and again of those who do, not everyone who has had a remarkable spiritual experience wants to talk about it. So probably a much larger proportion than a third of people do in fact sometimes experience exceptional and uplifting states of mind. All the questions that this raises remain, but they become more pressing and of wider significance.

In particular, the question whether it is rational to trust such experiences becomes more urgent. Should we dismiss them as aberrations of no significance, like momentarily mistaking a leaf on the tree for a bird sitting there, or should we accept them as what they seem to be, occasional fortunate glimpses of a reality beyond the physical? This is the question discussed in Chapters 11 and 12. I still maintain that the principle by which we live all the time is to accept what appears to be so, as being indeed so, unless we have some positive reason to doubt it. This is the principle of critical trust which is implicit in all our dealings with our environment. I hold that this principle implies impartially to all our experiences, not only sensory but equally religious. They both face the same test: do we have some positive reason to distrust them?

The discussion now focuses on the differences between sensory and religious experience. These are principally that sense experience is compulsory, religious experience not; sense experience is universal, religious experience not; and sense experience is uniform around the world, religious experience not. It is these that I examine at length in Chapter 11, concluding that these differences are appropriately related to differences in the objects of the experience. In the end, the only reason we have for distrusting religious experience, when winnowed by our wider experience, is the naturalistic assumption of our culture. And this is only an assumption, peculiar to our modern industrialised societies.

Part of this discussion, the non-uniformity of religious experience within different cultures and religions, raises the whole disputed question of the relation between the religions, with their different and often incompatible sets of beliefs. Here I suggest the pluralistic hypothesis that I have developed and defended at length in *An Interpretation of Religion* (1989, 2nd edn 2004) and elsewhere. This starts from the observable fact that although the belief-systems of the religions are often very different, and indeed mutually contradictory, the moral and spiritual quality of the lives within them is, so far as we can tell, more or less equal. How can we account for this? Not by the traditional belief of each religion – affirmed more strongly in some than in others, and more strongly in some periods than in others – that it alone is the one true faith, uniquely superior to all the others. This does not account for the facts on the ground. We have instead, I suggest, to postulate an ultimate transcendent Reality, whose nature is beyond understanding in human terms (transcategorial), and which is being humanly apprehended and responded to within different cultural contexts as the various world religions. This suggestion, in so far as it is accepted, requires development within each tradition in gradually filtering out those doctrines that entail its claim to unique superiority. But it has the advantage of being true to the observable facts of human life.

The other main challenge to the cognitive character of religious experience comes from modern neuroscience. Most neuroscientists (like most other scientists) share the naturalistic assumption of our culture. They are therefore materialists, believing that nothing exists but matter – including of course the matter constituting human brains. Materialism is implicit in our Western, and beyond, cultural assumption, and is explicit among scientists. It follows from this that there is not, because there cannot be, any supranatural environment enclosing and interpenetrating our natural environment, with religious experience as a rare glimpse of it. Such experiences must therefore be explained in purely material terms, as some kind of neural malfunction. In Part II of this book the arguments for and against these explanations are examined in some detail, but are too complex to be adequately summarised here.

I hope I have shown that the neurological case against religious experience is not proven. What is proved is that for everything going on in consciousness something is correspondingly going on in the brain. There is a complete consciousness–brain correlation. But I point out that correlation is not identity. Indeed, the identity thesis faces formidable problems. We may be conscious of a complex scene around us, involving colours, sounds and smells, and bodily pressure or discomfort or pain. But no part of the brain has any of these qualities. The corresponding electro-chemical brain states *may* cause the conscious state; they may be indispensable to it; but are they actually identical with it? Surely not. Indeed the leading neuroscientists today admit that the nature of consciousness remains a sheer mystery. I have quoted V.S. Ramachandran of the Center for Brain and Cognition at the University of California at San Diago (himself a materialist) as saying, 'despite two hundred years of research, the most basic questions about the human mind ... remain unanswered, as does the really big question: What is consciousness?' (*Phantoms in the Brain*, 1998, p. 14). The C word is the great elephant in the materialist's room!

So all the issues discussed in this book remain current and alive. I hope that this reissue may help to stimulate thinking and continued discussion.

January 2010   John Hick

Foreword

It is a great honour to be asked to write the foreword for this new issue of *The New Frontier*. John Hick is undoubtedly the most important of the philosophers of religion of the last 30 years. His work is always scholarly, yet always accessible, and this is particularly the case in this book which engages with a range of complex theory drawn from neuroscience. His engagement is, as ever, subtle and complex, drawing upon his knowledge of the many different world religious traditions and faiths, the practices of philosophy and the theories of neuroscientists.

Hick's approach to the philosophical discussion of religion has always emphasised the role that religion can play in constructing a meaningful human life, and there is a humane quality to his writing that makes engaging with the ideas that he presents more than simply an academic exercise. He encourages his reader to contemplate the depths of human experience, and as such his work is defined by a genuine commitment to the lived-experience of belief, not just with how religious beliefs and practices might best be presented to a philosophically minded audience. This makes his work of importance for all who seek to understand what it is to be a human being. Most importantly, his answer to this question involves the development of a contemporary spirituality that speaks not just to academics, but to a much wider readership, hungry for religious nourishment.

When this book appeared in 2006 it was significant for emphasising an important dimension in the science and religion debate. The debate is no longer simply about the tensions between these two areas as they seek to represent and understand the external world. Contrary to some popular critics of religion, the current shape of this debate is not primarily the dispute between evolutionists and creationists. Many theological positions, including Process thought, have long argued that belief in God is not necessarily a bar to accepting the scientific worldview expressed in evolutionary biology. The debate has now taken a rather different turn that in many ways relates to the concern with the subjective that dominates much public discourse in Western societies. If social policy has moved from an emphasis on how to create the external conditions for economic equality to a concern with how to ensure the emotional well-being of its citizens, a similar turn to the inner realm of the individual can be discerned in the science and religion debate. Now an important aspect of the discussion revolves around the attempt to understand the nature of human consciousness: can consciousness be reduced to the processes of the brain, or is there room for what philosophers have traditionally called 'the mind', something that transcends the physical brain and which cannot be reduced to it?

Some philosophers – myself included – might be tempted to shift the debate in a different direction, arguing that religion and science are speaking different languages and that religion cannot be understood apart from recognising its kinship with art and poetry. Religion is, like art and other forms of creativity, part of the human attempt to make meaning, to construct narratives about our lives that speak to our hearts and that enable us to locate ourselves in a world which often seems at odds with our hopes and desires. If science seeks to describe the world, religion seeks ways of understanding our place in it. For the religious, this involves thinking seriously about the way in which we orientate ourselves in the world, and, particularly, how our fallible human relationships might be transformed.

This kind of approach, which focuses on the emotional, non-cognitive, aspects of religion, is not without its problems, and, as always, reading Hick's work confronts me with the failings and pitfalls of such ideas. A method which seeks to distance religion from science can fail to acknowledge the impact of the 'scientism' that denotes the attitude of some contemporary scientists. In scientism, the sphere of science is extended so that it becomes a method for explaining absolutely everything: often to the detriment of a deeper understanding of the mystery and beauty of human life and experience. Hick addresses the problems of such an overreaching methodology head-on. His careful analysis of the findings of neuroscience leads him to challenge the attempt to make any straightforward identification between the brain and the mind. Something is lost if this identification is accepted unthinkingly. But what could have become a rather dry defence of the difference between human consciousness and the physical brain becomes, in Hick's hands, something altogether more significant. His concern is with the effect that reducing the mind to the brain has for the interpretation of religious experience. If religious experience can be reduced to (apparently delusional) processes in the brain, it cannot be understood as something cognitive, as an experience that tells us something about the nature of the universe and the reality of the divine. Hick's defence of religious experience as an authentic phenomenon reveals the limitations and unproven assumptions of much neuro-science, but it does more than that as Hick uses this discussion to open up important questions about what a meaningful contemporary spirituality might look like.

In developing the form a contemporary spirituality might take, Hick challenges both scientific and religious fundamentalisms. If he exposes the failings of scientism, this does not mean that he will countenance the oppressive forms that religion can take. He is particularly damning of Christian literalism which he dismisses as 'theologically crude'. There can be no return to an exclusivist model of religion. Instead, he considers the benefit of thinking about religion not in its institutional forms but as the inner spiritual response to what he calls 'the Transcendent'. Emphasising this aspect of religion is to be welcomed, for it leads us away from debates about the failings of religious institutions and their power structures to something altogether more humane and personal. Hick's concern is not with establishing the differences between the world's religious traditions, with a view to determining which offers 'the best path' to the Transcendent, but with considering where their similarities might lie and how these might best be built upon. Emphasising the spiritual realm enables creative connections to be found and used in developing a pluralistic vision of the religions.

Hick's approach relies upon seeing each of the religions as concerned with providing responses to the stresses of finitude, including suffering and death. Each, he argues, offers the real possibility of 'a limitlessly better existence'. Each, in this sense, is concerned with providing a path to salvation. Identifying a common concern does not mean, however, that he ignores difference or indeed that he does not address the complexity of any one faith tradition. Different spiritual approaches are to be found between adherents of any one religion. Identifying the different paths possible within world faiths means that the religions are not treated as amorphous masses whose key practices and claims could be reduced to 'all Christians think this' or 'all Muslims think that'. Instead, Hick seeks to identify the benefits of accepting a pluralistic perspective where a range of different insights into the divine can be explored and used in the construction of a contemporary spirituality. The insights of the mystics from a range of traditions become partic-ularly important for this endeavour, for they challenge the dogma of established religion and provide frameworks for the kind of spiritual thought and practice that Hick wishes to advocate.

In developing this contemporary spirituality a number of themes stand out. Principally, Hick does not reduce religion to a form of moral practice. He may consider the way modern sainthood involves political commitment and liberating action, but this is not sufficient to make a complete identification between religion and morality. Why? Because, he argues, religion is concerned with exploring 'a further dimension of meaning'. The importance of the religious perspective cannot be reduced to the structures of the moral life. The religious perspective adds something that cannot be reduced to morality. This claim suggests something important about the way a religious perspective provides a framework for thinking about the nature of the world. What does it mean to be alive in a world like this? What kind of stories might enable us to make sense of this world and our place in it? There is a richness in the religious perspective, when it is articulated through the spiritual dimension, that allows for the deepening of our experiences and our relationships with others.

To think in these terms is to emphasise the practical aspect of the position that Hick is expounding. Rather than leave his reader to decide how the ideas of this book might structure a contemporary spirituality he suggests specific areas for our attention. This includes 'cosmic optimism'; the sense that it is possible to find a way of living in this world that, while taking seriously the reality of suffering, acknowledges the possibility of finding 'a new orientation centred on the Transcendent'. The universe is such that the good life is possible. Prayer and meditation have a particular role to play in cultivating the mindset which will support this orientation, and practices from a range of religious traditions and perspectives are offered to support this development. What is particularly appealing here is that Hick is prepared to offer his own spiritual practice and his reflections upon it in order that the reader might have an insight into what such practice involves. The spiritual dimension that emerges is grounded in the cultivation of mindfulness, where the self is located in the world and is open to that world.

This profound book confronts views of human being which would reduce it to rather mechanistic and superficial processes. Religion, understood through the spiritual dimension, becomes something which can support an altogether richer understanding of the meaningful human life. This book will stand many readings, for it challenges its readers to think seriously about the role that religion might play in the future. Hick's vision is of a religion that does not constrain human possibility but which deepens our engagement with life in this world. He reminds us of how precious a thing it is to be able to reflect, as conscious beings, upon our lives, our relationships, and our place in the cosmos. For an age which can at times seem only interested in the trivial and the superficial, this is an important corrective that challenges lazy thinking, but also, more importantly, provides inspiration for those committed to a spiritual path suited to the contemporary world.

Professor in the Philosophy of Religion   Beverley Clack
Oxford Brookes University

Part I

1
Religion as Human Institutions

Rather than begin with any of the scores of definitions of religion offered over the years from different standpoints – sociological, anthropological, psychological, philosophical, theological – it will be more useful to begin with two important distinctions. One is historical, between pre- and post-axial religion, and the other, within the latter, between on the one hand the human religious institutions and, on the other, their living heart, for which we have no satisfactory name but which I shall call both spirituality and mysticism. Each term is appropriate when understood in a certain way, and each can also be misleading. I will clarify in the next chapter the way I want to use them.

Pre-axial religion

The axial age or era was first identified by Karl Jaspers (Jaspers 1953), who dated it from roughly 800 to roughly 200 BCE.[1] For millennia before that the implicit overarching human world-view had remained essentially unchanged, though with a gradual movement through what is today called primal or archaic religion to larger state religions expressing the same basic outlook.

Nineteenth- and early twentieth-century anthropologists, such as Edward Tyler, Robertson Smith, Andrew Lang, James Frazer, R. R. Marett and others, were able to observe primal societies in Africa, Australia, Central and South America and elsewhere before contact with the outside world had significantly affected them. The anthropologists found – and the same is true of early state religions such as that of the Aztecs – that primal religion was basically concerned to keep the existing order of things, the life of the tribe or state and it's environment, steady and in balance. Humanity and the rest of the living world were seen as

3

a single whole, and for most purposes primal people seem to have been aware of themselves, less as autonomous individuals, and more as parts of the living social organism.

Humans have always had a sense of the numinous, the mysterious, and a tendency to experience the natural in terms of the supra-natural. This natural religiousness is indicated by the earliest known methods of burial, which suggest a belief in some kind of afterlife, and was also expressed in a sacralising of the environment, with mountains, trees, rivers, rocks, clearings, the sky inhabited by spirits, ancestors, gods who had to be served as local patrons or placated as dangerously unpredict-able powers. Life was precarious, and the function of the tribal, and later national, rituals and sacrifices was to ensure that the seasons came round again, the harvest was abundant, the rains came when expected, the warriors were strong and the women fertile. Life was accepted as it is without any comparison with the idea of a radically better possibility. It was, in Stanner's phrase, 'a one-possibility thing' (Stanner 1979, 515).

Primal religion continues today as the underlying but living substrate on which, particularly in Africa, the world faiths of Christianity and Islam have later been superimposed. It preserves values that had been largely lost within the major traditions in their modern forms, but are still potentially present within them and are now beginning to be recovered in an increasingly serious awareness of our interrelationship with the rest of the world of which we are a part. This ecological concern has been demanded by the impact of global warming, the alarming depletion of the earth's non-renewable energy sources, the destruction of rain forests and the continuing elimination by humanity of other animal species. We are tragically engaged in cutting off the branch on which we are sitting. In this situation the gift of primal religion to the modern world is a reminder of our unity with the whole of nature and our continuity and kinship with all life.

The axial age

In a band of time centred around the mid-first millennium BCE – from roughly 900 or 800 to roughly 200 – in much of the world, from China to Greece, there was an extraordinary outburst of new spiritual insights embodied in great religious figures.[2] India produced the basic Hindu texts, the Upanishads, and, towards the end of this period, the *Bhagavad Gita*, perhaps the most widely influential of Hindu scriptures today, and Gautama, the founder of Buddhism, and Mahavira, the founder of Jainism; in China, Confucius and the *Tao Te Ching* (traditionally attributed to the shadowy figure of Lao-Tzu), the basis of Taoism, and Mencius and Mo-Tzu; in Palestine many of the great Hebrew prophets, I and II Isaiah, Jeremiah, Amos and Hosea; and in Greece Pythagoras, Socrates, Plato and Aristotle.

However, the history is more complex than a narrow focus on the axial age would suggest. The Vedas are of earlier but of undated origin. Around 1375 BCE the Egyptian pharaoh Amunhotep IV imposed a form of monotheism in the exclusive worship of Aton, with himself as the son of Aton and taking the name Akhenaton. This did not, however, survive beyond his own life. Zoroaster, once placed within the axial period, is now thought to have lived much earlier, around 1000–1200 BCE. Behind the Moses saga there was probably an historical figure living around the thirteenth century BCE. Abraham, supposedly living sometime earlier in the second millennium BCE, is, however, much less securely historical – quite possibly a number of traditional stories from various periods became fused together under one name. But whether or not naming an historical individual, the figure of Abraham is often used to bring Judaism, Christianity and Islam together under a common ancestry as 'children of Abraham' (e.g. Kuschel 1995). This is a positive use; but it also has the negative side-effect of categorising the Abrahamic faiths over against the eastern forms of religion. There are in fact considerable overlaps there with the mystical strands of the monotheisms.

Some writers have wanted to extend the axial period forward to include Jesus and the rise of Christianity, and some to go yet further to include Muhammad and the rise of Islam. But this is a mistake. Within the last thirty or so years the profound Jewishness of Jesus has been rediscovered and made central to our understanding of him (e.g. Vermes 1973 and 1993; Sanders 1985; Charlesworth, ed., 1991). He was a radical reformer within the Judaism of his day, attending the synagogue, frequently referring back to the Torah, sharing the apocalyptic hope of many of his contemporaries and possibly – though not certainly – seeing himself as the expected messiah of the Jews. His teaching about a loving God and about how to live in relation to God was not new. But his influence has, of course, been truly immense, both because of the extraordinary power of his personality, the fame of his healings and the impact of his moral teaching and, after his death, through the Pauline understanding of him which successfully carried the transformation of the Jesus of history into the Christ of faith into the wider world, his presentation as the unique divine saviour of the world. Islam also stands firmly within the Abrahamic tradition, the Qur'an having its own versions of the stories of many biblical figures, including Adam, Abraham, Aaron, Enoch, Isaac, Jacob, David and Goliath, Ezra, Ishmael, Elisha, Job, Jonah, Noah, Lot, Sheba, etc., with Jesus being revered as one of the greatest of the prophets: 'Jesus, son of Mary, illustrious in this world and the next' (Qur'an 3:45). Muslims are taught to say, 'We believe in God and what has been sent down to us, and what has been revealed to Abraham and Ishmael and Isaac and Jacob and their progeny, and that which was given to Moses and Christ, and to all other prophets by the Lord. We make no distinction among them, and we submit to Him' (Ibid. 2:136). Islam sees itself as a new and final chapter in this long religious story. The more recently founded Sikh faith draws heavily on both Hindu and Muslim sources, and the Baha'i faith on Islam, thus all having their roots, though at one or two removes, within the axial age.

The new axial insights

It was the transforming idea of a radically better possibility that emerged during the axial centuries. The great figures who launched the new movements that have developed into the world religions experienced an overpowering awareness of reality transcending the human and the material which brought with it the real possibility of a radical transformation of human life. These individuals did not of course spring up without the already existing context of a society ready for their message. The growth of cities, division of labour, the development of writing within cultures that provided opportunity for speculation and debate, all constituted environments in which new spiritually challenging and revolutionary claims could be heard. China, India, the Middle and Near East and Greece, the scenes of these paradigmatic moments of religious creativity, were alive with a turmoil of often conflicting ideas.

During this axial period, extending as it did over a span of centuries, the sense of being a unique responsible individual gradually spread from an elite, the kings and priests, to the many. Individual conscience and individual religious insight were often expressed in critical or prophetic stances over against the existing traditions and authorities. The idea of the dead persisting as hollow shades in a dim underworld was gradually superseded by the belief in an individual moral judgement beyond death, with the contrasting fates of heaven and hell. And this moral judgement applied to all alike, kings as much as commoners, serfs and slaves. Religious experience, which is to be our main concern, began to be more than the inner reflection of communal ritual orchestrated by priests and shamans. The new spiritual insights, released from the confines of a tribal or national religion and made available to the individual, were now potentially universal in significance, thus making possible the great world faiths. But arising as they did within the existing religions their initial impact was inevitably as movements of reform within those religions.

This reform sometimes had far-reaching social implications. The Buddha rejected the caste structure of India, seeing all humans as equally capable of attaining enlightenment, and likewise rejected the priestly system of sacrifices; and the Buddhist emperor Ashoka (third century BCE) affirmed the equality of the different religions of his empire. Among the great Hebrew prophets First Isaiah (eighth century BCE) repeatedly criticised the Jewish establishment, preaching that the prevailing social injustices were an affront to God; while Amos (eighth century) and Jeremiah (seventh century) proclaimed the unpopular message that Israel and Judah's subjection to the Assyrian empire was a divine punishment, calling for national repentance. Jesus preached the imminent coming of God's kingdom on earth, with the end of Roman rule and of the power of the priestly elite in Jerusalem, thus becoming a dangerous influence who incurred the Roman death penalty. Muhammad attacked the prevailing polytheism of the Arabia of his time, thereby undermining the lucrative pilgrimage trade to the many gods of Mecca and thereby drawing upon himself the dangerous enmity of the ruling commercial elite, so that he had to flee with his first followers to Medina.

Religion as institution and religion as spirituality/mysticism

Remaining now in the post-axial period, the religions have both an outer and an inner aspect. The distinction was introduced into the modern discussion by Wilfred Cantwell Smith, the Canadian historian of religion who founded the Center for the Study of World Religions at Harvard.[3] The terms he used were 'the cumulative traditions' and 'faith', the former being what I have called institutional religion and the latter the inner aspect which is so hard to name. Roger Haight, SJ, likewise describes faith as 'a universal form of religious experience ... that entails an awareness of and loyalty to an ultimate or transcendent reality ... Faith in its primary sense is an intentional human response, reaction, act, or pervasive and operative attitude' (Haight 1999, 4). However, the word 'faith' seems to me, regrettably, to be too strongly associated in too many peoples' minds with holding beliefs not on evidence but 'by faith' (as in 'we believe that the world is round because of the evidence, but we believe by faith that God exists'); and so instead of 'faith' I shall use 'spirituality' and 'mysticism', though well aware that they too can carry unhelpful associations with them. But we have to make do with what we have.

The outer aspect of religion consists of contraposed socio-religious entities cumulatively developed by a multitude of cultural, economic, geographical, climatic, historical and political influences taking them far beyond their originating impulse. Pre-axial religion was already to some degree organised, but only locally. Referring to the world faiths that we know today, Cantwell Smith has shown that this conception of religions as organized institutions with their own fixed boundaries, related as potential or actual rivals, is a distinctively western and comparatively modern way of thinking.[4] What he calls the cumulative traditions – institutionalised forms of religion – include not only scriptures, hierarchic priesthoods, liturgies, moral codes, political affiliations, but also creeds and theological systems, all of which inevitably show a range of human-all-too-human influences in their development over time. The fingerprints of our 'fallen' human nature are all over them. As a result they reflect not only the best but also the worst of human characteristics. And so we find that, as powerful players in history, they have not only contributed a great deal of good but are also responsible for a great deal of harm to humankind.

The institutional balance sheet

On the one hand the religions have been instruments of social cohesion, maintaining the unity of a tribe or a nation by providing communal rituals and shared identity-defining stories handed down from generation to generation. These stories, sagas and myths refer to specific strands of history but constitute for each community an all-encompassing 'grand narrative' which binds society and generations together, providing frameworks of meaning for the lives of hundreds of millions of people. The religions have also challenged their members with moral ideals, and have supported and comforted them in the sufferings and amid the anxieties and vicissitudes of life's recurrent personal and social crises. Further, the religions have constituted the foundation of civilisations and been instrumental in the development of language, education and science. They have been responsible for the creation of hospitals and universities, and have inspired literature, music, painting, sculpture, architecture. So there is a great deal on the positive side of the balance sheet.

But on the other side they have not only been instruments of social cohesion but also of social control by a dominant class. As a very minor but typical expression of this, in England in 1381 there was a Peasant's Revolt led by Wat Tyler ('When Adam delved and Eve span/Who was then the gentleman?'). The revolt was put down with ruthless violence and bloodshed, and the official chronicle of the time records that 'God sent remedy by the hand of the most renowned man, Sir William Walworth, the then Mayor... who by the favour of divine grace mortally pierced [Tyler] in the breast'. God was on the side of the powers that be. A thousand other examples could be cited. Again and again a ruling class has in effect claimed privileged access to the deity who has ordained their own earthly power – hence 'the divine right of kings'. Again, the religions have embodied, and in varying degrees still embody, the age-old male dominance over women. And they have divided people into rival groups, validating and intensifying almost all human conflicts, as we see so tragically in many parts of the world today. God has, according to those who claim his blessing, been on both sides of every war, perhaps the most recent explicit examples coming from the American Civil War (1861–65), of which one account is aptly called Gods and Generals, for the generals on both sides repeatedly appealed to divine guidance and intervention. Further, as well as inspiring so many valuable human activities, the religious institutions have also sometimes distorted or subverted them. The origin of modern science in Christian Europe is a classic case. It has been argued that this was made possible by the Christian teaching of the unity and intelligibility of nature as a divine creation. But this is doubtful, for that is equally the teaching of the other monotheisms, and in different ways of the non-theistic faiths as well. The rise of modern science in Europe seems to have resulted from a confluence of cultural streams, the existing Christian tradition and the Renaissance rediscovery of the ancient Greek spirit of free enquiry. But from the time of Copernicus, through the controversies about the age of the earth and biological evolution in the nineteenth century, the churches' united response to the self-propelling advance of science, as soon as its discoveries conflicted with established dogma, was always to oppose and seek to suppress it. Even today there is strong fundamentalist resistance to the teaching of biological evolution in some states of the USA.

Again, while the religions have produced and nourished a succession of great philosophers and theologians, the monotheisms have also restricted the search for truth and new understanding by threatening and punishing thinkers who failed to conform to accepted ideas.

Thus within Islam al-Hallaj was executed for his mystical teaching; and today reforming thought, though increasingly widespread, is still widely discouraged. Within Judaism Spinoza was excommunicated by the Jewish community of Amsterdam; and today Jewish Orthodoxy still often denies the validity of other branches of Judaism. Within Christianity heretical movements such as the Cathars were suppressed by the Church with pitiless violence; the internal struggles between Catholic and Reformed Christians were played out in Europe in the prolonged wars of religion, causing tens of thousands of violent deaths and the widespread destruction of towns and cities; thousands of innocent women were burned as witches; and even within the same sub-tradition Servetus was burned at the stake in Calvin's Geneva for arguing that the doctrine of the Trinity is not scripturally based. And in the twentieth century, with its escalating technology – the most violent century ever – the appallingly destructive wars have all been, with the exception of Japan, between the traditionally and still basically Christian peoples of Germany, Poland, France, Britain, Russia and the United States.

The 'Eastern' faiths of Hinduism, Buddhism, Taoism, Confucianism have generally been more peaceful and tolerant, but by no means entirely so. Gregor Paul has traced the themes of peace and war in classical Chinese thought, for in China there have been plenty of intra-Chinese wars, but 'in China, religious beliefs or religious zeal were never, or almost never, decisive, when it came to the question of war and peace. In more than 3,000 years of Chinese history, there have been no religious wars comparable to those that have occurred in Jewish, Muslim, Christian and Hindu history. In particular, there were no aggressive, or missionary, religious wars' (Paul 2004, 75). In the case of Buddhism, whose basic outlook and teaching explicitly excludes violence and hatred, the twentieth century has seen striking lapses from this. For example, the Zen form of Buddhism was used by some to justify Japanese aggression on the Asian mainland. 'Certain Zen figures supported growing Japanese militarism in the 1920s and 1930s by directing Zen practice as a preparation for combat, and a large meditation hall was erected in Tokyo for this purposes' (Ives 1992, 64), though other Zen figures, such as Ichikawa Hakugen, strongly criticised this (ibid., ch. 4). In the long-running violent conflict between Buddhist Sinhalese and Hindu Tamils in Sri Lanka some Theravada monks have provided the Sinhalese government with a religious sanction (Schmidt-Leukel 2004). In modern Burma and Thailand also Buddhism has been involved in sanctioning war (Ling 1979). Within 'Hinduism' (a collective name for the many different streams of Indian religion) war is a familiar topic. The *Mahabharata*, of which the *Bhagavad Gita* is a part, chronicles dynastic wars involving the gods, both male and female, as protagonists. The twentieth century saw relentlessly bitter and bloody conflict between Hindus and Muslims on the border between the Indian Punjab and Pakistan at the partition of India in 1947, and recurrent outbreaks of Hindu–Muslim communal violence have marred the subcontinent since, with a particularly damaging peak in the destruction by a resurgent Hindu nationalism of the Ayodha mosque in 1992. And yet at the same time the influence of the greatest peacemaker and practitioner of the power of non-violence, Mahatma Gandhi, has exerted a still continuing influence far beyond India. Martin Luther King, Cesar Chavez, Lech Walensa, U Thant and very many less-well-known figures are among those who have acknowledged Gandhi's powerful influence in their lives, and other major figures, such as Nelson Mandela and Desmond Tutu in South Africa and Thich Nhat Hanh in Vietnam, have lived out the same positive and healing insight into human nature.

However, if we try to arrive at a 'bottom line' in this complex profit-and- loss account, we find that the goods and evils flowing from religion are of such different kinds as generally to be incommensurable, so that it is not really possible to reach any straightforward verdict. We can only paint the mixed black-and-white picture which history displays. The world religions all teach love and compassion, each has it's own formulation of the Golden Rule, each includes great examples of self-giving love for others, and yet each has been used to validate and justify large-scale violence and merciless atrocities.

But 'large-scale violence and merciless atrocities' have not always been connected with religion – one thinks of Stalin's deliberate elimination of millions of Russian peasants and of his Gulag Archipelago for dissidents, Hitler's attempt systematically to murder the Jewish population of Europe, Pol Pot's Cambodian killing fields, Treblinka and other smaller examples.

The 'scientific' study of religion

Religion as institution is the subject-matter of the academic study of religion. The historians of religion, and the anthropologists and sociologists who study religion, necessarily focus on it's outer and visible aspects. Emile Durkheim, for example, studying Australian aboriginal societies in the late nineteenth century, concluded that its totem functioned as a symbol both for its god and for the tribe itself as a reality greater than and having authority over the individual, and concluded that god was society in the guise of the sacred totem (Durkheim 1963). His analysis of the religion of a particular primal tribal society is convincing but he, and many others after him, made the mistake of generalising it to explain religion as such: the overarching authority and power of society have been projected by the religious imagination as the idea of God. However, this theory does not explain either such non-theistic and basically individualistic faiths as Buddhism or the important element of prophetic challenge to society among both them and the monotheisms. Such oversimplifying generalisation is indeed characteristic of all the various reductionist sociological and psychological theories. They have a valid insight into some one particular aspect of religion and then uncritically assume that they have thereby discovered the essential nature of all religion. Thus Freud, believing that we need to personalise the forces of nature in order to be able to deal with them (Freud 1961, 16–17), saw God as a buried infancy memory of one's father, so that 'at bottom God is nothing other than an exalted father' (Freud 1955, 147). It is no doubt true that a good father – but not all fathers are good! – provides a child's first model of the heavenly Father. But Freud forgot, or was barely aware of, Buddhism, Taoism, Jainism, etc. It is of course a sound psychological insight that religion often functions as a comforting myth; but it would be a gratuitous mistake to generalise this into an explanation of religion as such. Much in the great world faiths is far from comforting, much is profoundly challenging, and much is by implication socially revolutionary.

Again, anthropologists and sociobiologists have explored very fruitfully the ways in which religious belief systems and their accompanying practices have been affected by geography and climate. For example, the nomadic herding communities of the ancient Near East tended to think of the divine as male, while the settled agricultural communities of ancient north-west India tended to think of the divine in female terms, as mother earth. And so the great monotheistic religions that originated in the Near East have worshipped a male God, while the Hindu traditions see the ultimate reality of Brahman as manifested equally in male and female deities.

There are also innumerable sociological studies of particular religious communities around the world, examining them as historical phenomena. It is appropriate that they should do so, and it is natural that such work should constitute the bulk of the academic study of religion in the universities. This often includes belief systems as well as patterns of behaviour. But valuable, fascinating and indeed indispensable though this is, it does not touch the inner side of religion. If we think of the Buddhist idea of likening belief systems to fingers pointing to the moon, so that to focus on the pointing finger is to miss the moon itself, we can say that the entire history and phenomenology of religions is our academic study of the finger, or many different fingers – but not of the moon, the religious reality itself. For the inner side of religion, to which we turn presently, is not open to this kind of study, although psychologists have sought to explain it, and now the neurosciences have become highly relevant, as we shall see. But among historians of religion the relatively few who have sought to take serious account of its inner as well as outer aspect include some of the greatest, such as Mircea Eliade, Wilfred Cantwell Smith and Annamarie Schimmel.

To conclude, since the axial period it has been possible to distinguish between religion as institution and communal practice, and the inner mystical or experiential dimension of religion. And it is within this mystical dimension that we must look for the kinds of religious experience in which we are to be interested here.

2
Spirituality and Mysticism

But this institutional aspect of religion, so ambiguous in its value, is only half the story. The other aspect comes under the general heading of spirituality and mysticism. The general twentieth-century concentration on the remarkable and extraordinary in this area was heavily influenced by William James's monumental *The Varieties of Religious Experience*. This continues to be an indispensable and highly accessible and fascinating book, as widely read now as when it was first published over a hundred years ago. But we do not need today to focus to the same extent on those more dramatic cases.

'Spirituality' and spirituality

Within the Anglo-American analytic philosophical tradition today it is barely acceptable to speak of spirituality but quite permissible to speak of mysticism, concerning the epistemology of which a good deal of work has been done.[1] This is focussed upon the rare and extraordinary experiences of some of the great mystics. But the range of religious experience is much wider than this, and to encompass it we shall also have to make use of 'spiritual' and 'spirituality', even though they are today used so extremely loosely. One meaning is that used by the sociologists,where

> Survey after survey shows that increasing numbers of people now prefer to call themselves 'spiritual' rather than 'religious'. Terms like spirituality, holism, New Age, mind-body-spirit, yoga, feng shui, chi and chakra have become more common in the general culture than traditional Christian vocabulary. Even a cursory glance around the local bookshop or a stroll around the shopping centre leaves little

doubt that Christianity has a new competitor in 'the spiritual market-place'. (Heelas and Woodhead 2005, 1)

This is clearly an aspect of what Charles Taylor calls 'the massive subjective turn of modern culture' (Taylor 1991, 26), and which historians trace to the influence of modern philosophy since Descartes's 'I think therefore I am', focussing on the individual self. In fact, I think, that many other social and economic factors have also affected the intellectual history of the modern world, with philosophers reflecting rather than creating the subjective turn.

I am going to refer to this New Age spirituality as 'spirituality', to distinguish it from what I mean by the inner aspect of religion, by which I mean the individual's response to the Transcendent. Although this remains to be argued for later (chs 11 and 12) I am assuming here for our present purpose that there is such a reality.

To gain an objective assessment of the prevalence of 'spirituality' today in one country, Britain, two sociologists, Paul Heelas and Linda Woodhead, with a team of assistants conducted an empirical survey of the 'spiritual' and 'religious' life of a particular community, Kendal, a flourishing town in the north-west of England.

They distinguish between what they call 'subjective-life spirituality' and 'life-as religion'. The former includes acupuncture, the Alexander technique, aromatherapy, art therapy, astrology, chiropractice, circle dancing, flower essences therapy, GreenSpirit groups, herbalism, hypnotherapy, inter-faith groups, massage, the Iona community, pagan activities including contemporary witchcraft, palm reading, play therapy, osteopathy, psychic consultancy, rebirthing, reflexology, reiki, crystal gazing, Sai Baba groups, Sea of Faith groups, spiritual healing, Tai chi/Chi kung groups, Tarot card reading, walking labyrinths, women's spirituality groups, Wild Women groups, yoga and more – a very wide spread. And by 'life-as religion' they mean organised religion based on belief in a God who is worshipped and whose will is sought to be discerned – though with wide variations of outlook and practice within the churches. Their basic distinction is thus between 'spirituality' as therapy, self-improvement, seeking happiness in a variety of ways, without any transcendent reference, and 'religion' as relation to the Transcendent (conceived as a personal God) and occurring within organised ecclesiastical bodies.

This classification has, however, its limits, because there is considerable overlap between the two categories. Some of the practices listed above – the social engagement of the Iona community, the thinking of the Sea of Faith movement, inter-faith activity and services of healing – are also present within the churches, and indeed mainly so in the case of the Iona Community; and there must be many church members who also participate in a number of the other listed 'spiritual' activities, some now often part of mainstream medical practice – such as acupuncture, use of the Alexander Technique, massage, osteopathy and chiropractice.

The Kendal project involved first identifying the places of worship of all the denominations represented in Kendal, Anglican, Catholic, Methodist, United Reformed, independent Evangelical, Mormon, Jehovah's Witnesses, Christadelphian, Salvation Army, Spiritualist, Christian Scientist, Quaker and Unitarian; and the various places where 'spiritual' groups met, concentrating particularly on Infinite Tai Chi, Rainbow Cottage and Yoga at the Kendal Leisure Centre, though recognising that 'spirituality' in their sense is found much more widely than in these venues, with small unnamed groups meeting in private houses and also many one-to-one therapy sessions. They visited and participated in the activities of selected 'spiritual' groups and churches, and then issued an extensive questionnaire. The detailed results with statistics and analysis are published in Heelas and Woodhead's *The Spiritual Revolution*.

Some of the statistics from the Kendal project are interesting. From the questionnaire addressed to those involved in the 'spiritual' groups:

In answer to the question 'Do you believe in any of the following?' the greatest number of respondents (82.4 per cent) agree with 'some sort of spirit or life force pervades all that lives', with 73 per cent expressing belief in 'subtle energy (or energy channels) in the body'. Presented with a range of options and asked to select the statement which best describes their 'core beliefs about spirituality', 40 per cent of respondents equate spirituality with 'love' or being 'a caring and decent person', 34 per cent with 'being in touch with subtle energies', 'healing oneself and others' or 'living life to the full'. Spirituality, it appears, belongs to life-itself ('subtle energy in the body' which serves to keep us alive) and subjective life ('love', 'caring'). It seems that spirit/energy/spirituality is understood to dwell within the life of participants, an interpretation that is supported by the finding that very few associate spirituality with a transcendental, over-and-above-the-self, external source of significance. Just 7 per cent of respondents agreed that spirituality is 'obeying God's will'. It appears, then, that rather than spirituality serving to dictate the course and nature of life from beyond the self, it is experienced as being integral to life: 'pervading' or flowing through life, bringing life alive. (Heelas and Woodhead 2005, 25)

So the basic distinction between what Heelas and Woodhead think of as spirituality and what they think of as religion hinges on the absence or presence of reference to a transcendent reality. But this is not as clear a criterion as it may seem. Belief in 'a transcendent reality' is equated in the above quote with 'obeying God's will'. This limits transcendence to the God of much traditional Christianity, whereas for many today 'God' often functions simply as place holder for a higher Reality of some kind.

The participation numbers in Kendal showed that on the particular Sunday in 2000 when a precise count was carried out 2209 people (adult and younger) attended the 25 churches and chapels, constituting about 7.9 per cent of the population of the town; and on a count spread out over a longer period Heelas and Woodhead reckoned that in a typical week about six hundred people took part in 126 separate New Age or holistic activities, constituting 1.6 per cent of the population.

This shows a much larger participation in what they call 'religion' than in 'spirituality'. However, their time-flow conclusion, including also wider evidence from the United States and other available sources, was that 'we have found robust evidence of a pattern: a correlation between subjective-life spirituality and growth on the one hand, and between life-as religion and decline on the other' (ibid., 9). There are other researchers who have concluded that while a genuine concern for the deeper issues of life and death and the meaning of our existence are as widespread as ever, they have largely migrated outside the churches. The BBC's 'Soul of Britain' survey in 2000 found that 76 per cent of the population were prepared to say that they had some kind of spiritual experience.[2] But according to another, 1992, survey church members were less likely, at about 53 per cent, to report spiritual experiences than the public as a whole.[3] This is bad news from an ecclesiastical point of view. But, again, much depends on what is to be counted – is the ecstatic experience of the participant in a Pentecostal church a spiritual experience? And is this 'mainstream'?

But 'spirituality' is also very commonly used even more widely than Heelas and Woodhead's understanding of it. At the time of writing I find a report of the closing of a Jaguar car factory in Coventry UK in which the factory is described as 'the spiritual home of Jaguar' – because it had been there so long and had become a symbol of the Jaguar brand. A catalogue of new books, under the heading 'Explore your spirituality' advertises one on the meaning of the stars for your life. More sinisterly, a newspaper report refers to the 'spiritual leader' of a Satanist cult in Milan, calling itself The Beasts of Satan.[4] On another day a headline runs 'Hate campaign awaits Bin Laden's "spiritual ambassador in Europe"'.[5] When stretched this far, the word becomes so vague and indefinable as to be of no serious use.

Further, the 'shift from religion to spirituality' runs alongside a continuing widespread professed belief in God. This varies from country to country. In the USA a Harris Poll taken in 2003 found that 79 per cent of Americans believe in the existence of God: of these 66 per cent are 'absolutely certain' of this; 9 per cent do not believe in God; and 12 per cent are not sure. Among those raised as Protestants 90 per cent believe in God, among those raised as Catholic 79 per cent, among Jews 48 per cent. Within these overall figures there were a number of variations. In the USA belief in God is highest in the Midwest (82%) and the South (82%), lower in the East (75%) and the West (75%). Belief tends to increase with age from 71 per cent of those aged 25–9, to more than 80 per cent for the age groups over 40, including 83 per cent of those aged 65 and over. (This may account for the fact that while there are few young people in many churches, those churches nevertheless continue, though diminishingly, to renew their congregations with older members.) Women (84%) are more likely then men (73%) to believe in God; African Americans (91%), Hispanics (81%) and whites (78%). Of those with no college education 82 per cent are more likely to believe in God than 73 per cent of those with postgraduate education. The Harris Poll reckoned that its results have a 95 per cent accuracy for the total population, plus or minus 3 per cent.[6] The Poll also found that far fewer attend the churches than profess belief in God – only about 26 per cent of believers in God in the USA every week, 36 per cent once a month or so, and 55 per cent only a few times a year.

In Britain the proportion of believers in God is much lower. A British Social Attitudes Survey by the National Centre for Social Research in 1998 found that 21 per cent have no doubt that God exists, 23 per cent have doubts but nevertheless believe, 14 per cent sometimes do and sometimes do not believe in God, 14 per cent believe in a Higher Power of some kind but not a personal God, 15 per cent are agnostic, and 10 per cent are atheists (and 3% unknown). The situation is probably much the same in other west European countries.

But it is important to remember that much depends on what people mean by 'God'. Certainly those classified as believers do not all believe in the same God, in the sense of having the same, or even a very similar, concept of God. But even in today's western Europe some kind of reference to a transcendent reality, predominantly thought of in personal terms, does still seem to be very common.

Spirituality/mysticism

The spirituality that I want to discuss in this book is not that described in the Kendal project, although there is an overlap at some points. What I want to examine is the 'inner aspect of religion' in the sense of religious experience or mysticism. The term 'mysticism', however, also needs some clarification. The writings of the great mystics of each tradition sometimes consist in their attempts to describe their own experiences, and sometimes in developing a mystical theology or philosophy. It will be enough to give one example of each within the Christian tradition. In spite of the fact that his name is largely unknown outside scholarly circles, the writings of Pseudo-Dionysius, thought to have been a Syrian monk writing around 500 CE, have probably been more influential than any other within the Christian tradition apart from St Paul. He wrote in the name of the Dionysius, or Denys, the Areopagite, who was converted by St Paul (Acts 17:34), thereby giving himself a near Pauline authority. (This is not the only example of such authorial concealment among Christian and also Jewish writers of the period.) Such was his influence that he was cited as an authority by Aquinas some 1700 times; and the thirteenth and early fourteenth centuries, the period recognised by Bernard McGinn in his multi-volume history of western mysticism as *The Flowering of Mysticism*, saw a 'Dionysian renaissance' (McGinn 1998, 86). Dionysius's writings show a strong neo-Platonic influence, and it was this that made Martin Luther reject him as the impostor whom Erasmus had already suspected. But the relevant point at the moment is that this great Christian mystic, whose 'influence on the Latin West was to be more powerful than that of any other Eastern [i.e. Eastern orthodox] mystic', as McGinn says (Ibid., 157–8), did not offer descriptions of mystical experience, but wrote several fairly slim volumes of mystical theology, emphasising in particular the total ineffability of the ultimate divine reality. And Christian mystics generally, prior to the thirteenth century, typically produced works of biblical exegesis in which they sought to bring out the mystical meaning of the texts but did not usually speak of their own mystical experience. In Dionysius's case, he does hint at 'experiencing the divine things' (Lubheid [trans.] 1987, 85) and writes of the moment when the mind 'is made one with the dazzling rays, being then and there enlightened by the inscrutable depth of Wisdom' (Ibid., 109). But there is no developed account of his own experiences.

In contrast to this, the late-fourteenth- and early-fifteenth-century English mystic, Lady Julian of Norwich, in her *Showings* or *Revelations of Divine Love*, describes in detail her powerful experiences, beginning with an initial vision when a priest held a crucifix before her as she lay ill and thinking herself close to death: 'suddenly I saw the red blood trickling down from under the crown, all hot, flowing freely and copiously, a living stream, just as it seemed to me that it was at the time when the crown of thorns was thrust down upon his blessed head'.[7] She describes this as a 'corporeal sight' (130), distinguishing it from the 'spiritual sight' of

> something small, no bigger than a hazelnut, lying in the palm of my hand, and I perceived that it was as round as any ball. I looked at it and thought: What can this be? And I was given this general answer: It is everything which is made. I was amazed that it could last, for I thought that it was so little that it could suddenly fall into nothing. And I was answered in my understanding: It lasts and always will, because God loves it: and thus everything has being through the love of God. (130)

She continued to have a series of visions, some external and some inner, over several days, some comforting and some frightening, but together giving her an overwhelming sense of the love and goodness of God as mediated through the figure of Jesus. There are two versions of her book, the Short Text written soon after the experiences, and the Long Text written some twenty years later in which she repeats her account of the experiences but adds her own very interesting reflections on them. As to their basic meaning, 'do you wish to know your lord's meaning in this thing? Know it well, love was his meaning. Who reveals it to you? Love. Why does he reveal it to you? For love'.[8] Her reflections in the Long Text are brilliantly original and radical.[9] Whereas she had been taught that humanity lies under the wrath of God and can be pardoned only by Christ's atonement to appease the divine anger, she says that 'for anything that I could see or desire, I could not see this characteristic [of wrath] in all the revelations . . . I saw [God] assign to us no kind of blame . . . our Lord God cannot in his own judgment forgive, because he cannot be angry'.[10] She also broke with the long (and still continuing) tradition of speaking of God as male: 'As truly as God is our Father, so truly is God our Mother', and she even spoke of 'our true Mother, Jesus'.[11] She also hinted at a belief in universal salvation,[12] carrying to its logical conclusion her famous refrain, which recurs several times in her text, 'All shall be well, and all shall be well, and all manner of thing shall be well.'

Julian was part of the new phenomenon of women mystics who based their teaching on direct religious experience. Bridget of Sweden, Catherine of Siena, Catherine of Bologna, Catherine of Genoa, Margaret and Christina Ebner in the Rhineland, Collette of Corbie and Joan of Arc in France, Hadewijch of Antwerp, Marguerite Porete in northern France, Margery Kempe as well as Julian in England. There were also major male mystics – Meister Eckhart, John Tauler, Ruusbroec, Walter Hilton, Richard Rolle, Ramon Lull – who, however, wrote mainly in the area of mystical theology. The anonymous *Cloud of Unknowing* is a work of mystical theology and the anonymous *Theologica Germanica* is devotional, though also containing profound mystical thinking. Whereas earlier, women's voices were seldom heard, in this period they played a leading role in the emergence of experiential writing. This also brought them under suspicion, not only because of a deep-seated patriarchal culture but also because a claim to direct experience of God bypassed the Church's teaching authority and gave them an independent standing outside ecclesiastical control. Most were watched suspiciously by the Church. Marguerite Porete was burned at the stake. Quite likely Julian of Norwich escaped censure because her writings were not widely known in her life time.

Unitive mysticism

William James says that 'overcoming all the usual barriers between the individual and the Absolute is the great mystic achievement. In mystic states we both become one with the Absolute and we are aware of our oneness' (James 1979, 404). Or in Christian, Jewish and Islamic terms, union with God. In some sense of 'union' or 'oneness' this is undoubtedly correct, but it is not easy to define this sense. If we press questions which were not in the minds of pre-modern writers, it is clear that within the monotheisms 'union' has almost always been intended in a metaphorical rather than a literal numerical sense. Indeed, I shall question later whether it is logically possible for a literal numerical unity to be experienced in this life.

For the clearest example of the unitive claim we turn to advanced advaitic Hindu practitioners. The Advaita Vedanta philosophy is well summarised by the modern Hindu scholar Radhakrishnan: 'The ego belongs to the relative world, is a stream of experience, a fluent mass of life, a centre round which our experiences of sense and mind gather. At the back of this whole structure is the Universal Consciousness, Atman, which is our true being' (Radhakrishnan 1953, 91). And the Atman is itself finally identical with the ultimate and eternal reality of Brahman. The great advaitic (non-dualist) Shankara (around 700 CE) used the famous analogy of empty jars. If you break the jars what remains is the air no longer divided by the jars. In *The Crest-Jewell of Discrimination* Shankara (or possibly one of his disciples, because the book's authorship is not certain) says, 'The air in the jar is one with the air everywhere. In like manner your Atman is one with Brahman' (Shankara 1978, 80). And he describes the unitive experience:

> His mind was completely absorbed in Brahman. After a while, he returned to normal consciousness. Then, out of the fullness of joy, he spoke: The ego has disappeared. I have realized my identity with Brahman and so all my desires have melted away... The treasure I have found there cannot be described in words. The mind cannot conceive it. My mind fell like a hailstone into the vast expanse of Brahman's ocean. Touching one drop of it, I melted away and became one with Brahman. And now, though I return to human consciousness, I abide in the joy of the Atman. (Shankara 1978, 113)

The reason why I question this and other similar accounts, when taken literally, is that to lose one's individual identity completely, like a drop becoming part of the ocean – a familiar simile in mystic literature – would be to lose the individual continuity of consciousness and memory in virtue of which the mystic would later be able to report the experience. How could someone remember being in a state in which he or she no longer existed as a distinct individual? There must, surely, have been a continuing strand of consciousness to enable them later to speak about it, while still enjoying something of its bliss. Is it not then more likely that having passed beyond the ordinary self-centred state to an ego-transcending awareness, the mystics's consciousness is filled with the ultimate universal reality which, according to the advaitic philosophy, we all are in the depths of our being? And they speak metaphorically of the experience as ceasing to exist as a separate consciousness while being totally merged into the infinite? This is indeed compatible with Shankara's account, for he says that 'it cannot be described in words...The mind cannot conceive it', and then there follows the simile of the hailstone dropping into the ocean.

I suggest, then, that the unitive language of Advaita Vedanta is not to be construed literally, as reporting a total extinction of the individual memory-bearing consciousness, but metaphorically, as expressing a usually brief but vivid awareness of the limitless reality in which we are rooted, an awareness whose quality is a profound *ananda*, happiness, and whose continuing effect is a considerable degree of liberation from the domination of the ego. This profound happiness of the experience is affirmed again and again by Shankara as he speaks of 'the highest bliss' (39), 'the Atman, which is endless joy' (103), and of the liberated person being 'illumined when he enjoys eternal bliss' (104). It is a liberation from ego-concern. This is important because, as we shall see in the next chapter, it is not only the intensity of the experience at the time but also it's long-term effects in the experiencer's life that characterises what the religions regard as authentic experience of the Transcendent.

I believe that a similar analysis must apply to unitive mysticism within the monotheistic traditions. Within Christian mysticism the language of union is freely used: Pseudo-Dionysius, who we have already met, writes of 'the most divine knowledge of God, that which comes through unknowing, is achieved in a union far beyond mind' (Pseudo-Dionysius 1987, 109); the ninth-century John Scotus Eriugena speaks of 'ineffable unity' (McGinn 1994, 116); the fourteenth-century Meister Eckhart says that God 'is light and when the divine light pours into the soul, the soul is united with God, as light blends with light' (Eckhart 1941, 163); and his disciple Henry Suso says that the mystic 'disappears and loses himself in God, and becomes one spirit with Him, as a drop of wine which is drowned in a great quantity of wine' (Underhill 1999, 424); while yet another fourteenth-century mystic, John Ruusbroec, speaks of 'unity without a difference' (Ruusbroec 1985, 265).

However, I believe that the notion of unity is nevertheless being used here metaphorically, not literally. For Christian belief maintains a fundamental distinction between the eternal Creator and the creature. The unity experienced by the mystics is not a unity of being but a union of wills in which the human is fully conformed to the divine. As Bernard of Clairvaux explains, 'The union between God and man is not unity...For how can there be unity where there is a plurality of natures and difference of substance? The union of God and man is brought about not by confusion of natures, but by agreement of wills' (Butler 1967, 114). And many of the mystics who use the language of unity also warn against a literal understanding of it. Thus Ruusbroec says, 'Nevertheless, the creature does not become God, for this union occurs through grace and through a love which has been turned back to God. For this reason the creature experiences in his inward vision a difference and distinction between himself and God' (Ruusbroec 1985, 265). Suso likewise says that the human person's 'being remains, but in another form, in another glory, and in another power' (Underhill 1999, 424). And St John of the Cross insists that the soul's 'natural being, though thus transformed, remains as distinct from the Being of God as it was before' (St John of the Cross 1958, 182).

Walter Stace maintained that in such disclaimers the Christian mystics who used unitive language were submitting to 'the menaces and pressures of the theologians and ecclesiastical authorities' (Stace 1960, 232). He believed that the mystics' experiences themselves would have led them to affirm a strict numerical identity with God but that the orthodox doctrine of an ineradicable distinction between Creator and creature, reinforced by the all-powerful authority of the Church, prevented them from drawing the logical conclusion from their first-hand experience. However, I agree at this point with Nelson Pike (Pike 1992, 211–12) that it is much more likely that they were sincere in their disclaimers of literal unity, for the mystical moments which they report occurred within the context of a religious life in which they were daily praying to God as their creator and as one with whom they lived in an I–Thou relationship of love, adoration and obedience. In their 'unitive' experience, structured as is all cognition by the experiencer's own conceptual resources, their consciousness was completely filled by the divine presence – but it was still their own individual human consciousness. The poet W. H. Auden was right when he said the theistic mystics are presumably 'trying to describe . . . a state of consciousness so filled with the presence of God that there is no vacant corner of it detachedly observing the experience' (Woods 1980, 385). But they never suppose that they have literally become identical with God.

And the same is true, although there is no space to develop this here, of the very fruitful theology of the Eastern Church, originally influenced by Neo-Platonism, in which humanity's divinisation or deification (*theosis*) is seen as the purpose of the spiritual life. We do not literally become God, but are to progress from what Irenaeus called the 'image' of God, which is our rational moral personhood, to the 'likeness' of God, which is our ultimate complete spiritual transformation.

We find a similar situation within the Sufi mystics of Islam. The tenth-century CE al-Hallaj used something like the drop in the ocean simile when he wrote in one of his poems,

> Thy Spirit is mingled in my spirit even as wine is mingled in pure water.
> When any thing touches Thee, it touches me. Lo, in every case Thou art I.
>
> (Nicholson 1979, 151)

This could be construed in various ways, but when he proclaimed, 'ana al-haqq', I am The Real, or the Truth, that is, God, he was executed for blasphemy. Or was he? A leading authority, Annemarie Schimmel, says that 'political and practical problems certainly played an important role' (Schimmel 1987, 174). There has also been much debate as to exactly what he intended by these words. He (with an earlier Sufi, al-Bistami) *may* have been affirming unity with Allah in the sense of a strict numerical identity. But even so, al-Hallaj is not evidence for Stace's theory, since he did not bend to community pressure to express himself more acceptably. Another great Sufi poet, Rumi, also used the wine and water simile:

> With Thy Sweet Soul, this soul of mine,
>   Hath mixed as Water doth with Wine,
> Who can the Wine and Water part,
>   Or me and Thee when we combine?
>
> (Underhill 1991, 426)

But I think it is clear that such poetic language is not to be understood literally. Even in *fana*, the full self-naughting which is the end of the mystical path, the conscious person still exists in this world: as Rumi says, 'The spirit becomes joyful through the I-less-I' (Chittick 1983, 193). Another tenth-century Sufi, and great Islamic theologian, al-Ghazali, says that the mystics,

> after their ascent to the heavens of Reality, agree that they saw nothing in existence except God the One . . . Nothing was left to them but God . . . But the words of lovers when in a state of drunkenness must be hidden away and not broadcast. However, when their drunkenness abates and the sovereignty of their reason is restored – and reason is God's scale on earth – they know that this was not actual identity. (Zaehner 1957, 157–8)

Further, Sufi mysticism is essentially love mysticism – God's love for us and our answering love for God – so that al-'Arabi can say that 'the greatest union is that between man and woman, corresponding as it does to the turning of God toward the one He has created in His own image, so made him His vice regent, so that He might behold Himself in him' (al-'Arabi 1980, 275). And mutual love presupposes two personal centres of consciousness. I think that this, together with the manifestly poetic mode in which the Sufis always expressed themselves, supports al-Ghazali's reading of them.

The Jewish mystics have been less influential within Judaism than the Sufis within Islam, though in the medieval period they achieved great heights. The mystics of the Kabbalah proliferated into many schools and strands of tradition which defy any unitary characterisation. Some of them undoubtedly used the language of unity. Thus the thirteenth-century CE Abraham Abulafia declared that 'he and He become one entity' (Idel 1988, 60). And Rabbi Isaac of Acre used a variation of the familiar simile of the drop and the ocean: the soul and God 'become one entity, as if somebody poured out a jug of water into a running well, that all becomes one' (Scholem 1955, 67). There is, however, disagreement about whether their unitive language should be understood literally or metaphorically. I suspect, metaphorically. If literally, the counter-argument that I offered above in relation to advaitic Hinduism will also apply here. But Gershom Scholem, a leading authority on Jewish mysticism, warns that 'Even in this ecstatic state of mind the Jewish mystic almost invariably retains a sense of the distance between the Creator and his creature' (Scholem 1955, 60).

It seems to me, then, that while it could be, as many strands of mystical thought teach, that our ultimate state will be one of total absorption (or re-absorption) in the Ultimate, the Real, this must lie far beyond this present life.

3
What Is Religious Experience?

What do we mean by religious experience?

Key terms in epistemology have been used over the years in different ways, so that it will be well to begin with some definitions. Because of the variety of usages, these will be stipulative, saying what in this book I mean by certain words. However, these definitions are not novel or eccentric and they will I think be acceptable to most readers.

To be conscious is to be experiencing. Religious, like all other forms of experience, consists in modifications of consciousness. And *an* experience, as a particular moment or episode which we single out, is a momentary or prolonged modification of consciousness. To say that it is subjective is just to say that it is, like all our other experience, a part of our stream of consciousness. Many elements within this are caused by the impact of our physical environment, as when we see, hear, touch, taste something. Many are created by ourselves as we deliberate, calculate, speculate, invent, compose, decide. These two normally go on at the same time, when we are both perceiving and thinking. Again, when we dream the mind creates its own content of consciousness (the qualia), as it also does when, awake, we project a hallucinatory image of something that is not physically there. And our central question in this book is going to be whether some or all religious experience is veridical and, if some, how the veridical is to be distinguished from the false.

A natural formal definition of 'religious experience' would be that it refers to any experience, veridical or not, that is structured in terms of religious concepts – such as God, Brahman, nirvana, angels, miracles, divine condemnation, divine forgiveness, etc., etc. – or consists in religious images such as the figure of Christ, the Virgin Mary, Krishna, an angel or a devil, heaven, hell, purgatory, etc. But this definition in terms of the use of religious concepts will prove to be too restrictive, closing off necessary questions. If there is veridical religious experience, is awareness of the supra-natural reality necessarily and exclusively structured by religious concepts? It could turn out that, in a thoroughly secular culture which rejects religious ideas and beliefs, the Transcendent nevertheless impacts people's minds and affects their lives in moral or political rather than religious terms. More about this in Chapter 4.

The kinds of religious experience

The modern discussion of religious experience has generally focussed on its more striking and dramatic forms of voices, visions, transforming 'peak experiences', claims to an experienced unity with the Ultimate. William James's famous book is full of fascinating speculations as well as a wealth of striking examples,[1] some of which I shall use. In addition, I shall refer to religious literature through the centuries and contemporary cases collected by the Religious Experience Research Centre.[2]

There are many levels of intensity and of effect on the experiencer (or experient), and I shall sometimes use the term mysticism for the higher and more transforming levels. But we must begin much lower down, for the greater part of religious experience occurs below the level of the dramatic or highly charged and sometimes life-changing forms that tend to be recorded and discussed. There are more common, generally vaguer, but still significant moments in the lives of ordinary people who may not necessarily think of themselves as religious, moments of awe and a sense of transcendence when looking up into a cloudless night sky and feeling the mystery of this vast universe of galaxies or, among natural scenery, sensing a value that is somehow within but also beyond the landscape, or in moments of profound peace during prayer in a church, synagogue, mosque or temple, or at home, or when reverencing the statue of a god in India, or of the Buddha or a Bodhisattva in a Buddhist temple, or of Christ on the cross, or the Virgin Mary or a saint, in a Christian church, or again when being in the presence of extraordinary acts of self-sacrificing goodness and compassion, or yet again in listening to great music, which is untranslatable into the language of insight and emotion. In some of these cases explicitly religious ideas structure the experience, but even when this is not the case there is often an inchoate sense that there is something more than matter, something more to life and the universe than simply the changing patterns of physical particles, a feeling that 'there are more things in heaven and earth than are dreampt of' in a purely physicalist or materialist philosophy – that there is a further spiritual dimension of reality.

A transformed world

Turning to explicitly religious forms of experience, these occur in (at least) four different modes. One is a distinctive way of experiencing aspects of the natural world, or the natural world as a whole. A second is the sense of presence, whether of God or of an angelic being or of a surrounding and indwelling more ultimate supra-natural reality. A third consists in religious visions and auditions, both inner and outer. And a fourth, already discussed, is the experience of unity with God or with the Ultimate reported by mystics within each of the great traditions.

Jonathan Edwards provides a well-known theistic example of the first mode:

> The appearance of everything was altered; there seemed to be, as it were, a calm, sweet cast, or appearance of divine glory, in almost everything. God's excellency, his wisdom, his purity and love, seemed to appear in everything; in the sun, moon and stars; in the clouds and blue sky; in the grass, flowers, and trees; in the water and all nature. (James 1979, 248)

As a typical modern example of nature mysticism of a non- or semi-theistic kind:

> One day years ago I went for a walk in the fields with my dog. My mind suddenly started thinking about the beauty around me, and I considered the marvellous order and timing of the growth of each flower, herb and the abundance of all the visible growth going on around. I remember thinking 'Here is mind'. Then we had to get over a style and suddenly I was confronted with a bramble bush which was absolutely laden with black glistening fruit. And the impact of that, linked with my former reasoning, gave me a great feeling of ecstasy. For a few moments I really did feel at one with the Universe or the Creative power we recognise. I know it was a feeling of oneness with something outside my self, and also within. I must have been confronted with the source of all being, whatever one should call it. I have often told my friends about it, though it seems too sacred

to talk about. The experience has never been forgotten. It was quite electric and quite unsought. (Female aged about 30. Maxwell and Tschudin 1990, 52).

Here are a few other brief extracts out of the large number on record. A woman aged 19 on holiday in Cornwall walking along the cliffs: 'I was part of something bigger and absolutely beyond me. My problems and my life didn't matter at all because I was such a tiny part of a great whole. I felt a tremendous relief. I was aware of my eyes not only looking at, but feeling, the beauty of everything that was there for eternity' (ibid., 47). And a man, age not known:

I was lying under a tree thinking rather deeply about love and the joy it brings. Suddenly . . . I seemed to be filled with the rays of the sun. This experience lasted for about three minutes. It is interesting to note that my behaviour pattern has changed since this experience. I feel a lot more peaceful and happier within myself, and look upon life as being a spiritual evolution within a material body. (Ibid., 49)

We can presume that the same kind of experience occurs to a more or less equal extent in the East as in the West, although I am not aware of any published collection of ordinary peoples' reports from other traditions, comparable with the (British) Religious Experience Research Centre, that might be able to confirm this.[3] However, within Mahayana Buddhism – the northern form of Buddhism found in China, Japan, Tibet, Korea and Central Asia generally – the *satori* or *kensho* experience is in some ways akin to that of Jonathan Edwards. For its astonishing claim, based on direct experience, is that *samsara* (the familiar transitory world of pleasure and suffering, hoping and fearing, striving and desiring, birth and death) is identical with *nirvana* (the ego-free state of puri-fied awareness, joy and compassion). Our ordinary experience of the world is everywhere haunted by *dukkha*, variously translated as unsat-isfactoriness, suffering, woe; but in *satori*, enlightenment, the same world is experienced quite differently. 'The essence of Zen Buddhism consists in acquiring a new viewpoint on life and things generally', says D. T. Suzuki, the great exponent of Zen to the West (Suzuki 1956, 83). He says, 'Zen . . . opens a man's mind to the greatest mystery as it is daily and hourly performed . . . it makes us live in the world as if walking in the Garden of Eden . . . I do not know why – and there is no need of explaining – but when the sun rises the whole world dances with joy and everybody's heart is filled with bliss' (Suzuki 1964, 45, 75). The central philosophical concept, developed in the Madhyamaka or Middle Way, is *sunyata*, emptiness. But this emptiness is not nothingness. In *satori* the world becomes empty of everything that the mind projects in its activity of cognition, revealing the world as it is in itself. In the words of the Buddha, 'Because it is empty of self or of what belongs to the self, it is therefore said: "The world is empty"' (Woodward 1956, 29). When devoid of the effects of the ego point of view, the whole world shares the eternal buddha-nature. The Kyoto philosopher Keiji Nishitani says that the ancient saying 'True Emptiness is Wondrous Being' is 'usually acknowledged as expressing the core of Mahayana Buddhism' (Nishitani 1982, 183). A Zen monk gives his first-hand account of the *satori* experience:

> Enlightenment [*satori*] is an overwhelming inner realization which comes suddenly. Man feels himself at once free and strong, exalted and great, in the universe. The breath of the universe vibrates through him. No longer is he merely a small, selfish ego, but rather he is open and transparent, united to all, in unity. Enlightenment is achieved in *zazen* [the Zen form of meditation], but it remains effective in all situations of life. Thus everything in life is meaningful, worthy of thanks, and good – even suffering, sickness, and death. (Dumoulin 1963, 275)

The sense of presence

Many ordinary Christian worshippers say that in church, or in their private prayers and devotions, they are sometimes conscious of being in the unseen presence of God. They are vividly aware of the divine love for them; or of a divine call to do some particular thing, such as visit someone they know to be in need of comfort and support, or to give money to an organisation working in some disaster zone or amid desperate poverty; or are aware of a divine command to apologise and make amends to someone whom they have wronged – and then subsequently they have experienced a sense of divine forgiveness. Or, much more dramatically, a man during a walking tour with his family in France:

> [A]ll at once I experienced a feeling of being raised above myself, I felt the presence of God – I tell the thing just as I was conscious of it – as if his goodness and his power were penetrating me altogether. The throb of emotion was so violent that I could barely tell the boys to

pass on and not wait for me. I then sat down on a stone, unable to stand any longer, and my eyes overflowed with tears. I thanked God that in the course of my life he had taught me to know him, that he sustained my life and took pity on both the insignificant creature and on the sinner that I was . . . (James, 1979, 84).

Equally dramatically, in a semi-theistic mode, a 58-years-old woman speaks of 'the most shattering experience of my entire life' when

Without any sense of perception (except that I do seem to recollect an impression of light and darkness), I was made aware of a Reality beyond anything that my own mind could have conceived. And that Reality was a total love of all things in heaven and earth. 'It' enclosed and accepted everything and every creature: there was no distinction of its love between the star, the saint and the torturer. (Maxwell and Tschudin 1990, 61)

In addition to such experiences – a large number of which have been recorded, as well as an undoubtedly much greater number of unrecorded examples – of being in the vast surrounding presence of cosmic goodness and love, whether referred to as God or as It, there are also numerous cases of a finite presence, usually thought of as an angel, or deva – a god with a small g. My own former doctoral supervisor, the late Henry Price, then Wykeham Professor of Logic at Oxford and a powerful and penetrating philosophical intellect, told me and a few others of a vivid experience of presence, which we were not to make public during his lifetime. One morning, finding himself in an unusually tranquil and peaceful frame of mind, he was sitting in his drawing-room facing the empty fireplace when it gradually dawned on him that there was someone else in the room, though no one else was physically present. He was aware that the visitor, with whom he conversed in an exchange of thoughts, not spoken words, was very good and wise, sympathetically understanding him, and kindly disposed towards him. The visitor assured him that God deeply loved his human creatures, including himself. This made a profound impression on him. After a period of quiet reflection he became aware that the visitor was no longer there. The 'conversation' had, he thought, probably lasted about a quarter of an hour. The after-effect was overwhelming for the rest of that day, which he said was the happiest he had ever known, and it lasted pervasively but less intensively for the rest of his life.[4] As with all other cases, the final question is whether such moments constitute a contact with transcendent reality, experienced in a form made possible by the experient's own mind, or is pure self-delusion. This will be the subject of later chapters.

Visions and auditions

Turning now to the third form of experience, visions and auditions, visions of Christ naturally tend to take the form of the traditional depictions of Christ in stained-glass windows and medieval paintings, which have varied from the stern majestic ruler of the universe to the gentle and kindly Light of the World, or, in today's films, varying from the powerful and authoritative leader and teacher to the tortured and crucified figure in *The Passion of the Christ*. The recorded contemporary experiences of visions of Jesus are generally of the white, robed, bearded, long-haired Christ of much popular art. From the Maxwell and Tschudin collection from the Religious Experience Research Centre's files: 'The figure, Jesus Christ, glided onto the centre of the road while we were on the rough pavement. We were spellbound as the figure walked up and we were walking down. We could see the white gown with a broad, twisted girdle around his waist, knotted and falling on his left side . . . ' (78); or again,

> I was busily occupied one morning in cooking the lunch and with no other thoughts in mind, when suddenly there was a blinding flash of light and standing at my side was a white-robed figure. I knew it was Christ when I saw the pierced hands and feet, but did not see his face. The amazing brightness all around me was indescribable and I was filled with such *overwhelming* joy that I cannot find words to express all I felt. (79, italics original)

Again, the late Anglican Bishop, Hugh Montefiore, born into a distinguished Jewish family, reported in his autobiography:

> I was sixteen years old at the time, and it happened to me about 5 pm one dark wintry afternoon in 1936. I was sitting alone in my study in School House at Rugby School – all older boys had studies of their own: pillboxes, really. What happened then determined the whole future pattern of my life. I was, as I remember, indulging in a rather pleasant adolescent gloom. I suddenly became aware of a figure in white whom I saw clearly in my mind's eye. I use this expression because I am pretty sure that a photograph would have showed nothing special on it. I heard the words 'Follow me'. Instinctively

I knew that this was Jesus, heavens knows how: I knew nothing about him. Put like that it sounds somewhat bare; in fact it was an indescribably rich event that filled me afterwards with overpowering joy. I could do no other than follow those instructions. I found that I had become a Christian as a result of a totally unexpected and most unusual spiritual experience, although that was not how I would have put it at the time. I was aware of the living Christ, and because of that I was aware of God in a new way. People ask me why and when I decided to convert. I did not decide at all; it was decided for me. (Montefiore 1995, 1)

This account raises questions in my mind, which I now wish that I had asked him about. Could a 16-year-old boy at Rugby, even a Jewish boy, know *nothing* about Jesus? Assuming that he did not attend the school chapel, must not Christian ideas, including beliefs about and images of Jesus, nevertheless have become familiar to him through his studies of literature and history? Quite commonly, in retrospective accounts of religious experiences, as indeed of any other striking experience, a certain amount of interpretation almost inevitably enters into the description. This does not in any way invalidate the account, but it reminds us to be alert to the possibility of an interpretive element within it. Another understanding of Montefiore's vision, which does justice to its power for him, is that it was a 'threshold' experience, when thoughts that had been building up in the unconscious suddenly flood into consciousness. (St Paul's experience on the Damascus road would be another and much more powerful example of the same psychological effect.)

Both outer and inner visions and auditions occur within many traditions. For example, Fr Klostermeier reports a Hindu Swami telling him of his vision of Krishna: 'He was about fourteen years old. Krishna met him, coming out of a rice field . . . Krishna smiled at him and embraced him. The contact electrified and changed him. "Since then I had no other thought but to serve only Krishna, and I became a sadhu" ' (Klostermeier 1969, 31). And as an example of an inner vision, the still influential nineteenth-century Hindu mystic Ramakrishna described a vision which came to him when meditating in a temple:

It was as if houses, doors, temples and everything else vanished altogether; as if there was nothing anywhere! And what I saw was an infinite shoreless sea of light; a sea that was consciousness. However far and in whatever direction I looked, I saw shining waves, one after another, coming towards me. They were raging and storming upon me with great speed. Very soon they were upon me; and made me sink down into unknown depths. I panted and struggled and lost consciousness. (Isherwood 1965, 65)

Again the question remains: in such experiences are people becoming aware, though always in culturally conditioned forms, of a supra-natural reality that is there all the time, or are such experiences among the more exotic examples of human self-delusion?

Some rarer forms of religious experience

The central focus of this book is on the religious or transcendental or numinous experience of 'ordinary' people, whether they think of themselves as religious or not. According to all the published research approximately a third of the population have either once or more than once had such experiences. In the United States a 1975 National Opinion Research Center inquiry in which people were asked 'Have you ever felt as though you were close to a spiritual force that seemed to lift you out of yourself?' found that 35 per cent of those asked said that they had, and a Princeton Research Center (a subsidiary of Gallop Polls) survey in 1978 also recorded 35 per cent. In Britain at the same time a National Opinion Poll of a sample of 2000 reported 36 per cent. (For detailed tables for different age groups, religious affiliations, educational backgrounds, etc., see Hay 1982, ch. 8). In the majority of cases each individual reported only one such experience in the course of their life, although some reported several. All such surveys are limited in scope and are also subject to problems of definition. But nevertheless it does seem likely that something like a third of these populations has experienced awareness of a 'spiritual' dimension to reality of which we humans are sometimes, usually only fleetingly, conscious.

This concentration on 'ordinary' religious experience is at the expense of attention to a number of other rarer but extremely interesting phenomena, particularly NDEs, near death experiences; OBEs, out of the body experiences; mediumship; claimed memories of previous lives; ESP, extra-sensory perception or telepathy; and other phenomena studied by parapsychology (psychical research).[5] Some of these have potentially far-reaching implications. For extra-sensory perception, the reality of which is in my opinion well established, is incompatible with the prevailing naturalistic assumption of our culture. So also, if the planned hospital experiments to test their reality succeed, are OBEs. I do not omit a discussion of such phenomena here out of a lack of interest in parapsychology (see Hick 1976), but because this is not where the science/religion debate is at present focussed, and I would like to contribute something to that debate.

The relation between the inner and outer aspects of religion

I shall try in later chapters to justify the belief that religious experience is (in many cases) our human response to a reality beyond as well as within us. In the West we most naturally speak of God. But as used within the Western monotheisms this carries with it the strong connotation of a limitless all-powerful divine Person with such attributes as loving, commanding, judging, accepting, condemning, punishing, revealing, who is the creator of everything other than him/herself and who acts purposefully within the history of the universe and in the history of some one particular section of humanity, as recorded in their scriptures. This is the anthropomorphic concept of the Ultimate modelled on our own human nature but magnified to infinity and purified of all limitations and defects. But if we are looking at religion globally we also have to take account of quite different concepts and experiences of the Ultimate. In the predominantly non-theistic religions of Buddhism, Jainism, Taoism/Confucianism and some forms of Hinduism the ultimate reality is not conceived as a personal God but as an ultimate reality beyond the distinction between the personal and the impersonal. We therefore need a term for the final focus of religious concern which encompasses both the theistic and non-theistic understandings of it. I shall speak of Ultimate Reality, or the Ultimate, or the Transcendent, or the Real, this last because it has a degree of resonance with some uses of both the Sanscrit *sat*[6] and (among some of the Sufis) the Arabic *al Haqq*.[7]

There is a two-way relationship between the outer reality of the religious institutions and the inner reality of spirituality or mysticism. On the one hand, religious institutions are the natural and inevitable creations of inherently social beings, and human responses to the Transcendent were communal before becoming individual. We all need human companionship and the comfort of a supporting community. And within the great organised institutionalised religions, despite all their moral failures, there has nearly always been space, sometimes ample space, for the spiritual life. On the other hand, sometimes there has been very little, and when this falls below a certain level the institutions become simply humanly created organisations which have too often been intolerant forces, destructive of the human spirit. Nevertheless, the spiritual life depends upon the continuing institutions for preserving scriptures and the accumulated wisdom of the past, for methods of prayer and meditation that have been handed down through the generations, and for mutual fellowship and easy communication between like-minded people. So these two aspects of religion, spirituality and the institutions, are mutually dependent. But the spiritual life, the transforming personal response to the Ultimate, is the living heart of religion. The institutions are necessary, but religiously secondary; and when they make themselves primary as absolute authorities they almost inevitably become dangerous centres of power and repression.

When we stress the priority of the spiritual and experiential over the institutional a different conception of religion from the standard Western understanding of it becomes possible. We see this different way of thinking in China prior to the Maoist revolution, when it was quite normal to be a Buddhist, a Confucian and a Taoist. Again, in Japan today great numbers of people practise both Buddhism and Shinto to meet different needs in their lives. And in India the many different strands of religious thought and practice that are brought together under the name of Hinduism, such as the Vaishnavite and Shaivite streams of devotion, are not so much rivals as regional variations. People do not argue about which of the many gods is the true God, because they all are, as different manifestations of the ultimate reality of Brahman. On this other conception of religion the different faiths are not seen as bounded entities set over against one another, but more as fields of spiritual force or spheres of spiritual influence – the influence emanating from the teachings of the Buddha, the influence emanating from the teachings of Confucius, the Taoist influence emanating from the *Tao Te Ching*, the influence coming from the teachings of Jesus, and of the Qur'an. Now while one cannot belong simultaneously to two organisations with mutually exclusive memberships, one *can* live within two or more overlapping spheres of spiritual influence. The same person can respond to the wisdom and can use some of the spiritual practices – such as different forms of prayer and meditation – that come from a variety of sources; and indeed many, and probably a growing number of us today, are doing just that. In this model of religion the institutions have an important function in preserving historic memories and providing communal symbols and rituals. But they are no longer closed socio-religious entities whose professional priesthoods and hierarchies protect their exclusive claims against those of other such entities. For while religious institutions almost inevitably divide humanity, the inner openness to the Ultimate that I am calling spirituality, or mysticism, does not split people into opposing groups. Spirituality does indeed take characteristically different forms within the different traditions, but these differences are complementary rather than contradictory.

The central question remains, again, how can we hope to determine whether this inner side of religion is authentically cognitive of reality, or is a form of self-delusion? But prior to that it is necessary to ask how the distinction is drawn within the religions themselves – for they have never accepted as genuine by any means all religious experience claims within their own traditions.

4
'By Their Fruits You Will Know Them'

From the sublime to the ridiculous

Religious experience in the broad sense of any experience structured by religious concepts covers an enormously wide range from the sublime to the ridiculous and beyond that to the positively evil. We have seen some examples of the sublime. As an example of the ridiculous:

> After I felt the call of God to trust Him for everything I was in the RAF as an aircraft mechanic. After a short time I was posted to the Far East and during the trouble we were required to keep up a fighter umbrella. This meant that I had to decide which aircraft to service first and which had to be left to the last. Imagine a line of fighters as one taxies to the far end and one to the other. We were short staffed in my trade. I trusted God to guide me to the right plane and in my mind came a quiet voice. I obeyed the code letters and raced to that aircraft. As I did, my heart was filled with joy to the brim. After the trouble was over I worked it out to 360 aircraft checked without the mistake of servicing the wrong one. I can write a small book on how God has guided me and also fill it with everyday happenings which I know come from our Maker, not the subconscious. (Maxwell and Tschudin 1990, 116)

To categorise this as ridiculous is of course to adopt a point of view. The aircraft mechanic is operating with a popular understanding which enables believers to manipulate God by believing that God is manipulating them. Such people are projecting the image of a God who intervenes on earth in detailed ways in the lives of the faithful, who is assumed in this case to approve of war as a way of settling disputes and who was on Britain's side of this particular conflict, feeding the mechanic with information in support of the military operation. To those who cannot believe that there is such a God it seems evident that the mechanic's technical knowledge and experience enabled him to recognise the aircraft that he judged to be in most urgent need of attention – the same judgement, whether correct or not, assuring him afterwards that he had always made the right decisions.

Not ridiculous, but peculiar, if not pathetic, are such experiences as this: 'Pilgrims yesterday flocked to a flat where images of Jesus, St Peter and St Paul are said to have appeared on a wardrobe. Valeriu Junie, 66, claims to regularly see the figures at his home in Drobeta, Romania. Priest Vasile Nahaiu said, "Jesus was there. It's a miracle".'[1]

More famously, and moving to the morally dangerous, the Hebrew scriptures record a divine revelation, 'Thus says the Lord of Hosts ... [G]o and smite Amalek, and utterly destroy all that they have; do not spare them, but kill both man and woman, infant and suckling, ox and sheep, camel and ass' (1 Samuel 15:3. Cf. Deuteronomy 7:2). The writers of 1 Samuel and Deuteronomy had a conception of the God of Israel which was morally far below the later Hebrew understanding of him as 'merciful and gracious, slow to anger and abounding in stead-fast love ... For as the heavens are high above the earth, so great is his steadfast love toward those who fear him; as far as the east is from the west, so far does he remove our transgressions from us' (Psalm 103:8, 10–11), and from this later point of view the commands of the tribal warrior god must be seen as a reflection of human genocidal savagery rather than as a message from God. The Qur'an has nothing quite so extreme, but it gets close in a reference to the battle of Badr: 'And the Lord said to the angels: "I am with you; go and strengthen the faithful. I shall fill the hearts of infidels with terror. So smite them on their necks and in every joint and incapacitate them" ... It was not you who killed them, but God did so. You did not throw what you threw [i.e., sand into the enemies' eyes], but God, to bring out the best in the faithful by doing them a favour of his own' (Surah 8:12). And there are dangerous cults today, such as the Japanese Aum Shinrikyo (aka Aleph, and not to be confused with the much older and respected Shinrikyo faith), whose members put nerve gas in the Tokyo underground; the Order of the Solar Temple with its mass suicide in 1994 in the USA; the Branch Davidians, with the disastrous Waco, Texas, siege and slaughter. There are also sects that are more weird than dangerous, such as the Raelian cult in Canada, receiving messages from extraterrestrials on planet Elohim, who some-times supposedly abduct earthlings. And others in both categories spring up from time to time around the world.

On the individual level, a newspaper has a headline, 'God told me to kill boys, says mother'. This was a woman in Texas who stoned two of her children to death, 'driven to kill by a message from God'.[2] She was eventually found not guilty by reason of insanity; but she experienced her insane thoughts in terms of her concept of God, bringing this under our broad definition of religious experience. But in a powerful statesman such projections of one's own ideas onto God can be dangerous on the world scale. President of the USA George W. Bush is reported to have said, 'I am driven with a mission from God ... "George, go and fight these terrorists in Afghanistan". And I did ... "George, go and end the tyranny in Iraq". And I did'.[3]

Such examples make it evident, from a religious point of view, that religious experiences as such are not always authentic. This is of course a particular standpoint within religion, one that rejects the concept of the ultimate reality as an all-powerful disembodied divine person who is specially interested in some one particular individual or section of the human race, who intervenes in earthly history on their behalf, and who is capable of love but also of hatred, cruelty and injustice. Rejecting that image, we see many instances of experiences structured by religious concepts that express the experiencer's own prejudices, hatreds, naivety or insanity. It is clear, then, that the religions need criteria by which to separate the wheat from the chaff.

Within the monotheisms

Such criteria have in fact been developed, particularly in relation to mystical experience with its claim to an authority by-passing that of the ecclesiastical authorities. The great medieval Christian mystics, for example, were acutely aware that not every vision and audition comes from God. St Teresa of Avila is a good example. In her case the auditions were heard in her mind: 'Though perfectly formed, the words are not heard with the bodily ear; yet they are understood much more clearly than if they were so heard, and, however determined one's resistance, it is impossible to fail to hear them' (Teresa of Avila 1960, 233). Her visions were likewise inner visions. For example, 'Christ revealed himself to me, in an attitude of great sternness, and showed me what there was in this that displeased Him. I saw Him with the eyes of the soul more clearly than I could ever have seen Him with those of the body' (99).

Teresa's experiences were controversial at the time both because they came independently of the Church hierarchy and because they motivated her in her considerable practical achievements. She reformed one of the Carmelite orders, founding a new convent in Avila to embody her reforms and then 17 more elsewhere in Spain, against continuous male ecclesiastical and political opposition. Her mystical experiences were therefore challenged by many within the Church establishment; and such challenges were possible because it was accepted within the monasteries and nunneries that visions and auditions sometimes come from the devil instead of from God. The first test was tradition-specific, namely, conformity to orthodox teachings. For Teresa, the devil was a real malign force who 'can play many tricks', so that 'the soul must be convinced that a thing comes from God only if it is in conformity with Holy Scripture' (Ibid., 239). But this was not sufficient by itself.

Convinced that her revelations did not conflict with scripture, Teresa appealed to ordinary common sense as a second criterion. This was long before the discovery of the capacity of the unconscious mind to present material to consciousness with such force that it seems to come from outside. But for her, the fact that she could not help hearing the divine message, that its power was such that she could not ignore it, and that she could not summon it at will, were valuable supporting evidence. She was here using her reason. Likewise, in the case of some of the Sufis, we saw earlier (p. 25) how al-Ghazali used his reason – for 'reason is God's scale on earth' – to recognise the metaphorical rather than literal nature of the language of numerical union with God.

But the even more important universal criterion, common to all the great traditions, both theistic and non-theistic, has always been the observable spiritual and moral fruits of the experience in the individual's life. It was this that was decisive in Teresa's becoming recognised as a saint. In the New Testament Jesus, telling his followers how to distinguish true from false prophets, said, 'Are grapes gathered from thorns, or figs from thistles? So, every sound tree bears good fruit, but the bad tree bears evil fruit. A sound tree cannot bear evil fruit, nor can a bad tree bear good fruit . . . Thus you will know them by their fruits' (Matthew 7:18, 20). This was how Teresa authenticated her own experiences. In reply to those who were sceptical about her auditions she used this telling argument:

> I once said to the people who were talking to me in this way that if they were to tell me that a person whom I knew well and had just been speaking to was not herself at all, but that I was imagining her to be so, and that they knew this was the case, I should certainly believe them rather than my own eyes. But, I added, if that person

left some jewels with me, which I was actually holding in my hands as pledges of her great love, and if, never having had any before, I were thus to find myself rich instead of poor, I could not possibly believe that this was a delusion, even if I wanted to. And, I said, I could show them these jewels – for all who knew me were well aware how much my soul had changed: my confessor himself testified to this, for the difference was very great in every respect, and no fancy, but such as all could clearly see. As I had previously been so wicked, I concluded, I could not believe that, if the devil were doing this to delude me and drag me down to hell, he would make use of means which so completely defeated his own ends by taking away my vices and making me virtuous and strong; for it was quite clear to me that these experiences had immediately made me a different person. (265)

And it was because this was observably the case that she had the spiritual authority to carry through her reforms. Teresa was one of the rich company of 'love mystics' concerning whom Louis Dupres says that, 'By no coincidence did most love mystics become "saints", that is, persons who, by heroic virtue, learned to love without possessiveness' (Dupres 1987, 255).

Within Islam the criterion is again practical – faithfulness in prayer, almsgiving, fasting during Ramadan, undertaking the pilgrimage to Mecca if one can once in one's life. But

> Piety does not lie in turning your face to East or West: piety lies in believing in God, the Last Day and the angels, the Scriptures and the prophets, and disbursing your wealth out of love for God among your kin and the orphans, the wayfarers and mendicants, freeing the slaves, observing your devotional obligations, and in paying the zakat (alms) and fulfilling a pledge you have given, and being patient in hardship, adversity, and times of peril. (Qur'an, 2:176–7)

And among some of the Sufis, spiritual progress is from 'Yours is yours and mine is mine', through 'Yours is yours and mine is yours too', to 'There is neither mine nor thine' (a Turkish Muslim saying).

Within Buddhism

The same pragmatic test, 'by their fruits you will know them', operates among those who experience religiously within different traditions around the world. For example, during Gautama Buddha's lifetime a large number of monks and nuns and laypeople, both men and women, experienced the full enlightenment of *nirvana*[4] (Horner 1957, 490–1), and in one of the Discourses of the *Majjhima Nikaya* (Horner 1954, 379–82) the Buddha tells his disciples how to recognise whether someone is or is not a genuine Tathagata, 'a fully Self-Awakened One', who has attained to *nibbana* (*nirvana*). The test lies in their behaviour. This must be free from the 'defilements' of, to quote one of the lists, 'malevolence, anger, malice, hypocrisy, spite, envy, stinginess, deceit, treachery, obstinacy, impetuosity, arrogance, pride, conceit, indolence' (Horner 1954, 46). For a Buddha (an Enlightened One) will have followed successfully the Noble Eightfold Path, the first element of which is ethical conduct: truthfulness; avoiding malicious gossip and abusive language; peaceful conduct; not destroying life, including animal life; not stealing or dealing dishonestly with people; refraining from 'illegitimate' sexual intercourse; not making a living in ways that harm others such as trading in lethal weapons or poisons or intoxicating liquors – to which no doubt today the tobacco and leisure drug industries must be added. And it must be true of them that 'This venerable one refrains not out of fear' but out of the gradual ending of the self-centred cravings which lead to such behaviour (Ibid., 380).

The other elements of the Eightfold Path are less open to others' observation: right effort, meaning a mental effort to cultivate good and avoid bad thoughts and attitudes, and right mindfulness, developed in the practice of meditation. Meditation is central to the path to enlightenment. We shall come later to the relation between this and brain activity, but it is relevant to note here that the plasticity of the brain is such that the two forms of Buddhist meditation which have mainly been studied by contemporary neurophysiologists, Zen and Tibetan, are correlated with an enhanced activity in the area of the brain associated with equanimity, happiness and compassion (the left prefrontal lobe). James Austin, in his massive study, *Zen and the Brain*, adds that this is a long-lasting effect expressed in 'Subsequent persisting positive changes in attitude and behavior. The experience [of *kensho*, the Japanese word for enlightenment] changes the way the subjects think about themselves and about the rest of the world, and it transforms their behavior' (Austin 1999, 543). There are two possibilities: (1) that the altered pattern of cerebral activity produces the altered state of consciousness, the brain being part of the continuous causal system of the material world; and (2) that we have the freedom to make deliberate mental efforts which cause changes in the pattern of neural activity. Which of these is correct is a major question to be examined.

This persistence of the enlightened state, reflected in the individual's life, connects with another, common-sense, criterion used by the Buddha. One has to ask, 'Has this venerable one been possessed of this skilled state for a long or only for a short time?' (Horner 1954, 380). If only for a short time, one should suspend judgement. True enlightenment does not show itself in a momentary experience or in a brief period of euphoria but in a continued and consistent life expressing the profound transformation of freedom from ego-concern leading to openness to all life, expressed in compassion (*karuna*) and 'loving-kindness' (*metta*).

Individual and social fruits

During the pre-democratic centuries, indeed millennia, when political power and responsibility were concentrated in the hands of a tribal chief or a local or national ruler, the fruits of religious experience, including the epoch-making new insights of the great religious founders, necessarily occurred in the transformation of individuals, but not directly of society. This was true of Gautama Buddha. The wider social fruits of individual enlightenment would come only as more and more people came to live in the spirit of compassion (feeling with and for others) that it produced. But Gautama himself did not seek to lay down rules for the governance of society beyond the *Sangha*, the community of monks and nuns.

The Buddha did, however, criticise on religious grounds the caste system of Indian society, the four main castes (each with many sub-castes) being the brahmins, nobles, merchants and workers. In Discourse 93 of the *Mijjhima Nikaya* there is a dialogue between Gautama and a brahmin (or brahman) representative, sent to ask if he really does, as reputed, deny the superiority of the brahmins and teach the equality of the four castes. As always, Gautama uses the Socratic method, beginning 'What do you think about this, Assalayana?' He asks concerning each of the four castes in turn, if one of their members 'made onslaught on creatures, took what had not been given, wrongly enjoyed pleasures of the senses, were a liar, of slanderous speech, of harsh speech, a gossip, malevolent in mind, of wrong view', would they 'at the breaking up of the body after dying arise in the sorrowful way', that is, in a lower world? The answer is Yes, and the same for each of the other castes. And so Gautama asks, 'In reference to this then, Assalayana, on what

authority do the brahmans say, "Only brahmans form the best caste?"'
(Horner 1957, 342). And in the end Asalayana comes to see that, by the
practical test which they all recognise, people of the different castes are
all equal.

To a significant though limited extent we see a social application
of Buddhist principles in the policies of the emperor Ashoka, third
emperor of India in the Maura dynasty, who reigned for 36 years some
two centuries after the death of Gautama. Having waged a bloody and
destructive war and been shocked by it's carnage and devastation, he
resolved to renounce violent conquests (without, however, disbanding
his army), and converted to Buddhism. His Edicts, carved on rocks,
require an equal respect for all the religions within his empire. In the
Edicts Ashoka is referred to by the honorific title Beloved-of-the-Gods,
and the twelfth of the Fourteen Rock Edicts reads:

> Beloved-of-the-Gods honors both ascetics and the householders [lay
> people] of all religions ... Beloved-of-the-Gods does not value gifts
> and honors as much as he values this – that there should be growth
> in the essentials of all religions. Growth in essentials can be done
> in different ways, but all have as their root restraint in speech, that
> is, not praising one's religion, or condemning the religion of others
> without good cause. And if there is cause for criticism, it should be
> done in a mild way. It is better to honor other religions for this reason.
> By so doing, one's own religion benefits, and so do other religions,
> while doing otherwise harms one's own religion and the religions
> of others. Whoever praises his own religion, due to excessive devo-
> tion, and condemns others with the thought 'Let me glorify my own
> religion', only harms his own religion. Therefore contact (between
> religions) is good. One should listen to and respect the doctrines
> professed by others. Beloved-of-the-Gods desires that all should be
> well-versed in the good doctrines of other religions. (Dhammika
> [trans.] 1993)

He did, however, encourage the Buddhist missionary movement outside
his realm, the Theravada Buddhism of Sri Lanka being a result. Ashoka
showed a genuine concern for the welfare of his subjects, instituting
a more humane legal system (though stopping short of abolishing the
death penalty), providing free medical aid, and having banyan trees
planted for shade, mango groves, and watering places and shelters along
the trade routes to make travel easier. In the last of the Seven Pillar
Edicts he calls for 'harmlessness to living beings and non-killing of living

beings'. In various Edicts this includes animals. In the third Rock Edict there is provision for medical treatment of animals as well as humans. The fifth of the Minor Rock Edicts lists a number of species that are not to be killed, including parrots, wild ducks, squirrels, deer and bulls, but in the seventh Edict it is added that 'The Dhamma regulations that I have given are that various animals are to be protected. But it is by persuasion that progress among the people through Dhamma has had a greater effect in respect of harmlessness to living beings and non-killing of living beings.' There has, however, been dispute as to whether the non-killing principle, applied to animals as well as humans, was a deliberate ban on animal sacrifices which 'must therefore be seen as a massive blow to the Brahmans' (Schmidt-Leukel 2004, 49) or not (Basham 1987, 468).

The present Dalai Lama, though prevented by the Chinese occupation of Tibet from influencing the governance of his own country, exhibits the same impartial concern for all, and in traditional Buddhist mode advocates changing the world by changing the minds and hearts of its inhabitants. 'Human history', he says, 'is in a way the history of human mental thought . . . Tragedy, tyranny, all the terrible wars, all those negative things have happened because of negative human thought . . . World peace must develop out of inner peace' (Dalai Lama 1990, 102–3). He is here following the teaching of the Buddha. There is a Sutta in the *Majjhima Nikaya* (no. 56) in which Gautama is debating with an adherent of the Jain religion about which is the most evil element in a wicked deed: is it evil action, evil speech, or evil thought? The Jain maintains that the action itself is worst; and here many in the modern world would agree with him. Gautama, in contrast, maintains that it is the evil thought that is most important. For evil speech and evil actions flow from evil thoughts, and if there were no evil thoughts there would be no evil speech or evil actions.[5]

What, however, about the much larger institutional evils in national societies and in the global society? These include both the economic structures within a country that result in extremes of wealth and poverty, and today the global north–south divide in which the economic policies of the rich nations often undermine the economic development of the poor countries; the failure to moderate a consumption of energy that causes the global warming which threatens future generations; the suppression in too many countries of basic human rights. Are these evils susceptible to the Buddhist approach of seeking to address hearts and minds and thereby change human attitudes? I would say that in the long run this is the only hope for humanity, but that more immediately all forms of direct action by governments and individuals to persuade the nations of the earth to co-operate in sane long-term policies are also imperative.

For Jesus, as for Gautama, the immediate fruits were individual rather than political. In his case there were two reasons for this. One was that, like Gautama, he lacked political power and responsibility; and the other was that he seems to have expected an early divine intervention to end the present age and establish God's rule in a transformed world. The Kingdom was finally to come on earth, and his hearers were living in the last days ('Truly, I say to you, there are some standing here who will not taste death before they see that the Kingdom of God has come with power', Mark 9:1). This was linked in the mind of the Church with Jesus' own second coming in triumph as the Messiah to rule over his Kingdom.

However, unlike Gautama, Jesus' preaching of the imminent inbreaking of the Kingdom of God had the political implication that Roman rule would soon end, and with it the power of Rome's clients, the puppet government and the Jerusalem priesthood. This seems to have been the cause of his execution as a politically dangerous charismatic preacher in the sensitive moment of a Passover season in Jerusalem. In the course of Paul's letters we see the expectation of the second coming gradually fading as the End receded further and further into the future. It was only after the conversion of Constantine in the fourth century that Christianity began to wield a decisive influence as the religion of the Roman empire, the Church gradually becoming an integral part of the imperial power structure. But Jesus himself, believing that the present age was about to be ended by a dramatic divine intervention, never needed to think about the practicalities and inevitable compromises, the judicious balancing of differing interests, the commercial regulations, the definition of crimes and laying down of penalties, which the governance of nations requires.

Although many present-day Christians in the West assume that Jesus preached our modern liberal democratic values, much of his teaching belonged to a radically different cultural world and is either problematic, or at best ambiguous, when brought forward into our world today. His teaching as relayed in the Gospels contains a great deal that is permanently challenging, inspiring, uplifting and universally relevant – particularly the moral teachings collected in the Sermon on the Mount in chapters 5–7 of Matthew's Gospel. But his teaching also contains much that we have tacitly to ignore. The modern preacher, whether consciously or unconsciously, uses the New Testament selectively. For Jesus did not support democracy (which did not exist and naturally he never mentioned); or the sanctity of family life (the bonds of family were superseded by his message – e.g., Matthew 12:46–50, 10:37; Mark 3:31–5); or a liberation theology of resistance to oppressive rule (he said 'Render to Caesar the things that are Caesar's', Matthew 22:21); or the abolition of world poverty (he told a rich young man to 'sell what you possess and give to the poor', Matthew 19:21, on the assumption that 'you always have the poor with you', Matthew 26:11); or even an unambiguously universal divine love (he says, according to Mark, that he taught in a way that many could not receive so that they 'may indeed hear but not understand; lest they should turn again, and be forgiven', Mark 4:12); and his teaching was full (particularly according to Matthew's Gospel) of threats of a purely punitive, rather than reformative, torment for the wicked after death (e.g., Matthew 8:12, 11: 20–4, 13:41, etc.), and, particularly in John's less historically reliable Gospel, that all who do not believe in him were damned (e.g., 'He who believes in the Son has eternal life; he who does not obey the Son shall not see life, but the wrath of God rests upon him', John 3:36. See 6:46, 8:24). There are, however, also different and conflicting sayings to offset some of these, so that in practice most of us in the churches today take from Jesus' teaching what we regard as valuable while leaving aside whatever does not fit our modern liberal democratic principles or our ideal picture of Jesus as universal love incarnate.[6]

In his lack of the need to be concerned about the governance of society Jesus' situation was like Gautama's but quite unlike that of Muhammad in seventh-century CE Arabia. Here the new religion began as a reform movement attacking the existing polytheism and proclaiming a strict monotheism. However, this had serious commercial and political implications for the merchants, and for the priesthoods with their system of sacrifices, which attracted caravans of pilgrimages and trade to Mecca, thereby provoking powerful resistance by the Meccan establishment. As a result the new faith, originally based on the suras revealed in Mecca before the emigration to Medina, inevitably developed into a new state, based in Medina and then again in Mecca after Muhammad's triumphant return there. And so in the Medinan suras, revealed within an existing organized Muslim community, there are many detailed rules for the ordering of social life. Likewise the Judaism of the Torah, with its 613 mitzvot, laws for the details of daily life, was always directly concerned with the shape of society; and the message of some of the great prophets also carried profound and challenging political implications. Christianity was different in that Judaism and Islam were involved almost from the beginning in regulating the life of society, whereas

Christianity only became politically involved after several centuries. Today, in another very different historical situation, the New Testament teachings of Jesus are widely used to promote the modern humane liberal agenda of reducing world poverty and the great gap between the living standards of the developed north and the developing south, seeking to establish basic human rights and freedoms, opposing the destructive corporate greed of the arms and tobacco industries, working to preserve the earth's atmosphere against the global warming caused by the lavish waste of energy in the richest countries. All this can be said to be in the spirit of Jesus' teaching but transferred into a very different world.

In this new situation we see the emergence of the phenomenon of the 'political saint'. By a saint, or mahatma (great soul), I do not of course mean a perfect human being, for there have never been any – if indeed the idea of a perfect human being is a coherent concept – but a man or woman who has to a great extent transcended self-concern so as to embody, incarnate, to a significant degree the universal values of unselfish love or compassion for others, which create human harmony and enable human fulfilment. During the pre-democratic centuries, when power was concentrated in the hands of emperors, kings, local barons and war lords, saintly individuals typically lived in monasteries and nunneries or in solitary hermitages, and were not involved in the affairs of their nation. If they were activists, like St Benedict, or St Teresa, their efforts were directed to reform within the Church. In the case, however, of some of the great Hindu reformers, their teaching transcended, and thereby undermined, the caste system. Thus Kabir in the fifteenth century CE wrote:

> It is needless to ask of a saint the caste to which he belongs;
> For the priest, the warrior, the tradesman, and all the thirty-six castes are seeking for God.
> It is but folly to ask what the caste of a saint may be;
> The barber has sought God, the washer-woman, and the carpenter . . .
> Hindus and Moslems alike have achieved that End, where remains no mark of distinction. (Kabir 1977, 45–6)

But with the greater spread of political power and responsibility, saints (including some but by no means all of those canonised by the Catholic Church) or mahatmas have emerged whose faith has drawn them directly into the life of the world. The greatest of these has been

Mahatma Gandhi, and the subsequent list includes Vinoba Bhave in India, Martin Luther King in the USA, Tich Nhat Hanh in Thailand, archbishop Oscar Romero in El Salvador, archbishop Helda Camara in Brazil, Dag Hammerskjold in Sweden and the United Nations, Nelson Mandela and Desmond Tutu in South Africa. These are only some of those who have made a mark in history, and there are innumerable other 'ordinary' men and women who devote themselves in organised ways to countering the effects, and attacking the causes, of third-world poverty and the degradation of the environment, and to supporting the cause of the oppressed and the unjustly imprisoned and tortured. While the spirituality of the solitary individual and of the enclosed community continue to make a necessary but invisible contribution to the welfare of the world, typically today the fruits of the religious way of experiencing life, whether or not expressed in religious terms, are to be found in dedicated social action.

The conclusion to all this is that the universal criterion of the authenticity of religious experience consists in its moral and spiritual fruits in human life. It is by their fruits that you will know them. This fact distinguishes a global recognition of the significance of religious experience from a moral relativism which requires and indeed permits no criterion of authenticity.

Part II

5
The Neurosciences' Challenge to Religious Experience

The contemporary naturalistic world-view

What is the connection between the work of the neuroscientists, studying the internal architecture and workings of the brain, and the thesis of this book, namely, that religious experience (with all the important distinctions and qualifications in Chapter 4 and to come) can rationally be accepted, by those who participate in it, as awareness of a transcendent reality or realities?

We need first to be aware of the naturalistic world-view which dominates modern Western thought and that rules out the possibility of any such supposed realities. This is present as an unquestioned assumption in innumerable remarks by influential scientists. For example, 'On the one hand our lives seem so important – with all those cherished highly personal memories – and yet we *know* [my italics] that in the cosmic scheme of things, our brief existence amounts to nothing at all' (Ramachandran 1998, 176). That we *know* this should, in the ordinary use of know, mean either that it is self-evident or that we have compelling reason to believe it. But it is not self-evident, and we have no compelling reason to believe it; its status is that of a fundamental article of faith.[1] It is the prevailing uncriticised assumption, or background paradigm, within the scientific community and hence the general public. Indeed the philosopher John Searle, himself a materialist, says that 'There is a sense in which materialism is the religion of our time, at least among most of the professional experts in the fields of philosophy, psychology, cognitive science, and other disciplines that study the mind' (Searle 2004, 38). In contrast, Steven Rose, Director of the Brain and Behaviour Research Unit at the Open University UK, thinks that the same scientific community is 'still trapped within the mechanistic reductionist mind-set within which our science has been formed' (Rose 2005, 215). But mind-sets, pervasive assumptions – we do not see them, but see everything through them – have changed over the centuries and will continue to change in the future. Even today those for whom the naturalistic faith is their default position do not include anything like all humans or all modern Westerners or even all modern Western scientists.

In relation to the mind/brain issue there are both a hard, or materialist, version of naturalism according to which the universe – in the sense of all that is – consists exclusively of matter, and also the soft naturalism which recognises the existence of a non-physical consciousness which reflects but, however, has no influence over the matter constituting our brains. The challenge to religious experience of the neurosciences can presuppose either hard or soft materialism and is compatible with both, and both will be examined here. In the present chapter we are looking at the materialist, or physicalist, version.

The physicists' conception of matter is developing all the time, the solid 'billiard ball' atoms of the nineteenth century having long since been superseded by molecules, congregations of atoms each consisting of protons and neutrons and a cloud of electrons, down to quarks; and the whole system possibly ultimately consisting of the mysterious entities called 'strings' – a metaphor, for when they come to most funda-mental issues the physicists today speak largely in either mathemat-ical or metaphorical terms. But materialist naturalism does not depend upon whatever may eventually turn out to be the definitive analysis of matter – if we ever have one. For it is the view that the physical or material universe, however composed, constitutes the totality of reality. In its application to the mind/brain issue this view is advocated by the philosopher Daniel Dennett:

> The idea of mind as distinct . . . from the brain, composed not of ordinary matter, but of some other, special kind of stuff, is dualism, and it is deservedly in disrepute today . . . The prevailing wisdom, variously expressed and argued for, is *materialism*: there is only one sort of stuff, namely matter – the physical stuff of physics, chemistry, and physiology – and the mind is somehow nothing but a physical phenomenon. In short, the mind is the brain. (Dennett 1991, 33, italics in original).

And the same assumption prevails among very many, indeed most, of the relevant scientists. To quote Rose again, 'for many neuroscientists, to ask how the brain works is equivalent to asking how the mind works, because they take almost for granted that the human mind is somehow embodied within the 1500 grams of densely packed cells and connections that constitute the brain' (Rose 2005, 2).

The seventeenth-century philosopher René Descartes, who advocated a mind/body dualism, is seen as the great misleader who took a disastrously wrong turning at the beginning of the modern period, only corrected in the twentieth century. In 1949 Gilbert Ryle in his at one time much-discussed book, *The Concept of Mind*, caricatured Descartes's dualism as 'the dogma of the Ghost in the Machine' (Ryle 1949, 15–16); and a stream of subsequent writing is typified by the title of a book by the neurologist Antonio Damasio, *Descartes' Error*. In correcting Descartes's supposed error, mind/brain identity rules out a God or gods, a transpersonal Brahman or Dharmakaya or Tao, the survival of human consciousness beyond bodily death, and realms of existence other than the physical universe. And, closer to home, it entails that the successive moments of human consciousness, including those modifications of consciousness that constitute religious experience, are identical with the electro-chemical activity of the brain, which is in turn part of the seamless causal continuity of the natural world.

The connection of the mind/brain identity theory with religion and religious experience is put comprehensively by the science writer Rita Carter, 'Either mind/consciousness/God – call it what you will – is at the root of all things OR matter goes right down to the bottom and mind is just some special physical state or process' (Carter 2002, 44). For, as she says, 'Anyone who accepts the classic materialist model as a complete and accurate description of reality is forced, if they think about it, to take the [mind/brain identity] view' (Ibid., 44). Her book describing the workings of the brain is accordingly called *Mapping the Mind* (1998).

Religious materialism?

Carter is right to hold that a consistent materialism is incompatible with any belief in a transcendent divine reality. Despite this, some writers nevertheless try to put a religious gloss on it. There are recent books whose titles suggest that they are defending religion but which assume a physicalist understanding of the mind. Some now speak of neurotheology. For example in *Why God Won't Go Away* by the neurophysiologists Andrew Newberg and Eugene d'Aquili, the God who won't go away is the *idea* of God produced by various states of the brain. Concerning the mind/brain relationship, they say that 'brain creates mind, and the

two are essentially the same entity, seen from different points of view'
(Newberg and d'Aquili 2001, 34. See also d'Aquili and Newberg 1999).

At first sight paradoxically, some theologians also endorse this physicalist view – on the ground that the Judaic-Christian tradition conceives
of the human person as an indissoluble body/mind unity – expressed
in the Bible in such ideas as the future bodily resurrection of the dead
and of 'a new heaven and a new earth' to be inhabited by transformed embodied souls; and at the popular level in pictures of heaven
or paradise, purgatory and hell. Medieval Christian artists let their
imaginations run riot in their paintings of the day of judgement, with
the damned being hauled down to hell by the devil and his cohorts.
Dante's *The Divine Comedy* begins in hell, and Milton's *Paradise Lost* likewise has an unforgettable picture of the fallen angels in their damned
state, all necessarily in bodily form. This conception of an indissoluble
mind/body unity is indeed extensively present in the Hebrew scriptures,
the Old Testament, though in the New Testament the contrary idea
of St Paul, the earliest and most influential of all Christian thinkers,
emerges. Referring to the future general resurrection of the dead he
says, 'It is sown a physical body, it is raised a spiritual body. If there
is a physical body, there is also a spiritual body... Flesh and blood
cannot inherit the kingdom of God' (1 Corinthians 15:44 and 50). Both
strands of thought have continued, unreconciled, through Christian
history to the present day. But even if the body/soul unity assumed
in most of the Old Testament, and continued in a major strand of
Christian thought, is granted it does not make the claims of either
Christianity or any other major faith compatible with physicalist naturalism. For neither the Western nor the Eastern traditions hold that
the ultimate reality, whether God, Brahman, the Tao, etc. is a *physical*
entity. (The Hindu philosopher Ramanuja's idea of the world as the
body of God may possibly, depending on the way it is understood,
constitute a quasi-exception.) The materialist dogma that nothing exists
but matter therefore has no place for any non-material ultimate reality,
except as a figment of the human imagination. It remains the case that
materialistic naturalism is radically incompatible with all of the great
world religions. The same is also true, as we shall see later, of 'soft'
naturalism.

Brain to consciousness causality

We are all familiar today with the fact that the human brain, with
its estimated hundred billion nerve cells, is the most complex object

in the universe as known to us. During the last fifty or so years the study of the brain has proliferated into a range of neurosciences – neurobiology now embraces neurophysiology, neuroendocrinology, neuropharacogenetics, neuropharmacology, psychometrics, producing neurotechnologies and connecting with the growing neurogenetic industry, leading to neuroeconomics and neuroethics.

Research has made tremendous advances in mapping the functions of different areas of the brain. This has been made possible by the electroencephalogram (EEG) and more recently by positron-emission tomography (PET), single photon emission computer tomography (SPECT) and yet other methods of scan. All this, and other procedures, has revealed a great deal – though what is unknown remains vastly greater than what is thus far known. The agreed large-scale finding is that of the four lobes of the cerebrum the occipital lobe is concerned with visual processing, the parietal lobe with movement, orientation, calculation and certain kinds of recognition, the temporal lobe with sound, speech, comprehension and some aspects of memory, and the frontal lobes with thinking, conceptualising and planning. There has of course been much more minute mapping than this, although the details do not concern us at this point. But while discovering the function of increasingly precise neural locations the neurophysiologists also stress that the mass action of relatively large areas of the brain is necessary for these more localised performances. For example, different aspects of an object, such as its shape, its colour, its motion, are initially registered in different areas of the brain and then coordinated in another area to produce our actual conscious awareness of the object. So the brain functions as a living whole, although within its total activity different areas specialise in different tasks.

Mood can also be shown to have its basis in the brain. As a dramatic example, surgeons applied a tiny electric current to a particular part of a patient's left brain while trying to locate the seat of her intractable epileptic seizures. She was conscious, and as the stimulus passed through a particular part of her cortex she started to laugh, and when they asked her what was so amusing she had no answer. They applied the current again and this time she suddenly saw something comic in an ordinary picture on the wall, a picture of a horse (Fried 1988, 650). So there is a part of the brain which, when stimulated, produces the conscious state of being amused.

But how does the brain produce the moments of consciousness that constitute religious experience? There are several possible ways.

One is by the fact that drugs can alter the chemistry of the brain. There are many undisputed examples. In a number of British and North American schools today there are a large number of children aged between about six and sixteen whose behaviour is sometimes barely controllable and even sometimes violent – apparently from 5 to 10 per cent of the age group. The labels Attention Deficit Disorder and Attention Deficit Hyperactivity Disorder have been invented for these behavioural problems. And a medically prescribed drug, Ritalin (methylphenidate), has been found to calm these children down, enabling them to concentrate better and so be less easily distracted from their school work. This is a clear case of chemicals directly affecting mental states and hence behaviour. Again, millions of people take Valium to banish or reduce a chronic state of depression, caused in some cases by a lack of serotonin in the brain. Popularly used 'recreational' drugs produce a 'high' which can be a temporary state of all-consuming euphoria. Some cannabis users report that when the drug is used by a group, individual concerns disappear to be replaced by a warm mutual affection. However, research is not yet conclusive on the important question whether cannabis can have long-term harmful effects on the brain, either for all or more likely for some particularly vulnerable category of users, and if so which and in what degree. In the case of the much more powerful ecstacy (MDMA) and cocaine, damaging long-term physiological effects are well established (see e.g. Austin 1999, 424). (Likewise excessive use of alcohol can irreversibly damage the liver, and nicotine the lungs.)

Back in the nineteenth century a number of scientists and philosophers experimented with nitrous oxide (N_2O) and William James famously reported on his own experience after inhaling it. He said that it can

> stimulate the mystical consciousness to an extraordinary degree. Depth upon depth of truth seems revealed to the inhaler. This truth fades out, however, or escapes, at the moment of coming to; and if any words remain over in which it seemed to clothe itself, they prove to be the veriest nonsense. Neverthless, the sense of a profound meaning having been there persists. (James 1979, 373)

And in a fuller account elsewhere of his own experience James tells how during his intoxications he wrote furiously, sheet after sheet of phrases 'which to the sober reader seem meaningless drivel, but which at the moment of transcribing were fused in the fire of infinite rationality'

(James, quoted by Austin 1999, 408). Here, then, is another example of the chemistry of a gas – another is carbon dioxide (CO_2) – temporarily changing the state of the brain so as to produce a form of 'religious' experience; and one which we can see in these cases to have been delusory.

But most of the published work on the cognitive and emotional effects of drugs, directly relevant to religious experience, took place in the 1950s and 60s before their use became illegal in the United States and Europe except for narrowly defined therapeutic purposes. In that earlier period such well-known psychologists as Charles Tart, influential writers including Aldous Huxley, Rosalind Heywood, Raymond Mortimer, the authority on mysticism R. C. Zaehner, the authority on world religions Ray Jordan, and a number of others reported on their own experiments with these drugs or carefullly discussed the reports of others.

Ray Jordan, for example, experimented with LSD (which can take effect in doses as small as 25–50 micrograms) and described his experience:

> I have realized that quite literally everything is Self, everything in the whole field of experience – both what is usually known as self and all that usually is not self (people, objects, sky, earth, etc.). This Self, which is everything is not the same as the ego-self. It is not that I, Ray Jordan, am everything, but that there is a more fundamental self which is everything, including Ray Jordan.

Again, in a different but related experience, ' "I" and "other" have become correlative existences, neither of which could be isolated but both of which interact interdependently' (Jordan 1972, 284–5). The first of these descriptions corresponds to aspects of advaitic Hindu, and the latter to aspects of some kinds of Buddhist, experience. The common feature in all these cases is ego-transcendence, something that is basic in some form to all the world great religions.

Returning to more precise scientific evidence, and following up the work of Hans Kornhuber and Luder Deecke in the 1960s, Benjamin Libet's much-discussed experiments in the early 1970s are relevant at this point. He found that in an experimental situation in which the subject is asked arbitrarily to chose a moment to perform a simple flick of the wrist, the time of the conscious decision being identified by the subject from a rapidly moving arm on a dial, some cerebral activity (the 'readiness potential') occurs approximately half a second (on average 550 msec.) *before* the conscious decision. Clearly this, by itself, would show that the brain activity caused the conscious decision, which is thus a delayed epiphenomenon of the brain activity. Rather than commenting on this here I shall return to it in Chapter 8.

God and the limbic system

This is the title of one of the chapters in Ramachandran's fascinating *Phantoms in the Brain*. The limbic system constitutes a large area of the brain within which it has long been known that temporal lobe epileptic seizures can cause some patients to experience vivid hallucinations, including hearing voices and seeing visions, sometimes of a religious nature. When the chaotic firing of a region of neurons expands to a certain point the patient may fall to the ground with muscles contracting in spasm – the 'grand mal' seizure. But epileptic seizures can be much more local within the brain and still often cause strong emotional reverberations. The nature of the emotional response can be anywhere within a wide range – elation and ecstasy, rage, terror and despair.

> But most remarkable of all are those patients who have deeply moving spiritual experiences, including a feeling of divine presence and the sense that they are in direct communion with God. Everything around them is imbued with cosmic significance. They may say, 'I finally understand what it's all about. This is the moment I've been waiting for all my life. Suddenly it all makes sense'. Or, 'Finally I have insight into the true nature of the cosmos'. (Ramachandran 1998, 179)

One researcher reports a patient 'whose seizures consisted of feelings of detachment, ineffable contentment, and fulfilment; visualizing a bright light recognized as the source of knowledge; and sometimes visualizing a bearded young man resembling Jesus Christ' (cited by Newberg and D'Aquili 2001, 444) – that is, Jesus Christ as traditionally imagined in Christian art, for no one knows what the historical individual looked like.

However, Dr Michael Persinger has reported that, without any epileptic seizure, by stimulating this same area, 'Typically people report a presence. One time we had a strobe light going and this individual actually saw Christ in the strobe. [Another] experienced God visiting her. Afterwards we looked at her ECG and there was this classic spike and slow-wave seizure over the temporal lobe at the precise time of the experience' (Persinger 1995). It seems, then, that the stimulation of the temporal lobe can produce in some people a sense of divine presence. Persinger has developed a helmet (a transcranial magnetic stimulator) to enable the researcher to stimulate this area, and Rita Carter reports that 'nearly all who have used it report the sensation of a presence. Many also see religious visions such as the Virgin Mary or Jesus' (Carter 2002, 288). She adds that 'Such storms may also be triggered by lack of oxygen or glucose (e.g., when the brain is exhausted or traumatized) or when a state of high anxiety suddenly gives way to one of relief. This may explain why people often "find God" at moments of crisis' (Ibid.).

All this has suggested to some that epileptic seizures in the temporal lobe, causing powerful hallucinations, may account for such major religious experiences as Jesus at his baptism seeing 'the spirit of God descending like a dove, and alighting on him; and lo, a voice from heaven, saying, "This is my beloved Son, with whom I am well pleased" ' (Matthew 3:16–17); or St Paul's experience on the Damascus Road in which he saw a blinding light and 'fell on the ground and heard a voice saying "Saul, Saul, why do you persecute me?" . . . And he said, "I am Jesus, whom you are persecuting . . . " ' (Acts 9:3–5); or St Teresa's or Julian of Norwich's and many other mystics' visions and auditions. Again, 'Some of these diagnoses suggest, for example, that the Prophet Mohammed, who heard voices, saw visions, and sweated profusely during his mystical interludes, may have suffered from a complex partial seizure' (Newberg and d'Aquili 2001, 111). And so the question is asked, are God and the religious significance of life products of local brain malfunctions?

Meditation and the brain

Other kinds of religious experience have also been studied by neurophysiologists. One such experience is the sense of self-transcendence in meditation. Newberg conducted experiments with eight advanced Tibetan Buddhist monks[2] whose brain activity he monitored during deep meditation with SPECT scans which detect the location of a radioactive tracer injected into the blood to show any increase or decrease of blood supply and hence of oxygen in different areas of the brain, indicating increased or decreased activity.

In the Tibetan monks there was an increased activity in the frontal lobe where the focussing of attention takes place. At the same time the amygdala (within the limbic system), the neural seat of anxiety and fear, became inactive. The monks were in a calm, serene and unstressed state.

A common aspect of meditation, when it reaches a certain point, is the sense that one is not an isolated unit but an integral part of a greater reality which both includes and transcends the immediate physical environment. Newberg and d'Aquili believe that they have discovered its neural cause. Towards the upper rear of the brain is the posterior superior parietal lobe whose function is to orient us in space. 'To perform this crucial function, it must first generate a clear, consistent cognition of the physical limitations of the self... it must draw a sharp distinction between the individual and everything else' (Newberg and d'Aquili 2001, 5). At the high point of the Tibetan monks' meditation there was a distinct decrease of activity in this area. Newberg's suggestion is that in the state of 'higher consciousness' this spatial orientation area is disconnected, intense concentration on the breathing having blocked it's normal input of sensory information. He asks,

> Would the orientation area interpret its failure to find the borderline between the self and the outside world to mean that such a distinction doesn't exist? In that case the brain would have no choice but to perceive that the self is endless and intimately interwoven with everyone and everything the mind senses. And this perception would feel utterly and unquestionably real. (Ibid., 6)

As Carter summarises, 'In meditation... the attention mechanism remains on, and in the absence of other things to illuminate, it latches on – if you like – to its own workings. In other words, "pure consciousness" is not exactly consciousness of nothing but consciousness of consciousness – the brain listening to itself' (Carter 2002, 288).

This 'self-transcending' effect, Newberg suggests, can occur in varying degrees:

> At low levels, this blockage results in mild unitary sensations, such as the feeling of unity and common inspiration shared by worshippers in a moving religious service. As we move along the continuum we find a progression of increasingly intense unitary states, characterized by feelings of spiritual awe and rapture. Where prolonged and rigorous rituals are involved, trance states may occur, featuring moments of ecstasy and hyperlucid visions. And at the farthest end of the continuum, where deafferentation would be most advanced, we

find the profound states of spiritual union that have been described for us by the mystics. (Ibid., 116)

Using the same monitoring procedure on several Franciscan nuns at prayer, Newberg and d'Aquili recorded similar neurological changes, but with a quite different conscious outcome.

[They] tended to describe this moment as a tangible sense of the closeness of God and a mingling with Him. Their accounts echoed those of Christian mystics in the past, including that of thirteenth-century Franciscan sister Angela of Foligno: 'How great is the mercy of the one who realized this union . . . I possessed God so fully that I was no longer in my previous customary state but was led to find a peace in which I was united with God and was content with everything'. (Ibid., 7)

And there are innumerable other similar accounts by Christian, Muslim and Hindu mystics of this type of experience.

Further hypotheses can be drawn in to fill out a more comprehensive naturalistic account of religious experience.

Concerning the sense of a divine, or angelic, or demonic presence, Persinger suggests that the sense of presence may occur when 'assymetrical temporal lobe hyperactivity separates the sense of self into two – one twin in each hemisphere. The dominant (usually left) hemisphere then interprets the other part of the self as an "other" lurking around outside' (Carter 2002, 290). This can be either good or evil, God or the devil. Persinger suggests that right hemisphere stimulation is associated with a sense of fear or dread, while stimulation of the left inhibits this – hence the presence of a benevolent being. The sense of presence then, he suggests, consists in a part of the left hemisphere of the brain being conscious of a corresponding part of the right hemisphere as a separate entity.

Putting a cluster of hypotheses together, Rita Carter summarises a comprehensive neurophysiological explanation of religious experience:

There seems, then, to be a plausible mechanistic account for each of the core qualities of mystical or spiritual experience. Put very crudely: 'pure' consciousness emerges when a tension is maintained in a perceptual vacuum; 'oneness' is created by the close-down of the 'boundary-making' parts of the self; ecstasy comes from turning off the right amygdala; and the sense of presence is formed by the splitting of the self system into two. (Carter 2002, 290)

The proposed – but as we shall see, contested – challenges of the neurosciences to religious experience can now be listed:

1. Epileptic seizures and frontal lobe stimulation by the 'Persinger helmet' cause religious visions.
2. Psychotropic drugs cause various forms of religious experience.
3. 'Pure' consciousness, consciousness of the Void, Emptiness, *sunyata*, is caused by consciousness continuing after the cutting off of all perceptual input.
4. The sense of unity with all reality is caused by closing down the awareness of the bodily boundaries of the individual.
5. The sense of the presence of God or of other supernatural beings is caused by a splitting of the 'self-system' into two, one half seeing the other half as a distinct entity.

All this constitutes a serious case for holding, in accord with the naturalistic philosophy, that religious experience is caused by entirely natural processes and is entirely – even if no doubt some times benignly – delusory.

6
Caveats and Questions

Religious experience as mental aberration

We must distinguish, first, between the kind of cases Ramachandran is discussing and the quite different kind studied by Newberg and others in their experiments with the Tibetan monks and other religious meditators. The monks are outstanding examples of authentically religious people; and what the experiments show is that it may well be possible to identify the neural correlates of their mystical states. In contrast, Ramachandran is a practising physician as well as an experimental neurophysiologist and is reporting on patients who have been referred to him for diagnosis and treatment of various kinds of abnormal and disabling conditions. But in the case of the very large majority of people who have had some kind of religious experience, significant enough for them to remember and record it – at least 30 per cent of the population[1] – we have no reason at all to think that any larger percentage of them than of the population as a whole has suffered from psychological or neurological abnormalities, and there is some evidence that the proportion is lower. These are not generally the kind of people who are most likely to come to the attention of a neurologist or psychiatrist.

It is important to establish this before coming specifically to God and the limbic system. For there are many sources for the view that there is no significant correlation between religious experiences and mental illness.

We should note first that outstanding religious experiencers, if they have lived in the public world, have very often been notably effective men and women. As W. R. Inge says, 'all the great mystics have been energetic and influential, and their business capacity is specially noted in a curiously large number of cases' (Inge 1899, xi). Teresa of Avila, as

I mentioned earlier, reformed a branch of the Carmelite convents and created 17 new ones. Ignatius Loyala created the Jesuit order. Catherine of Genoa was matron of a large hospital; Plotinus, St John of the Cross, Fenelon and Madame Guyon all showed considerable administrative abilities. Meister Eckhart was Provincial of the Dominican Order in Saxony and a professor at Cologne. The neuroscientist James Austin,[2] researching extensively into the neurophysiology of Zen experience, and basing his studies on a wide knowledge of the technical literature as well as his own direct observations, says that the ego, in the sense of 'each person's capacity to deal confidently with life in a mature, realistic, matter-of-fact way' is strengthened, not diminished, in the 'no-self' state that can be achieved by Zen meditation (Austin 1999, 35), and my own very limited experience has shown me that the roshis (Zen masters) whom I have encountered in Japan have been exceptionally powerful personalities. The Sikh mystic, Kushdeva Singh, whom I knew in Patiala in the Punjab, served his community selflessly as a commanding figure with great achievements which made him widely respected.[3] The Dalai Lama has been a continual influence in favour of world peace, of compassionate dealings between peoples, and of non-violent conflict resolution. Another Buddhist, the Zen monk Thich Nhat Hanh, has been a notable activist working for peace and social justice in Thailand.[4] The Truth and Reconciliation Commission in South Africa, conceived by Nelson Mandela and carried through with great patience and wisdom by Archbishop Desmond Tutu, has been an inspiring example of a new approach to reconciliation in the wake of profound and prolonged injustice.[5]

More broadly David Hay, commenting on the findings of several surveys of reported religious experiences, says that 'those who report religious experiences are more likely than others to be in a good state of psychological well-being . . . all the evidence to date suggests that those reporting religious experience are, if anything, more adequate psychologically than others' (Hay 1990, 57, 89).[6] This is endorsed by Newberg and d'Aquili who, despite their naturalistic understanding of religion, suggest that it has arisen because evolution 'has favored the religious capabilities of the religious brain because religious beliefs and behaviors turn out to be good for us in profound and pragmatic ways' (Newberg and D'Aquili 2001, 129). They say:

> A considerable body of research tells us this is true. Studies have shown that men and women who practice any mainstream faith live longer, have fewer strokes, less heart disease, better immune

system function, and lower blood pressure than the population at large.[7] ... Religion, it seems, is at least as good for the body as it may be for the soul, but the health benefits of religious behaviors do not end with physiology; a growing body of research is making it clear that religion can also be linked to superior mental health. This idea comes as a surprise to much of the modern psychiatric community that, still following in the footsteps of Freud, has long regarded religious behavior at best, as a dependent state and at worst, a pathological condition. Until 1994, for example, the American Psychiatric Association officially classified 'strong religious belief' as a mental disorder. New data, however, indicates that religious beliefs and practices can improve mental and emotional health in several significant ways. For example, research [referring to the sources cited in n. 7] shows that rates of drug abuse, alcoholism, divorce, and suicide are much lower among religious individuals than the population at large. It also seems clear that people who practice religion are much less likely to suffer from depression and anxiety than the population at large, and that they recover more quickly when they do. Other experiments have linked specific religious activities to positive psychological results; spiritual practices such as meditation, prayer, or participation in devotional services, have been shown to reduce feelings of anxiety and depression significantly, boost self-esteem, improve the quality of interpersonal relationships, and generate a more positive outlook on life. (Newberg and D'Aquili 2001, 129–30).

While there is reason to believe that this is broadly true, its causes may be various. The religious population on which most of this research is based is a rather limited sample – middle-class Americans who are accessible to researchers and respond to questionnaires. And while it is evident that to belong to the local community of a friendly church, synagogue, mosque, temple or vihara is emotionally helpful and conducive to psychological stability, the same will also be true of dedicated participation in the work of a political party or being part of a group of friends meeting regularly in a pub or as keen enthusiasts for a sport. It is also, however, the case that many religious rituals, particularly those involving the regular repetition of the same words, the same familiar movements and gestures, surrounded by the colourful symbols of an ancient tradition, particularly in the context of inspiring architecture, are likely to awe and uplift the mind; and the intense togetherness of a shared charismatic experience in a Pentecostal service (however primitive the presupposed theology); or again Muslims' participation in a large congregation of worshippers at the Friday noon prayers and at the great annual religious festivals, performing together with millions around the world the same ritual prayers, or taking part in what so many report to be the spiritually transforming experience of the pilgrimage to Mecca; and again, when both Muslims, Hindus and Sikhs take part in the life of their local mosque or temple or guruwara as a social as well as religious centre, or in one of the great religious gatherings at sacred rivers – in all such experiences individual's lives are enhanced and its quality raised. And it is now uncontroversial that meditation, with or without religious beliefs, is psychologically beneficial. Again, religious faith, often of a very simple kind, sustains the extraordinary fortitude and mutual caring of many suffering from endemic poverty and deprivation in Africa and other developing regions. In all these respects religion does seem to be a life-enhancing resource. But it is also true that it produces the all-too-numerous religious fanatics, who cause so much damage to others, and the oppressive effects over the centuries, and today, of many powerful religious institutions, large and small. The situation is complex, as we saw in Chapter 1.

The complexity is, however, clarified when we maintain the distinction, drawn in Chapter 4, between authentic and inauthentic religious experience in accordance with the long-term 'fruits' criterion. It must be added, however, that, paradoxically, much 'inauthentic' or very shallow religious experience may also be psychologically helpful. A good deal of purely formal communal worship – such as going to church purely out of habit or for the sake of social respectability – can produce at least the benign side effect of a supportive community. Once again, the situation is complex.

Religious experience and epilepsy

Returning now to Ramachandran, he reminds us that shooting a rapidly fluctuating and extremely powerful magnetic field, by means of the Persinger helmet that we met in the last chapter, onto certain parts of the brain may produce conscious experiences of, in the case of the septum (in the middle of the brain), intense pleasure, like 'a thousand orgasms rolled into one', and in the case of the left frontal lobe a sense of well being. Ramachandran believes that the left frontal lobe in particular, within the limbic system, is involved in religious experience because it is known that (as we saw in the last chapter) 'patients with epileptic seizures originating in this part of the brain can have intense spiritual experiences during the seizures and sometimes become preoccupied with religious and moral issues even during the seizure-free or interictal periods' (Ramachandran 1998, 175). It is clear that for him 'religious experience' means primarily the kind of abnormal cases that come to a neurologist's attention, a distorting fact to which I have already drawn attention.

It is a fact, but not a criticism, of Ramachandran – as also of most other neuroscientists who have written about religion – that, while he is a distinguished expert in his own field, his expertise does not extend to the quite different field of the study of religion. But the relation between neuroscience and religion is an interdisciplinary study in which we can all benefit from the work of others. To illustrate Ramachandran's naive presupposed understanding of religion and of religious experience, he says 'these patients enjoy the unique privilege of gazing directly into God's eyes every time they have a seizure. Who is to say whether such experiences are "genuine" (whatever that might mean) or "patholo-gical"? Would you, the physician, really want to medicate such a patient and deny visitation rights to the Almighty?' (Ramachandran 1998, 179). He shares the popular anthropomorphic image of God as an invisible Person who sometimes talks (whether in Hebrew, Arabic, English or some other language) to selected individuals, such as those epileptic patients who report that God speaks directly to them.

A great many professed atheists also share this naive conception of God. The God they don't believe in, and whose existence they go to so much trouble to disprove, is one that many thoughtful Christians don't believe in either. But probably no one outside Russia in its official atheist period has gone as far as Yuri Gagarin, the first astronaut, reporting from space 'I don't see any God up here'.

But if we apply the all-important criterion used by the world religions (see again Chapter 4), namely, the long-term moral and spiritual fruits of the experience in the experient's life, it is doubtful whether experiences in epileptic seizures were religious in anything more than the formal sense of being structured in terms of religious concepts. This is not to say that such 'religious experiences' may not have long-term effects on the individual's outlook. Ramachandran notes that 'The seizures – and visitations – last usually only for a few seconds each time. But these brief temporal lobe storms can sometimes permanently alter the patient's personality so that even between seizures he is different from other people', and he describes some of these long-term changes.

[They] give rise to what some neurologists have called 'temporal lobe personality'. Patients have heightened emotions and see cosmic significance in trivial events. It is claimed that they tend to be humorless, full of self-importance, and tend to maintain elaborate diaries that record quotidian [daily] events in elaborate detail – a trait called hypergraphia. Patients have on occasion given me hundreds of pages of written text filled with mystical symbols and notations. Some of these patients are sticky in conversation, argumentative, pedantic and egocentric... (Ibid., 180)

He goes on to describe one such case in detail. (Some theologians have also displayed such characteristics as writing at interminable length, being highly dogmatic, strongly authoritarian and self-important, and with an underdeveloped sense of humour!) But these traits do not indicate what the world religions themselves, in their careful discussions of how to discriminate in this area, would regard as genuine religious experiences. Indeed even in the case of religious experience in its broadest sense, and strong religious enthusiasm, the link with epilepsy may well not be as strong as many have supposed. Austin says that 'temporal lobe seizures may coexist with hyperreligiosity in a few patients, but the association does not appear to be one of direct cause and effect' (Austin 1999, 407).[8]

As in the focus on patients suffering from epilepsy, a focus on individuals given electrical stimulation to the brain can distort the general picture. Referring to Wilder Penfield's experiments with electrical stimulation to the outer layers of the temporal lobe, Austin comments, 'But most of his patients were epileptic. Normal brain is not responsive. When relatively *normal* brain tissue is stimulated, either rather little happens, or it happens inconsistently. In one large study of 1500 stimulations, euphoria and pleasant feelings occurred only once' (Austin 1999, 386, italics in original).

However, others, enlarging on the significance of epilepsy, have suggested, as we saw in the previous chapter, that the experiences of such crucial founding religious figures as Jesus, St Paul, Muhammad, were caused by epileptic seizures. This may possibly apply to some of the odder 'saints' and mystics through the centuries, some of whom were very odd – like St Simeon Stylites (fifth century CE) who lived for years on top of a pillar, and a number of other later Stylites, or those of several religions who have subjected themselves to painful flagellation and extreme austerities. But we have no reason to think that they were epileptic, and there are several reasons to doubt this diagnosis in the case of the great primary figures. The one for whom this is at least a plausible possibility is St Paul, because in his dramatic experience on the Damascus road he fell to the ground, and this could possibly have been a 'grand mal' epileptic seizure – though this remains no more than a possibility. But there is no reason at all to suppose that Jesus, Gautama Buddha, Mahavira, the writers of the Upanishads and of the *Bhagavad Gita*, Confucius, 'Lao-tzu', Mo-tzu, Zoroaster, the Hebrew prophets were epiletic. In the case of the prophet Muhammad, Newberg and D'Aquili say that he 'sweated profusely during his mystical interludes', suggesting that he 'may have suffered from complex partial seizure' which can cause sweating (Newberg and D'Aquili 2001, 111). According to some of the *hadiths* (post-Qur'anic stories about the prophet and his sayings, handed down through a variety of traditions) his early revelations were traumatic, painful and sometimes frightening. He believed himself to have been in the awesome presence of Gabriel, God's intermediary with humanity. According to some *hadiths* this made him shake, according to some to sweat. It is said that after receiving a revelation, even on cold days, sweat appeared on the Prophet's forehead. They also record that he became red faced (not a symptom of epilepsy), which might presumably cause the sweating.[9] There are 24 physical symptoms, one or other or several of which can appear, including shaking and sweating.[10] But the majority of the revelations came to him as linguistically clothed insights – not characteristic of epileptic seizures – which he accepted as divinely inspired, telling him how to proceed in a particular situation.[11] I think the appropriate conclusion is that he may indeed possibly have been epileptic, but that this is far from certain, and that it would be gratuitous to assume it. And the circumstances in which Teresa's and Julian's and most of the other famous mystic's visions and auditions occurred do not in any way suggest, or even offer any plausible possibility of, epileptic seizures. Further, as James Austin points out, 'Nor is everyone who shakes, quakes, or trembles having a genuine epileptic seizure' (Austin 1999, 407). It should also be remembered that there are people of deep religious experience who happen also to suffer from epilepsy, their epileptic experience having, however, no religious content or significance.[12]

Newberg himself does not accept that 'genuine mystical experiences can be explained away as the results of epileptic hallucinations or, for that matter, as the product of other spontaneous hallucinatory states triggered by drugs, illness, physical exhaustion, emotional stress, or sensory deprivation', for 'hallucinations usually involve only a single sensory system, [whereas] mystical experiences, on the other hand, tend to be rich, coherent, and deeply dimensioned sensory experiences'. Further,

> when hallucinating individuals return to normal consciousness, they immediately recognize the fragmented and dreamlike nature of their hallucinatory interlude, and understand that it was all a mistake of the mind. Mystics, however, can never be persuaded that their experiences were not real. The sense of realness does not fade as they emerge from their mystical states, and it does not dissipate over time. (Newberg and D'Aquili 2001, 112).

And Ramachandran adds that 'there are other neurological and psychiatric disorders such as frontal lobe syndrome, schizophrenia, manic depressive illness or just depression in which the emotions are disturbed, but one rarely sees religious preoccupations in such patients to the same degree' (Ramachandran 1998, 182).

Ramachandran's own conclusion about the relation between epilepsy and religious experience is – appropriately for a scientist – purely descriptive, namely, that 'there are circuits in the human brain that are involved in religious experience and these become hyperactive in some epileptics' (Ibid., 188), but he is clear that 'this has no bearing one way or the other on whether God really exists or not' (Ibid., 185). But even this conclusion still presupposes a specific and questionable concept of God, and the same applies to Persinger's reports from the use of his helmet.

We can, however, take it as established that both epileptic seizures, surgical interventions in the brain, and electrical stimulation of parts of it, do sometimes produce religious experiences in the sense of experiences formed in terms of religious images and concepts. But, as I pointed out above, by the religions' own criterion this does not mean that they are instances of authentic religious experience. We have to allow for the possibility of religious hallucinations as well as genuine moments of awareness of the Transcendent. After all, a blow to the head can make you see stars which are not physically there, and various drugs can induce much more complex hallucinations, but this does not show that there is no physical world that can also be perceived more or less correctly. Nor, likewise, does the fact that various physical causes can produce religious hallucinations show that there is no transcendent reality of which there can also be genuine forms of awareness. James Austin, sympathetic to religion while remaining a mind/brain monist, in his detailed investigation of religious experience and the brain says, 'So, in conclusion, evidence indicates that seizures remain fundamentally different from peak experiences, and there are no real grounds for confusing them with the extraordinary alternate states of absorption and insight-wisdom' (Austin 1999, 407).

Meditation and the brain

Newberg and d'Aquili's Tibetan Buddhist monks in a deep meditation designed to empty the mind of it's ordinary concerns and thereby open it to the Transcendent showed increased activity in the 'attention area' of the frontal lobe and a decrease in the amygdala, the neural seat of anxiety and fear. And meditators reporting a sense of oneness with the universe likewise showed a decrease of activity in the posterior superior parietal lobe, concerned with spatial orientation, and hence (on Newberg's theory) with the boundary between the self and the not-self. Given the accepted principle that every moment of consciousness has its neural correlates, the crucial question arises, Which produces which? Does the brain, as an integral part of the continuous causal system of nature, generate these conscious states, or does the prolonged conscious effort to achieve a certain mental condition produce its own neural correlates – the monks having trained themselves over a number of years to direct their attention upon their current breathing in order to transcend the ordinary ego-centred awareness which, they believe, shuts out a universal spiritual reality? Or again, in a materialist theory, did their brains, as part of the seamless ongoing system of nature, make them undergo this training? This would also involve everyone else, and indeed all human activity, being likewise programmed, leaving no place for freewill – a topic to which we shall come later.

It is relevant that Newberg and d'Aquili later 'broadened the experiment and used the same techniques to study several Franscisan nuns at prayer. Again, the SPECT scans revealed similar changes that occurred during the sisters' most intensely religious moments. Unlike the Buddhists, however, they tended to describe this moment as a tangible sense of the closeness of God and a mingling with Him' (Newberg and d'Aquili 2001, 7). This difference between the conscious states reported by Tibetan Buddhists and Catholic Christians is not readily reconciled with direct brain-to-consciousness causation. For their brains showed the same activity in the same neural area, and yet with different outcomes in consciousness, whereas if their experiences were simply reflections of the same neural state in totally brain-determined consciousnesses their effects should have been the same. Clearly there has been a wider cultural influence at work. This fits well the hypothesis, to be developed later, that a transcendent reality is accessed in authentic religious experience, but that (in accordance with the critical realist principle, to which we shall come later) this reality is not experienced directly but always through the screen of our varying human conceptual systems, in these cases Buddhist and Christian.

Drugs and religious experience

As we saw in the previous chapter, cannabis and other psychotropic drugs can produce an experience of euphoric ego-transcendence; and ego-transcendence is central to all the great religious traditions. But is this, in its drug-induced instances, a temporary (and sometimes helpful) retreat by shutting out the everyday world which causes so much stress and anxiety; or is it an openness to the transcendent reality in relation to which, according to the religions, we all exist and which finds an answering aspect of our own nature? This answering aspect is recognised by the religions as our being created in the image of God, or being indwelt by the Holy Spirit, or 'that of God in every person' (George Fox), or God being 'closer to us than our jugular vein' (Qur'an 50:16); or, in the non-theistic traditions, as our ultimate unity with the Brahman, or as our true nature as the universal Buddha nature.

Under the criterion discussed in Chapter 4, it seems evident that while drug-induced ego-transcendence opens the normal boundaries of individual consciousness, what it opens it to depends upon the psychological and 'spiritual' state of that individual at that time. Psychiatrists who have studied the effects of such drugs as cannabis (marijuana), ecstasy (MDMA), heroin, cocaine, LSD (lysergicacid diethylamide), peyote/mescalin emphasise the importance of set and setting, the user's total mental state and the social setting in which the use takes place. Charles Tart reported that 'in many d-ASCs [drug-altered states of consciousness], defences against unacceptable personal impulses become partially or wholly ineffective, so that the person feels flooded with traumatic material he cannot handle' (Tart 1975, 225). Or, as Aldous Huxley put it, mescalin, with which he experimented, can open the doors both of heaven and of hell.[13] For, like excessive alcohol, these other drugs are normally used as a temporary escape from the problems of daily life. They are not normally a stage in a fundamental inner transformation from natural self-centredness to a recentring in the Transcendent. For self-transcendence as such can also be evil, demonic, as in becoming part of a violent mob, or in following some fanatical self-appointed guru, prophet, führer, miracle worker, producing a dangerous insider-versus-outsider mentality and stimulating violent and destructive behaviour. According to the thesis of this book it is only self-transcendence in openness to the Transcendent – whether or not conceptualised in religious terms – that has long-term human and ethical value.

It may, however, be the case that in some circumstances a drug-induced self-transcendence does make possible a momentary glimpse of the fifth, spiritual, dimension of our nature. The religions speak of a sacred reality variously referred to as God, Brahman, Dharmakaya or Buddha-nature, Tao, etc., and it seems possible that the psychotropic (or psychedelic) drugs which produce an experience of ego-transcendence may sometimes constitute a window onto the Transcendent for that individual at that time, depending on his/her inner openness to that reality. The test, again, is the universal religious criterion of positive long-term fruits in the person's life. As Austin says, 'drugs which activate opioid receptors or serotonin receptors also help elevate mood. The person "feels good", at least for several hours. But Zen [about which he is writing] is concerned with *major enduring attitudinal change*' (Austin 1999, 351, his italics).

The context in which ego-transcendence takes place is thus all-important. The psychologist Walter Pahnke says,

> our evidence has suggested that careful preparation and expectation play an important part, not only in the type of experience attained but in later fruits for life. Positive mystical experience with psychedelic drugs is by no means automatic. It would seem that the 'drug effect' is a delicate combination of psychological set and setting in which the drug itself is the trigger or facilitating agent – i.e. in which the drug is a *necessary* but not *sufficient* condition. Perhaps the hardest 'work' comes after the experience, which in itself may only provide the motivation for future efforts to integrate and appreciate what has been learned. Unless such an experience is integrated into the ongoing life of the individual, only a memory remains rather than the growth of an unfolding renewal process which may be awakened by the mystical experience. (Pahnke 1972, 273)

It must, however, be stressed that 9 times out of 10 – or, more precisely, according to one careful investigation, 95 times out of 100 – drugs do not produce a positive outcome. Austin reports on data 'based on 206 drug sessions, and on interviews they [Masters and Houston 1966] had with another 214 persons. Their subjects had used either LSD – 25 of them, or peyote (which contains mescaline). Only 5 per cent of their psychedelic subjects underwent a fundamental, positive, integrative transformation: a mere 11 out of the original 206' (Austin 1999, 427–8). And referring to the powerful Zen experience of ego-transcendence leading to a greater caring involvement in everyday life, he says that 'when a psychedelic *drug* precipitated this kind of acute experience, it *rarely* went on to transform the person in the same radical way as did those other *spontaneous* religious experiences, occurring without the use of drugs, which would also have reached the integral level' (Ibid., 429–30, italics in original).

Pure consciousness

Newberg and D'Aquili found that when their Tibetan monk meditators reached their peak state, 'in virtually every case' their brains showed 'a sharp reduction' – which, however, on the next page becomes 'a slowing' – of activity in the part of the brain (the posterior superior parietal lobe) concerned with spatial orientation. This prompts them to speculate: 'Would the orientation area interpret its failure to find the borderline between the self and the outside world to mean that no such distinction exists?' (Newberg and D'Aquili 2001, 6), thus producing an experience of oneness with the universe. There are, however, several reasons to be sceptical about this speculation. First, Newberg and d'Aquili's theory treats this segment of the brain as though it were an autonomous intelligence engaged in a consciousness-producing interpretive activity, whereas our consciousness at any given time is not correlated with (or produced by) any one specialised area of the brain alone but by a much more extensive area, with the frontal lobes playing a crucial role. As Rose says, 'There is nowhere in the brain a site at which neurophysiology becomes psychology . . . if there were such an area, neuroscience has conspicuously failed to discover it' (Rose 2005, 154). Second, concerning the Zen experience which Newberg and d'Aquili describe as oneness with the universe, or in Zen terms 'emptiness', 'nothingness', 'the void', *sunyata*, Austin makes it clear (as do innumerable Zen writings) that this is an emptiness that is not nothing but, paradoxically, fullness! (Anyone seeking to understand Zen has to learn to live with such paradoxes.) 'Zen emptiness', he says, ' implies *no* mental constructs . . . [F]oremost among its meanings is the deep *emptying out from consciousness of the former subjective distinction and personal attachment* . . . this is a zero state of the personal psyche . . . It means that looking out, from inside the zero of this state, all things will then be perceived objectively, just as *they* really are' (Austin 1999, 570–1, italics in original). There is no reason to suppose that this is caused by a slowing of activity in the posterior superior parietal lobe, producing a blank consciousness. On the contrary, in Zen – this is its extraordinary claim – the material world is still there, but is experienced in a radically different way: *samsara*, the world of ordinary consciousness, is now identical with *nirvana*, the same world experienced from a non-ego point of view.

Again, I referred above to the fact that the SPECT scans on Franciscan nuns found the same neural changes as with the Buddhist monks, but with quite different outcomes in consciousness – for the nuns, the experience of an encounter with a personal God. This brings us to another suggested neural cause of religious experience. We met in the last chapter Michael Persinger's speculation that the sense of presence is caused by 'assymetrical temporal lobe hyperactivity' splitting 'the sense of self' into two, the dominant half then being aware of the other half as a separate being. Persinger's helmet, sending electrical impulses to selected areas of the temporal lobe, can produce this effect artificially, and Carter (citing a *Newsweek* article) says that 'nearly all who have used it report the sensation of a presence. Many also see religious visions such as the Virgin Mary or Jesus' (Carter 2002, 288). There may also, it seems, be the sense of an evil presence, the devil, or an 'incubus' (an oppressively haunting malignant creature).

Persinger's contribution at this point illustrates well the way in which so many neuroscientists, much better informed about their own subject – naturally enough – than about religion, tend to equate religious experience with unusual experiences structured in religious terms. They are mainly interested in the seeing of visions, the hearing of voices, and other such dramatic experiences. It certainly seems that local neural malfunctions and electrical stimulations produce some such experiences. But whether they are authentically religious is not determined by the character of the experience itself but by whether it contributes to long-term effects in the experient's life and, if so, the nature of those effects.

Further, visions of known individuals are not uncommon in circumstances in which it would be too great a coincidence to suppose that they are caused by random disturbances in the cortex. They are hallucinations – that is, there is no physical object occupying the space which the vision seems to occupy. But they are sometimes veridical hallucinations – that is, they express true information (in the cybernetic, not the propositional, sense of 'information'). For example, a loved person suddenly and unexpectedly dies and within the next twelve or so hours a relative or friend, who is unaware of the death, experiences a vivid vision of him or her at that time. This suggests an unconscious ESP (tele-pathic) connection between them such that the latter becomes aware, often in an unexplicit form, that a major trauma of some sort has been experienced by the former. Since, to establish this, normal communica-tion has to be excluded, many of the best authenticated cases come from the time before radio and the internet. For example, someone who is in England in the late nineteenth century has a sudden vision of a loved one in India who has just died in an unpredictable accident. They tell others of the vision, but only weeks later is news of the death received through the ordinary channels. There are many instances of this kind recorded in the *Proceedings* of the (London) Society for Psychi-cal Research, with further analysis being done since at Duke University, taking account of many factors, such as whether or not the experient has had other visions, etc.[14] The narrow time gap between the unpre-dictable traumatic event, usually but not always a death, and the distant person experiencing the vision makes it very unlikely that the vision was caused by an unconnected neural accident.

Many people, operating on a general sceptical principle, are not suffi-ciently impressed by cases of this kind to want to examine them in detail, however, and it must also be stressed that much the most common 'sense of the presence of God', to quote the title of John Baillie's classic book, does not consist in a claimed vision of God, but in a much more diffuse, though often powerful, sense of being in the presence of an all-encompassing benign or loving unseen presence, which they assume to be divine. Whatever its status, this experience, whether occurring in a place of worship or in solitary contemplation or amid the beau-ties of nature, does not fit the pattern of unusual neurological episodes proposed by Newberg and D'Aquili.

The alternative possibility, then, to a naturalistic understanding of religious experience as cultivated by the religions, is that this constitutes a wide variety of very different forms in which we can become vividly aware of, and affected by, a reality transcending and yet also immanent within our human existence.

These are caveats in assessing neuroscience's challenges to religious experience outlined in the last chapter. But more basically than all these considerations, that challenge presupposes either mind/brain identity or epiphenomenalism, and the full answer to it depends upon the outcome of the investigation of these options, and also of the difficult question of freewill, in the following chapters.

7
Mind/Brain Identity?

Most neurophysiologists work on some highly specialised area of brain research and are not particularly interested in the philosophical issue, as they see it, of the relationship between brain and consciousness. For it does not make any practical difference to them whether consciousness is identical with, or caused by, or only correlated with brain activity. But those who do concern themselves with this fundamental question distinguish between the easy problem and the hard problem. The easy problem – easy in principle – is to trace precisely what is going on in the brain when someone is consciously perceiving, thinking, willing, experiencing some emotion, creating a work of art, etc. The hard problem is to find out what consciousness actually is and how it is caused – assuming, as they mostly do, that it *is* somehow caused – by cerebral activity. This, says Steven Rose, is 'science's last frontier' (Rose 1999, 1). It is entirely appropriate for the physical sciences to explore every possible way of reducing consciousness to the material constituents and functions of the brain. But the possibility has to be faced that the attempt may be doomed to failure. In his most recent book Steven Rose seems to regard that 'last frontier' as a mirage. He says that his new position leads him

> to abandon both of the two simplest and commonest neuroscientific views about the mind/brain relationship, even though this will require me to recognise that some of my own earlier endorsements of these views [in e.g., Rose 1973] have been at best over-naïve and at worst simply mistaken. Neuroscientists by and large are not philosophers, the implicit assumptions of my discipline are rather coarse: either minds are 'nothing but' the products of brains, or 'mind language' is a primitive form of what is disparagingly called folk

psychology and it is time to eliminate it from scientific discourse. (Rose 2005, 88)

He proposes to 'transcend these over-simplifications' (Ibid.). This does not, however, as we shall see later, involve his abandonment of materialism.

Identifying the questions

It may be helpful at this point to have an overview of the questions to be asked. This will also function as a map of the argument to be pursued in this and the next three chapters.

First, is consciousness identical with brain activity? Is it, in Carter's phrase, 'some special physical state or process'? This is the mind/brain identity theory, known in its heyday in the philosophy of mind as central state materialism. I shall argue that this is totally implausible.

If that is so, is epiphenomenalism (consciousness as a temporary non-physical but non-executive by-product of cerebral activity), to which many naturalistic thinkers have moved, plausible? I shall argue that it is not.

If that is so, does consciousness have any executive power, exercised in free will? I shall argue that it does.

If that is so, non-physical mental processes are as real as the electro-chemical processes of brain function. This leaves open the possibility of there being other non-physical realities such as the religions speak of – God, Brahman, Dharmakaya, Tao, etc.

But each of this series of questions is in fact more complex than these brief formulations, and many other subsidiary issues will arise as we investigate them. We shall meet in particular the further ideas of emergence, complexification, dual attributes and functionalism.

The correlation = identity fallacy

Mind/brain identity is the theory that consciousness simply is neural activity. It consists without remainder in the electro-chemical functioning of the brain. A particular episode of conscious thinking, and the particular electro-chemical processes taking place in the brain at the same time, are not two distinct processes, one physical and the other non-physical, but are one and the same physical event. This is the materialist account of our mental life as a transient series of electrical discharges and chemical changes in the grey matter inside our heads.

This position is encouraged by the fact that it is possible to trace, with increasing precision, the neural correlates of conscious episodes. Indeed today we all – whatever our other differences – take it for granted that for every change taking place in consciousness there is a corresponding change taking place in some area of the brain. This applies as much to religious as to all other forms of experience. Newberg's Tibetan Buddhist monks in deep meditation, designed to empty the mind of it's ordinary concerns by concentrating on their current breathing, showed increased activity in the 'attention area' of the frontal lobe. And so on. So long as we stick to observed correlations, without engaging in further specu-lations such as we saw in Chapter 5, we are on solid common ground. The danger, however, that pervades much of the literature is to treat correlation as being the same as identity. For while there is an immense body of evidence for consciousness/brain correlation, to suppose that any accumulation of this, however extensive, is proof of their identity is a simple logical error. It should be obvious that, as Stephen Rose says, 'a correlation is a not a cause' (Rose 2005, 238)

Begging the question

We saw in Chapter 5 how some neuroscientists, such as Newberg and Ramachandran, speculate, very interestingly, beyond the accepted common ground. So do many contemporary philosophers of mind. For them it is important to set aside the testimony of introspection, in which the flow of consciousness of which we are directly aware seems to be different in nature from the physical changes known to be taking place at the same time in the brain. This appeal to the ordinary experience of us all is dismissed as 'the primitive psychological taxonomy of ordinary language' (Churchland 1988, 178), concerning which he says that 'we cannot expect that folk psychology represents anything more than one stage in the historical development of our self-understanding, a stage the neurosciences may help us to transcend' (Ibid., 144).

Developing this, Churchland says concerning the argument from (or, as I would rather say, the evidence of) introspection:

> But the argument is deeply suspect, in that it assumes that our faculty of inner observation or introspection reveals things as they really are in their innermost nature. This assumption is suspect because we already know that our other forms of observation – sight, hearing, touch, and so on – do no such thing. The red surface of an apple does not *look* like a matrix of molecules reflecting photons at certain

critical wavelengths, but that is what it is. The sound of a flute does not *sound* like a sinusoidal compression wave train in the atmosphere, but that is what it is. The warmth of the summer air does not *feel* like the mean kinetic energy of millions of tiny molecules, but that is what it is. If one's pains and hopes and beliefs do not *introspectively* seem like electrochemical states in a neural network, that may be only because our faculty of introspection, like our other senses, is not sufficiently penetrating to reveal such hidden details. (Ibid, 15)

This is a systematic begging of the question. In our ordinary introspective experience we see a red-coloured apple, that is, the visual field of which we are conscious contains the red-coloured shape that we call an apple. Our visual (and tactile if we touch it, olfactory if we smell it, gustatory if we taste it) awareness does not profess to tell us anything about the apple's inner atomic or chemical structure. Ignorance of this does not affect the character of the qualia, the content of our field of consciousness. Our direct awareness of this at a given moment is incorrigible, or infallible. It cannot be mistaken, although any inferences we may make from it can. And so the fact that, physically, the redness of the surface of the apple is (as Churchland correctly says) a matrix of molecules reflecting photons at certain critical wave lengths does not in any way render introspection 'deeply suspect' – and the same with his other examples. Introspection is awareness of the content of our consciousness, the visual etc. qualia, and this content remains the same whether we are aware or ignorant of modern physics. If we are knowledgeable about it, we can introspect that awareness too. So Churchland's argument that our direct awareness of the content of our own consciousness is unreliable because it is an awareness of the way the world appears to us, and not its inner physical and chemical structures, simply begs the question whether the qualia are identical with or only correlated with the neural activity.

The same question-begging is repeated later in his book when Churchland, after describing how the brain integrates the various sensory inputs when we see colours, odours, etc., adds: 'All this provides encouragement for the identity theorist, who claims that our sensations are simply identical with, say, a set of stimulation levels (spiking frequencies) in the appropriate sensory pathways' (Ibid., 149). The fallacious assumption, again, is that conscious sensations, sensory qualia, are identical with the neural events which make them possible – thus begging the question whether consciousness and brain activity are or are not identical. This is surprising in a distinguished philosopher of mind and can, I suppose, only be accounted for by his strongly dogmatic naturalism.

The identity theory

We can now turn directly to the identity theory. However obviously true this seems to a great many people, in fact it faces formidable difficulties. The basic problem is that not even the most complete account of brain function reaches the actual conscious experience with which it is associated. As Thomas Nagel argued in his famous 1974 article 'What Is It like to Be a Bat?' (Nagel 1974), when we know all there is to know about the bat's anatomy, physiology, mode of location by sound rather than sight, etc., we still – assuming that they have some level of consciousness – do not know what it is like to be a bat.

The point is often put in terms of the law of identity, namely, that if A is identical with B then they have the same attributes. But mental states are not located at some point in space, whereas brain states are; the conscious sensation of pain, for example, can be sharp or dull or throbbing, but no part of the brain itself goes dull or becomes sharp or starts throbbing. If I prick my finger, the attributes of my consciousness of pain certainly do not seem to be the same as the attributes of the firing of a series of neurons in my brain.

The most direct observations, beginning in the 1950s, have been made when surgery has been needed on the brain. It has then sometimes been possible to do very interesting experiments by asking the patient, who is awake (the brain itself containing no pain nerves), to report what is going on in consciousness as different parts of the cortex are stimulated. Suppose, then, a neurosurgeon has exposed a patient's brain and, with instruments registering its electrical activity, is tracing the successive coordinated firings of the neurons correlated with the patient's reports of what is going on in her mind. Suppose, for example, she is visualising a mountain scene with a blue lake in the foreground and pine trees beyond it growing in a green swathe up the lower slopes of a mountain range. Does it really make sense to say that the electro-chemical activity that the surgeon is monitoring with his instruments, taking place in the grey matter that he can see in front of him and can touch, literally *is* that visualised mountain scene which forms the content of the patient's consciousness? It makes sense, whether true or not, to say that the brain activity *causes* the conscious experience. It makes sense, again whether true or not, to say that there could be no conscious experience without that brain activity. But does it make sense to say that the brain activity literally is, identically, the visualised scene occupying the patient's consciousness? To me, that is counter-intuitive to the point of absurdity. Like the philosopher Jonathan Lowe, 'I do not consider the thesis that mental states "just *are*" physical states is even an intelligible one' (Lowe 1999, 235).

However, there is more to be said. For it has become clear in the philosophical discussions that what are apparently two different things *can* sometimes nevertheless be identical in spite of displaying different attributes. They can be the same thing described in different terms and perhaps in different relationships to ourselves. The identity of the morning star and the evening star is a standard example – they are both the planet Venus. Again, we all know what we mean in ordinary language by a flash of lightning in the sky. But that same phenomenon is described by the physicists as 'the massive, sudden discharge of the collective electrical charge generated by the movement of many slightly charged water droplets or ice crystals that form the clouds'. So, in spite of the fact that they are described quite differently and in entirely different terms, the lightning and the electrical discharge are in fact the same thing.

But does this help to make brain/consciousness identity plausible? It does not. When we take examples of two things which are both uncontroversially physical, like the morning star and the evening star, or a flash of lightning and a cloud-generated electrical discharge, we are begging the question – which is not whether two *physical* phenomena can be identical, but whether physical and *mental* phenomena can be identical. In the flash of lightning example, instead of taking the electrical discharge as the second term of the analogy we should take the conscious seeing of the flash of light. The question is whether that conscious episode is itself something physical.

But cannot this experienced flash be described on one level as neuron firings, mainly in the occipital lobe, and on another level as the conscious sensation of seeing a flash, so that the neuron firings and the conscious experience are the same thing described in different terms for different purposes? The answer is No. The question is how a conscious experience can be identical with a physical event in the brain, as distinguished from being precisely correlated with it; and to assume that the correlation constitutes identity simply begs that question. The belief that they are identical is not an experimentally established fact or the conclusion of a logically cogent argument but an affirmation of naturalistic faith.

The manifest weakness of the identity theory is sometimes concealed by the idea of dual attributes, the suggestion that cerebral events have two different sets of attributes, one physical and the other mental, requiring different languages for their description. So neurophysiological language and psychological language are two different ways of speaking about the same thing, namely, the functioning of the brain, but are selecting different attributes of it for attention.

This two-languages form of consciousness/brain identity is widely held today. As a recent example, Steven Rose, responding to the argument that there is a difference of kind between the neural activity taking place when we see the colour red and the conscious experience of seeing that colour, so that they are clearly not identical, says:

> It may be because I am philosophically tone-deaf, but I have never found this a very troubling question. It is surely clear that, granted enough knowledge of the visual system, we can in principle, and to some extent in practice, identify those neurons which become active when 'red' is perceived. (Indeed in animal experiments such neurons have already been identified.) This pattern of neural activity translates into the seeing of red, and seeing red is simply what we call in mind language the phenomenon that we call in brain language the activity of a particular ensemble of neurons. This doesn't seem harder to understand than is the fact that what we call a particular small four-legged furry mammal *cat* in English and *gatto* in Italian; the two terms refer to the same object in different and coherent, but mutually translatable languages. No problem. (Rose 2005, 215–16).

I am afraid that this *is* a symptom of philosophical 'tone-deafness'. The question is whether the conscious experience of red is identical with its neural correlates. And to appeal to the analogy of what is unproblematically the same *physical* object being differently named in different European languages is simply, yet again, to beg the question, which is whether events in consciousness are or are not the same physical events as electro-chemical events in the brain.

Functionalist theories are more ambiguous – or rather there are forms of functionalism that entail identity and others that are neutral as between monism and dualism. The former hold that we should not think of a state of consciousness in terms of mental characteristics but in terms of the role it plays in the organism's behaviour. This does not involve the identity of a particular mental state with a particular neural event, but holds rather that our ever-changing mental life as a whole is identical with the immensely complex and ever-changing life of the brain. And this identity is to be understood in functional terms. For example, a certain sensory input, say heat activating the pain nerves in the hand, interacts within a certain area of the structure of the brain to produce a certain output, the sudden withdrawal of the hand, and this process includes within it a mental state which is the sensation of pain. The mental state plays no causal role but is an epiphenomenon of the total set of bodily events. But this suggestion does not reveal what consciousness is. It merely tells us that it exists – which we already knew.

The other, dualistic, kind of functionalism, in contrast, allows a causal role to consciousness within the total input–output process and is thus a form of body/mind dualism. We shall come to this in the next chapter, but at this stage we are concerned with the identity theory.

A not often noticed point is worth making here. There is a question as to whether the identity thesis is a genuine scientific hypothesis. Most of us today accept Karl Popper's doctrine that while a large-scale scientific hypothesis can never be absolutely verified if true it can, at least in principle, be decisively falsified if false. But within the parameters of normal science there is no possible observation or experiment that could ever decisively contradict mind/brain identity if it is false, and accordingly it is not a scientific hypothesis. In moving from examples of two apparently different physical objects or events being the same object or event differently described to the idea that brain and consciousness are related in the same way, we have moved from a scientific hypothesis to a theory that is in principle unfalsifiable. That Venus appears at dawn in the east and after sunset in the west could be empirically falsified, if it were false, by for example sending up a satellite observer to trace its path. Likewise, that a flash of lighting is an electric discharge could be experimentally falsified by finding that there is no electrical activity taking place. But there is no way in which the idea that an electro-chemical event and a moment of consciousness are identical is falsifiable if false. The identity thesis is a theory stemming from a presupposed naturalistic philosophy, not a scientific hypothesis such that we can even imagine what could constitute its falsification if it is false.[1]

The only way in which mind/brain identity would become falsifiable is to recognise parapsychology as a genuine science.[2] For it is then possible that extrasensory perception (telepathy) or out-of-the-body experiences, which are incompatible with the identity thesis, might be authenticated. The dilemma for materialists, however, is that they do not allow research in these areas to be admitted as evidence.

The mystery of consciousness

Some philosophers of mind who lean strongly towards mind/brain identity are appropriately cautious about claiming too much. For example, Paul Churchland grants that 'a central mystery remains largely a mystery: the nature of *conscious intelligence*' (Churchland 1988, 1, italics in original). However, many other philosophers of mind are convinced, with a dogmatism that matches that of any medieval theologian, that consciousness is identical with cerebral activity. In contrast to this, in so far as the neuroscientists have turned their attention to the question, they are much less dogmatic. Indeed, there is now a widespread acceptance that the nature and status of consciousness remains a sheer mystery. And clearly if we do not know what consciousness is we cannot know that it consists in the electro-chemical functioning of the brain. Even Susan Greenfield, who speaks of 'the ripples in the brain that I argue constitute consciousness' (Greenfield 1999, 217) and who is well known for her TV advocacy of mind/brain identity, admits that 'I cannot at this stage describe exactly how a large number of neurons has the emergent property of consciousness' (Greenfield 1999, 220). Benjamin Libet of UCLA, whose experimental work has been widely discussed, says that 'There is an unexplained gap between the category of physical phenomena and the category of subjective phenomena . . . The assumption that a deterministic nature of the physically observable world (to the extent that it may be true) can account for subjective conscious functions and events is a speculative *belief*, not a scientifically proven proposition' (Libet 1999, 55–6). V. S. Ramachandran of the Center for Brain and Cognition at the University of California, San Diego, whom I have quoted earlier, says that 'despite two hundred years of research, the most basic questions about the human mind . . . remain unanswered, as does the really big question: What is consciousness?' (Ramachandran 1998, xvi). And Roger Penrose of Oxford, one of our most distinguished writers about science, adds that 'conscious actions and conscious perceptions – and, in particular, the conscious phenomenon of understanding – will find no proper explanation within the present-day picture of the material universe, but require our going outside this conventional framework to a new physical picture' (Penrose 1999, 14). He believes that this new physical picture will be found where the micro-physics of the quantum world merges into the macro-physics of the observable world, which includes the human brain. His hypothesis is that within the brain, it is to the microtubules in the cytoskeleton, rather than to neurons, that we must look for the place where collective (coherent) quantum effects are most likely to be found – and that without such quantum coherence we shall not find a sufficient role for the new OR [objective reduction] physics that must provide the non-computational prerequisite for the encompassing of the phenomenon of consciousness within scientific terms. (Penrose 1995, 406)

But this new physics is a hope, something that may or may not come about in the future, and the belief that if it does come about it will prove to be the key to the nature of consciousness is likewise only a hope. Again Steven Rose, Director of the Brain and Behaviour Research Group at the Open University, UK, concludes that 'the issue of consciousness lies beyond mere neuroscience, or even psychology and philosophy' (Rose 1999, 14), and in his most recent publication he adds:

Small wonder that, almost drunk with the extraordinary power of these new [neuroscientific] technologies, the neuroscientists have begun to lay claim to that final terra incognita, the nature of consciousness itself. Literally dozens of – mainly speculative – books with titles permutating the term 'consciousness' have appeared over the last decade . . . I remain sceptical. This book is definitely not about offering some dramatic new 'theory of consciousness', although that particular ghost in the machine is bound to recur through the text. Indeed, I will try to explain why I think that as neuroscientists we don't have anything very much useful to say about that particular Big C, and why therefore, as Wittgenstein said many years ago, we would do better to keep silence. (Rose 2005, 4)

While as a materialist he cannot resist invoking Ryle's dismissive phrase 'the ghost in the machine', he is frankly granting that to the neurosciences the nature of consciousness is a sheer mystery. And finally, Antonio Damasio, Head of the Department of Neurology at the University of Iowa College of Medicine, says, 'If elucidating the mind is the last frontier of the life sciences, consciousness often seems the last mystery in the elucidation of the mind. Some regard it as insoluble . . . [A]t the moment the neurobiological account is incomplete and there is an explanatory gap' (Damasio 1999, 14). But there is, surely, more than just a gap that a more complete knowledge of the brain may one day bridge, because no knowledge of the workings of the neural networks, however complete, can convert correlation into identity. And indeed Damasio himself is clear that he and his colleagues are researching the 'biological underpinnings' (Damasio 1999, 11) of consciousness, 'the neural architecture which supports consciousness' (Ibid., 15), but not consciousness itself.

And so it is absolutely not the case, in spite of being so widely assumed within our culture, that mind/brain identity is a scientifically established fact. Its status is that of an article of naturalistic faith. This faith is supported by the ingenious work of those philosophers of mind (this being one of the most active areas in philosophy today) who produce ever-more sophisticated theories, often with only token reference to the work of the neuroscientists, to avoid the conclusion at which so many neuroscientists have arrived, namely, that the nature of consciousness is a mystery. The fact that so many philosophers of mind proceed with only a minimal acquaintance with the work in the neurosciences is commented on by Steven Rose when he notes that 'through most of the past century even the most committedly non-dualist of philosophers have tended to be satisfied with merely rhetorical references to the brain' (Rose 2005, 197). This is recognised today by some candid naturalistic philosophers themselves, such as Michael Lockwood:

> I count myself a materialist, in the sense that I take consciousness to be a species of brain activity. Having said that, however, it seems to me evident that no description of brain activity of the relevant kind, couched in the available language of physics, physiology, or functional or computational rules, is remotely capable of capturing what is distinctive about consciousness. So glaring, indeed, are the shortcomings of all the reductive programmes currently on offer, that I cannot believe that anyone with a philosophical training, looking dispassionately at these programmes, would take any of them seriously for a moment, were it not for a deep-seated conviction that current physical science has essentially got reality taped, and accordingly, *something* along the lines of what the reductionists are offering *must* be correct. To that extent, the very existence of consciousness seems to me to be a standing demonstration of the explanatory limitations of contemporary physical science. (Lockwood 2003, 447)

Because the mind/brain identity theory has proved so difficult to sustain, many naturalistic scientists and philosophers have moved on to modifications of this under the overall name of epiphenomenalism, to which we come in the next chapter.

8
Current Naturalistic Theories

Epiphenomenalism

Within contemporary philosophy of mind the simple mind/brain identity thesis has now largely given place to a variety of more sophisticated naturalistic theories: emergent properties, dual attributes, functionalism. These are different forms of epiphenomenalism, the view that consciousness is a non-physical epiphenomenon produced by the functioning of the brain, but having itself no causal power and lasting only during the particular neural episode of which it is a by-product. As a rough analogy, while electricity is flowing through a light bulb it produces light, but stop the current and there's no light. Likewise, electricity flowing through the brain produces consciousness, but stop the current and there is no consciousness. So epiphenomenalism departs from identity theory in being a modified form of brain/consciousness dualism, though one in which the mental life has no volitional effect. It is a dualism in which the two elements have a very different status – the brain does things and consciousness simply reflects what the brain is doing.

The Libet experiments

I mentioned in Chapter 5 one of Libet's experiments in the 1970s which apparently supports epiphenomenalism. The subject was asked to make a simple flick of the wrist at an arbitrarily chosen moment, noting the moment of the conscious decision by the position of the moving arm on a dial; and Libet found that some cerebral activity (the 'readiness potential') occurred about 500 milliseconds *before* the flick of the wrist – suggesting that the conscious decision was a delayed epiphenomenal reflection of the neural activity.

Can this half second delay before the conscious volition be accounted for in any other way? Yes. The mind is much more than consciousness.

Although consciousness is the part of the mind of which we are directly aware, it is only the 'tip of the iceberg', and unconscious processes must also have their neural correlates. Many of our daily actions, not involving deliberate decision, are performed automatically, on autopilot – such as walking, or the spontaneous hand movements which many people make while talking. These do not involve conscious deliberation. But there is nevertheless a brief period of unconscious preplanning. The flicking of the wrist in Libet's experiment may well be an example of this unconscious preplanning, the neural correlate of which is measured by Libet as approximately 500ms.

Further, when this particular experiment is not taken in isolation but in the context of much other work, further interesting factors enter in. For example, there is ongoing discussion among experimental neurophysiologists about whether, as the theory of 'prior entry' claims, the subject's attention influences the perception of arrival times (e.g. Shore et al. 2001, 205f). This is compatible with another result of Libet's own work. He reported that when he applied stimuli to both the brain and the hand simultaneously, the touching of the hand was consciously experienced *before* the stimulation of the brain directly – although they had occurred at the same time. In other words, the message from the hand seems somehow to have been referred in consciousness backwards in time. Again, when he stimulated the appropriate part of the cortex directly, and then a fraction of a second *later* touched the hand, the hand stimulation was still reported as occurring first in consciousness. There seemed again to be a mental backwards referral in time which, according to Libet, 'would seem to raise serious though not insurmountable difficulties for the . . . theory of psychoneuronal identity' (Libet, Wright, Feinstein and Pear 1979, 364). As John Eccles explains,

The cortical activities evoked by some sharp stimulus to the hand in conscious human subjects took as long as half a second to build up to the level for giving consciousness; yet the subject antedated it in his experience to a time which was the time of the arrival of the message from the periphery onto the cerebral cortex, which may be almost half a second earlier. This is an extraordinary happening, and there is no way in which this can be explained by the operations of the neural machinery. It simply has to be explained by the manner in which the self-conscious mind becomes cognizant of the peripheral event by reading out from the neural machinery when its responses had developed to the necessary level of size and of action. (Eccles and Popper 1977, 476)

In other words, Libet, Eccles and others have interpreted the experiments as establishing the capacity of the mind to rearrange in consciousness the order of neural and sensory stimuli – which would support mind/brain dualism rather than either identity or epiphenomenalism.

Others, however, dispute this interpretation. A leading anti-dualist philosopher, Daniel Dennett, says that 'Libet's experimental procedures and his analysis of the results have been severely criticized. His experiments have never been replicated, which is reason enough in many quarters to remove his "results" from consideration' (Dennett 1991, 256); though he also goes on to offer a complex argument that even if Libet's experiments are accepted it is still possible to interpret them in a non-dualist way.

However, another experimental result further complicates the picture as it stands at the moment. Speaking of the mental activity of deliberately initiating physical action, Austin says, 'Suppose, for example, you decide to focus your attention on a visuospatial task. It will take as long as 80 to 130 milliseconds before its associated electrical potential shows up in the brain' (Austin 1999, 279).[1] In such cases, so far from the brain activity being registered before the mental decision, the mental decision occurs before any detectable neural event.

With the neurophysiologists disagreeing about the data, and philosophers about their significance, the appropriate conclusion thus far seems to be an unresolved question mark.

Consciousness as a social product

Wolf Singer, Director of the Max Planck Institute for Brain Research in Frankfurt, has explored the ways in which 'the brain constructs from the sparse and diverse signals of its sensors coherent models of its environment' (Singer 1998, 228). But he notes that, in addition to this, we can be aware of being aware, and he sees this self-awareness as arising in the neo-cortex. He says that 'Since the computations that underlie primary cognitive functions are carried out in the neocortex, one has to conclude that also the operations leading to meta-awareness, the awareness of perceiving, are due to cortical operations' (Ibid., 232). (Note his philosophically naive equation of 'carried out in' with 'due to'.) But he has to add that however complete our understanding of the neuro-cognitive process may become 'our perceptions of sensations and awareness as subjective, immaterial phenomena would still remain unsolved. There would still be no answer to the question of how it comes about that we experience ourselves as freely acting selves who are able to decide how to go about with our sensations and how to react to them' (Ibid., 233). For 'a particular state of neurons and the subjective experience of being conscious belong to different ontological categories [and] are defined within different description systems' (Ibid., 240). However, Singer does not conclude from this to a brain/consciousness dualism. He believes, apparently regarding this as an alternative, that the subjective phenomenon of consciousness is a social product.

While it is an important truth that social interaction is a necessary condition for distinctively human consciousness to come about, this fact is in itself neutral as between monism and dualism. It is clear that our human level of consciousness is linked with language, which is linked with society and culture. This was taught in the nineteenth century by Ludwig Feuerbach and then Karl Marx. In *The German Ideology* (written in 1845–46 but not published until 1932) Marx says:

> Language is as old as consciousness, language *is* consciousness that exists also for other men, and for that reason alone it really exists for me personally as well; language, like consciousness, only exists from the need, the necessity, of intercourse with other men . . . Consciousness is, therefore, from the beginning a social product, and remains so as long as men exist at all. (Marx 1970, 51)

And the twentieth-century Marxist psychologist, L. Vygotsky, whose work was suppressed during the Stalin era but has since become widely influential, says:

> Thought and speech turn out to be the key to the nature of human consciousness. If language is as old as consciousness itself, and if language is a practical consciousness-for-others, and consequently conscious-for-myself, then not only one particular thought but all consciousness is connected with the development of the word. The word is a thing in our consciousness, as Ludwig Feurbach put it, that is absolutely impossible for one person, but that becomes a reality for two. The word is a direct expression of the historical nature of human consciousness. (Vygotsky 1986, 256).

Friedrich Nietzsche, probably quite independently, came to the same conclusion in *The Joyful Wisdom* (1882).

Singer likewise argues that consciousness comes about through mutual communication, by brains becoming aware of other brains and aware that others are aware of them:

> the phenomenon of self-awareness – the experience of one's own individuality, the ability to experience oneself as an autonomous individual with subjective feelings – is to be seen as the result of social interactions, and hence of cultural evolution . . . I propose, therefore, that the subjective connotations of consciousness that give rise to the hard problems in the philosophy of mind have the ontological status of social realities, of realities that only come into existence through communication among brains . . . While our brains develop, our care-takers force us into an intensive dialogue during which we – our brains – acquire awareness of ourselves and realize that we are different from others, but we do not remember that this learning process took place . . . In conclusion, then, I propose two causes for the mysterious aspect of the phenomenon of self-awareness: first, its social origin, and, second, the amnesia for the acquisition process. (Singer 1998, 242–3)

And so, according to Singer, 'self-awareness and the subjective connotations of qualia can be understood as emergent properties of brains without having to take a dualistic position' (Ibid., 245). They are neural states produced by human interactions within society, culture and history.

But the move from the observation that consciousness requires a social context for it's development to the conclusion that 'the subjective connotations of consciousness . . . have the *ontological* status of social realities' (Ibid., 242, my italics) is not a valid inference. Singer is led to this because, having accepted that self-awareness and the subjectively experienced qualia 'transcend the reach of conventional neurobiological approaches' (Ibid., 245), he seeks some other naturalistic account of consciousness and finds this in the social reality of language and social interactions. But that the human level of consciousness has been made possible by our being social creatures, and has gone hand in hand with the development of language, does not mean that consciousness *is*, identically, any set of social interactions. We cannot legitimately identify the historical conditions that have made consciousness possible with consciousness itself.

Consciousness and evolution

But supposing, as all forms of epiphenomenalism require, that consciousness is devoid of causal power, is it not then totally redundant, since it can make no difference to an organism's behaviour? In that case, it cannot have come about because of any evolutionary advantage. If it makes no behavioural difference, but simply reflects the activity of the brain, how can consciousness have any survival value?

The neurophysiologist Antony Damasio, a materialist whose faith is that qualia 'will eventually be explained neurobiologically' (Damasio 1999, 9), nevertheless recognises the necessity of consciousness for everything that we value, and asks himself what part this can have played in the evolutionary process. On the one hand, he points out, the brain can nonconsciously and with great efficiency coordinate the activities of the heart, lungs, kidneys, the endocrine and immunological systems, and enable the organism to seek food, avoid danger, mate and generally live out its life within its own biological niche. This could only require, at most, what he calls the core consciousness that we share with many other species. But it is what he calls the extended consciousness found in humans, involving memory, language and intelligence, that makes possible creativity and civilisation. '[C]onsciousness', he says, 'is good for extending the mind's reach and, in so doing, improving the life of the organism whose mind has that higher reach . . . [T]he devices of consciousness handle the problem of how an individual organism may cope with environmental challenges not predicted in its basic design such that the conditions fundamental for survival can still be met' (Damasio 1999, 303). And so, he concludes, consciousness does have survival and evolutionary value.

However, when Damasio says that consciousness is 'good for extending the mind's reach', the *mind's* reach, is he not thereby going beyond the physical? Is he not tacitly acknowledging the fundamental distinction between mind/brain correlation and mind/brain identity? He is aware that he is only trying in his research to identify the cerebral activity which, as he says, 'is the neural architecture which supports consciousness' (Ibid., 15), constituting it's 'biological underpinnings' (Ibid., 11). He allows that, 'Armed with the data from all these high-powered scans . . . you may well obtain a remarkable set of *correlates* of the contents of the image in mind . . . You have an experience of something that is highly correlated with my experience, but it is an experience of something different. You do not *see* what I see when you look at *my* brain activity. *You see a part of the activity of my brain as*

I see what I see' (Ibid., 306, italics in original). Thus far he seems to be an epiphenomenalist, with consciousness having no executive power. But then he goes further. He speaks of our consciously *choosing* between available patterns of action. Mental '[i]mages allow us to choose among repertoires of previously available patterns of action' (Ibid., 24), and our activity is improved by 'purposeful preview and manipulation of images in mind and optional planning' (Ibid.). It seems, then, that for him the mind has the capacity to consider options and choose one line of action rather than another. In that case consciousness, at least in the case of the extended human consciousness, does have executive power. In order to fulfil the role that Damasio assigns to it, of reviewing a range of possible actions and choosing from among them, consciousness must be more than an epiphenomenal mirroring of brain activity.

Various other attempts have been made, along essentially the same lines, to find a biological value for consciousness within the evolutionary process. The philosophers Paul and Patricia Churchland have argued that we can explain the development of the large, complex human brain in evolutionary terms as having survival and reproductive value. They see consciousness as enabling the animal to respond more appropriately and effectively to its environment. Paul Churchland says that 'brains were selected for because brains conferred a reproductive advantage... because they allowed individuals to anticipate their environment...'(Churchland, Paul 1988, 76). Or as Patricia Churchland puts it, 'neurons are evolution's solution to the problem of adaptive movement' (Churchland, Patricia 1986, 14).

However, this is an explanation of the development of complex brains capable of responding in complex ways to their environment, but not of *consciousness* itself if, as they believe, consciousness cannot initiate action. The evolutionary value of highly developed brains cannot be invoked to explain the existence of consciousness unless consciousness makes a behavioural difference by exerting some executive power over the brain, and hence our actions. This is the crux of the matter. The point is made by Jaron Lanier when he refers to the theory that consciousness 'was evolved to focus mental attention in critical circumstances', adding, 'But such explanations can only make sense if consciousness has an effect' (Lanier 1999, 264). Is it not obvious that if consciousness has no executive power it cannot provide any evolutionary benefit?

Consciousness does, however, have a further extremely important function. It is the locus of enjoyment in personal relationships, of moral values, of the awareness of beauty, and the possibilities of creativity in science, philosophy and religion and the arts. Consider the kind of moral character that we esteem most highly, even if we so often fail to emulate it. It is not the person who is honest in order to avoid punishment, and it is not the human herd that sacrifices individuals for its own advantage. It is the person who is honest in character, and the group which risks its own safety to save an endangered individual. Prudential ethics can probably be explained in evolutionary terms, but can the higher morality of, for example, the self-sacrificing Captain Oates, a member of Scott's expedition to the South Pole in 1910, who, being severely frostbitten, went out into the antarctic snow to die rather than be a burden on his comrades trying to help him home? Very many comparable, if often less dramatic, examples of self-sacrificial action in the interest of others occur all the time, in both the horrors of war and the natural disasters of peace. It would take complex epicycles of speculation to avoid the powerful reality of self-transcending values that exist for humans only in virtue of our consciousness.

Consciousness as an emergent property

Another widely popular position today holds that mind is an emergent property of the brain. 'Emergence' is today something of a mantra throughout the science–religion debates. Here the idea is that when neural development reaches a certain degree of complexity its internal interactions constitute a new and higher-level reality – consciousness. This is not something additional to neural activity, but a new configuration of it. Steven Johnson offers the life of an anthill as an example of the emergence of a higher-level order out of the interactions of innumerable lower-level activities and interactions (Johnson 2002). The successfully organised life of an ant colony has not been arranged by any one ant or command structure of ants. But as the ants each perform their limited individual function, such as foraging for food and carrying it back to the colony, a complexly functioning society has come about without the awareness or intent of any of its parts. Likewise, it is suggested, consciousness has emerged naturally at a certain point in biological evolution out of the limited activity of billions of neurons as their interactions have become more and more complex in response to environmental challenges.

However, what is called the 'swarm intelligence' which we find in ants and other insects that live in colonies is accounted for in recent research in ways that do not require anything remotely comparable with the exercise of consciousness in humans. Ants exude a chemical called pheromone which attracts other ants and, when they disperse in search of food, the one to find it first returns with it first to the nest, thus doubling this pheromone trail, which in turn attracts other ants, who further strengthen the trail by using it, thus leading the whole colony to the source of food.[2] This looks like a new, emergent, order of ant 'intelligence', but it is not: it is a purely mechanical process developed in the course of evolution. It is futile to use it to try to illuminate the problem of how consciousness, so apparently different in kind from the physical brain, can be identical with highly complex brain functioning. This can only be done by begging the question. The life of the anthill is a complex physical reality, and the question at issue is whether the mind, like the brain, is also a complex physical reality. And so the analogy only explains consciousness by presupposing what it is supposed to establish, namely, identity or a form of epiphenomenalism.

Paul Churchland offers a more subtle view of consciousness as an emergent property of brain complexity, based on the idea of property dualism. According to this, there is no dualism of kinds of reality, physical and mental, but there is a dualism of kinds of property that a reality, the brain, has – physical properties and mental properties. Mental properties emerge in the brain as it attains a certain level of complexity. 'Examples of properties that are emergent in this sense', he says, 'would be the property of being *solid*, the property of being *colored*, the property of being *alive*' (Churchland 1988, 12). Being solid, coloured, alive, are indeed properties of matter. They explain what an emergent physical property is. But they do not show that consciousness is an emergent physical property. To assume that begs the basic question, which is whether consciousness is a property, of any kind, of the physical brain. Property dualism begs the basic question in favour of monism.

Others again seek to understand the nature of consciousness by analogy with the 'artificial intelligence' of computers. Igor Aleksander, Professor of Neural Systems Engineering at Imperial College, London, has studied the ways in which computers can be made to react to events in the light of their existing 'knowledge' (my quote marks) and also to learn from experience, thus acquiring new knowledge and even an individual 'personality' (my quote marks). He believes that 'the firing of artificial neurons could become just as meaningful to the machine as our own sensations are to us' (Aleksander 1999, 183). There can, he believes, be 'a neural net which enables it to be a dynamic artificial organism whose learned states are a meaningful representation of the world and its own existence in this world' (Ibid., 185). He approaches this through the idea of iconic learning, the process whereby the environment imprints itself upon the neural net, creating ' "echo-like" internal representations of what may be sensed by sensory neurons' (Ibid., 188). He suggests that this makes possible 'iconic memory', representations of self, and even freewill in the sense that 'there is sufficient non-determinism in a normally functioning neural system to make the organism itself "feel" that it can take freely arbitrary decisions' (Ibid., 194). So his conclusion is that consciousness 'is the ultimate masterpiece of iconically adapted firing patterns of parts of the brain' (Ibid., 198). He is right to put 'feel' in inverted commas, because a computer does not feel in the sense in which we do, and 'meaningful' should also have been in quotation marks. A computer feels free and is aware of meaning only in a 'so-to-speak' or metaphorical sense. Steven Rose emphasises that one reason for not seeing brains as 'nothing other than sophisticated computers, information processors, cognition machines' is precisely that they lack affect, emotion (Rose 2005, 54). As he says, 'The key feature which distinguishes brains/minds from computers is their/our capacity to experience emotion and to express feelings . . . [A]ffect and cognition are inextricable engaged in all brain and mind processes, creating meaning out of information – just one more reason why brains aren't computers' (Ibid., 102–3). A computer could be programmed to produce behaviour which simulates a human's responses of fear, anger, love, jealousy, compassion, but it is science fiction to imagine that the computer itself experiences these emotional states. For they do not arise simply from our reception and storage of information but also from our capacity to discern its meaning, and whereas a computer stores and manipulates information, 'our minds work with meaning, not information' (Ibid., 207).

There is an even more fundamental point to be made. The more successfully AI (artificial intelligence) demonstrates that computers, which totally lack consciousness, can model human intelligence, the more definitively it shows that the brain as a computer cannot explain the existence of consciousness. For they model human behaviour without being conscious. If we were essentially computers, consciousness would be a mysterious add-on with no function. If it does not exercise executive power, with conscious decisions affecting behaviour via the brain, consciousness becomes functionless and inexplicable. So far, then, from providing an argument for a physicalist account of consciousness, cognitive science progressively constitutes a powerful argument against it! This is something that many naturalistic thinkers have yet to take on board.

Returning now to the central affirmation of epiphenomenalism, the non-executive nature of consciousness, others have suggested that it may be a kind of spandrel – a term borrowed from architecture. When there are, for example, curved arches supporting a roof, the space between the arches and the wall is called a spandrel – the stone arches have been put there to serve a positive function, to hold up the roof, and the space between them is an incidental by-product of this. Likewise consciousness may be just an incidental by-product of the evolution of the brain, not itself serving any function, but existing as a kind of spandrel. So Carter says, 'Consciousness may . . . have appeared when certain cognitive mechanisms evolved, but only by virtue of them rather than for any purpose of its own' (Carter 2002, 92). But science requires more than a 'may have'; it requires some kind of explanation of how this happened, and none is on offer.

The spandrel metaphor reminds us that both neuroscientists and philosophers of mind often resort to metaphors when they have reached the limits of their disciplines. Thus Susan Greenfield speaks of 'the ripples in the brain that I argue constitute consciousness' (Greenberg 1999, 217), and Daniel Dennett speaks of the way in which language enables us to 'review, recall, rehearse, redesign our own activities, turning our brains into echo chambers of sorts, in which otherwise evanescent processes can hang around and become objects in their own right. Those that persist the longest, acquiring influence as they persist, we call our conscious thoughts' (Dennett 1996, 144). Again, Steven Rose, describing the interactions of neurons through their synaptic connections, says, 'Who its [a neuron's] neighbours are, who speaks to it via its synapses, and to whom in turn it speaks, determines the role of any neuron in the functioning of the organism' (Rose 2005, 148). This latter is a harmless use of metaphor, but those committed by Greenfield and Dennett (and many others) have provoked Raymond Tallis to introduce the term 'neuromythology'. He writes,

The power of neuromythology resides in the subtlety with which it juggles descriptive terms . . . The gap between the physical and the mental is bridged by describing end-organ events in rigidly physical terms, and events occurring more centrally in psychological terms . . . In short, electrochemical activity leaves the sense endings as physical events and arrives somewhere in the cortex as information. No explanation whatsoever is offered as to how this happens – and it cries out for explanation as all parties are agreed that the electrochemical activity remains electrochemical activity throughout. (Tallis 1999, 82–3)

The proper conclusion, I suggest, is that the various forms of epiphenomenalism are incapable of explaining the existence of consciousness. A completely non-executive consciousness could serve no function, and its emergence would be inexplicable.

Biological naturalism

The philosopher John Searle is well know for a distinctive position which he calls biological naturalism. The theory is both apparently simple and undoubtedly radical, and would solve in one move the entire tangled web of problems that have kept philosophers busy from the time of Descartes. The physical brain itself, or rather part of it, he says, is conscious. More precisely, 'Conscious states are realized in the brain as features of the brain system, and thus exist at a higher level than that of neurons and synapses. Individual neurons are not conscious, but portions of the brain system composed of neurons are conscious' (Searle 2004, 113–14. Subsequent Searle quotes are from this book). It is just a fact of nature that matter, in the form of certain patterns of neurons, is conscious: 'consciousness is a biological feature of the brain in the same way that digestion is a biological feature of the digestive tract' (115–16).

We know that consciousness exists because we are conscious. But in addition to this, he says, 'We know for a fact that all our mental processes are caused by neurobiological processes' (114). The causation is always from neural to mental processes, which are epiphenomena: they 'have no causal power in addition to those of the underlying neural biology' (114). He uses as an example the route by which the sense of thirst is caused, namely, by lack of water causing a saline imbalance in the system, producing a feeling of thirst; and 'My conscious thirst causes me to drink water' (114). '[T]he feelings [of thirst] themselves are processes going on inside the brain' (115). This is a good example of the way in which the impacts of the environment on our bodies cause modifications of consciousness and hence of behaviour. But Searle's assertion that '*all* our mental processes are caused by neurological processes' (114, my italics) is purely an assertion, and one which commits the question-begging fallacy of equating correlation with identity. It is uncontroversial that for everything going on in consciousness something correlated with it is going on in the brain, and also that there is a vast class of cases of one-way causation from brain to consciousness. The big question is whether there is also a class of cases of causation from consciousness to brain. Searle's theory rules this out by stipulative definition.

We must come later to the question of free will, but it makes a first appearance at this point, because the distinction between brain to consciousness and consciousness to brain causation arises in examples of behaviour caused, via the brain, by the capacity of consciousness to operate not only in terms of physical impacts but also of values, ideals, faith. As I write this I happen to be in a Muslim country during Ramadan, the month (which this year, 2005, falls in October) during which faithful Muslims fast by neither eating nor drinking between sunrise and sunset, a discipline which they find to be spiritually rewarding. Although the pangs of hunger subside after the first few days, thirst does not – and must be particularly intense in a hot climate like this (Egypt). What makes Muslims exercise self-control and refrain from eating and drinking is their religious faith. But a purely biological account of behaviour motivated by values and faith commitments would have to extend ultimately over all of human history, including religion, culture, the arts, creativity (in science as well as elsewhere) and morality.

It is worth noting the unsatisfactory nature of some of Searle's use of language. He complains concerning some other philosophers of mind that they 'fudge' by using vague phrases such as that neural activity 'gives rise to' or 'is the seat of' consciousness (112). But his own language is that 'All forms of consciousness are caused by the behavior of neurons and are *realized* in the brain system' (112, my italics); 'Conscious states are *realized* in the brain as features of the brain system' (113, my italics). But is 'realized' any less vague and fudged than the other metaphors?

However, Searle points out elsewhere (Searle 1984, 20–3) that water, which for the chemist is H_2O, a chemical combination which is not wet, is wet as experienced. At the micro-level it is not wet, and yet this same substance at the macro-level is wet. Analogously, at the micro-level of individual neurons the brain is not conscious, but the same substance at the macro-level is conscious.

This differs from the case that we saw earlier (p. 86) of lightning and electrical discharges in the clouds, which are the same phenomenon described in different terms. As I pointed out, this is a genuine scientific theory because it could be experimentally disproved if it were false. But, as I also pointed out, that two physical phenomena are identical does not show that a physical and a mental phenomenon can be identical. In Searle's case one of the two phenomena, the activity of a cluster of neurons, is indisputably physical while the other, consciousness, is mental. Searle's theory is that they are nevertheless identical. This is a genuine scientific theory which can in principle be experimentally confirmed or disconfirmed because it could be shown, if it is the case, that the behaviour of a particular constellation of neurons (its pattern of neuron firings and synaptic connections), when conscious, differs in a distinctive way from the behaviour of the rest of the brain. But the H_2O/water analogy does not address this problem because *all* H_2O is water, whereas according to Searle only certain areas of the brain are conscious. However, despite the intensive examination of the brain during the last fifty or so years no such difference between the ways neurons act and interact has been detected. Searle grants that 'the resulting phenomena [i.e. conscious thoughts] are complicated and the details of their neurobiological relations to the brain are difficult to understand and at present largely unknown. Once we have solved the relatively easy philosophical problem, we have very difficult neurobiological problems left over' (Searle 2004, 133). But these 'details' are not *largely* unknown: they are completely unknown. More than twenty years ago (Searle 1984, 22), Searle was saying the same, that, after solving the philosophical problem 'there are enormous empirical mysteries'; and nothing has happened since in neurophysiology to change the situation. Solutions to the philosophical problem are comparatively easy because, for the philosophically adept, speculation is easy. But the kind of evidence that could support his theory does not exist.

My conclusion is that there is no good reason why we should accept Searle's theory.

9
The Alternative Possibility

It is not a matter of controversy that altered brain states cause altered states of consciousness. But now we must look at the converse, the apparent causal influence of consciousness on the brain. For it is equally a matter of first-hand observation that we can consciously decide to initiate physical actions such as speaking or moving a finger, and it is *prima face* evident – given the complete brain/consciousness correlation that we all assume – that this mental volition produces the brain activity that produces the action. Because the experimental work has inevitably been concerned with physical actions most of the discussions have focussed on this. But conscious mental activity such as thinking out a problem, considering an argument or a theory and making a judgement about it, including philosophising about the mind/brain problem, making moral decisions, composing music, creating a character in fiction, are equally important. Kicking ideas about is as genuinely action as kicking a football about, and must also produce its neural correlates. The *prima facie* evidence is that there are causal links in both directions: the world as it impinges upon us causes changes in the brain which are reflected in consciousness, and conscious mental initiatives cause their correlative neural changes. The relationship between consciousness and the brain seems to be like that between two dancing partners who always move together but sometimes with one and sometimes the other taking the lead – though the analogy is incomplete in that our physical environment orientates us to itself via the senses through the brain while we are engaged in a thinking process or in acting purposefully in the world.

The plasticity of the brain

Unlike the inside of a computer, the brain consists of living tissue with a considerable degree of plasticity. It grows as part of the development of the body as a whole, and different areas of the brain are developed or allowed to atrophy according to use. In the early years there are uncommitted as well as committed areas so that in children up to the age of five or six if the left hemisphere, which controls speech, is damaged this function can be taken over by the intact right hemisphere. Again, 'Using modern brain imaging techniques, it was discovered that people who had been born blind and used braille throughout their lives had taken up the cortical areas that you or I would use for vision for processing touch . . . [So] the brain had been modified so that parts people normally use for vision are now used for touch' (Jeeves 2003, 19). Again, when stroke victims are able gradually to recover some of their lost abilities, this is done by constant effort, guided by physiotherapists, which forms new pathways in the brain to compensate for the damaged ones. In fact many of the millions of synapses between neurons are changing in strength all the time, with innumerable connections being established or lapsing from moment to moment in the ordinary course of life. It is now possible to grow living brain tissue in a culture and photograph its changing states through time. Steven Rose graphically describes what happens:

> [E]ven though mature neurons form a relatively stable, non-dividing cell population, their own shapes are not fixed but in constant flux. Under-time-lapse the dendrites can be seen to grow and retract, to protrude spines and then to withdraw them again, to make and break synaptic contact. In one study, in the region of the mouse brain that encodes information from the animals' whiskers, 50 per cent of dendritic spines persist for only a few days. If this be architecture, it is a living, dynamic architecture in which the present forms and patterns can only be understood as a transient moment between past and future . . . The brain, like all features of living systems, is both being and becoming, its apparent stability a stability of process, not of fixed architecture. Today's brain is not yesterday's and will not be tomorrow's. (Rose 2005, 146–7)

Further, we are able deliberately to make use of this plasticity. Work done at University College, London, produced a striking example of the way in which deliberate effort can affect the actual structure and functioning of the brain. A prospective London taxi driver has to spend the equivalent of a year or more gaining 'The Knowledge' by studying maps and travelling around the city until he knows where at least all the main streets are and the fastest route to them at different times of day. The researchers did MRI scans of London cabbies and compared them with those of a control group. They found that in the cabbies the posterior hippocampus, which is important for memory formation and for processing spatial information, was enlarged. Further, the fact that the enlargement continued as the cabbies became more experienced showed that the exam was not simply selecting people who already had a larger hippocampus. 'This suggests [the report says] that the hippocampus can undergo plastic changes to accommodate the increasing demand on spatial memory and spatial navigational capabilities that arise from working as a London taxi driver.'[1] The question, then, is: Do people become cabbies by their own free choice (within the range of choices that the circumstances of their lives offers) and deliberately make the necessary effort to acquire The Knowledge, this causing this continuous modification of areas of their brain activity; or does the brain itself, as part of a seamless nexus of physical cause and effect, do all this, the apparently freely made decisions and effort being simply reflections in the passive mirror of consciousness?

Brain plasticity observed in Buddhist meditation

There are many examples of the way in which mental effort produces new neural states. But the most interesting for our present purpose come from experimental work on advanced practitioners of Buddhist meditation. In Chapter 5 we saw that the meditative state is correlated with identifiable brain states. But other researchers go further than this. In *Zen and the Brain* James Austin reports the results of his observations and experiments with practitioners of zazen, the distinctive Zen method of meditation. He found that this modifies brain structure and function and makes possible a new form of consciousness. He says that the experience of *satori* or *kensho,* profound far-reaching enlightenment, is already there as a potentiality in the structure of the brain as 'innate, existing brain function, [which can be] rearranged into a new configuration' (Austin 1998, 23). Zazen produces a sense of unity with the totality of reality, an absence of any kind of anxiety or fear, a focussed 'mindfulness' and serenity, and kindness towards others.

Austin distinguishes between the pragmatic ego, which operates in everyday life and is not lessened but on the contrary strengthened by zazen, and the negative ego, the selfish self that, he says, 'Zen trainees first need to define, identify, and then work through. Not in ways that crush or deny their essential natural selves, but in ways that will simultaneously encourage the flow of their basic, ethical, compassionate impulses'

(Ibid., 35–6). They are uncovering, or recovering, what Zen calls the true original self, or in a typically paradoxical phrase 'your face before your parents were born', which is our buddha nature, now overlaid by the pervasive influences of our ego-deluded human society.

Austin observed this in the roshi, or Zen master, with whom he worked for about two years in Kyoto; and my own much lesser contacts with roshis in Kyoto and Tokyo, and with lay Zen practitioners, is entirely consonant with this. But I think of Zen, and particularly the very demanding Rinzai school of Zen to which these particular roshis belong, as macho-Buddhism, far too demanding for most of us. However, Zen is not the only path to the same end, and many Buddhists prefer the *satipatthana*, or mindfulness, meditation which is one of the methods taught in the Theravada tradition. In its first phase this is very simple and yet quite difficult. It is the opposite of meditation *about* some theme, like the method taught by such Christian masters of meditation as Francis de Sales, in which you imagine as vividly as you can some scene from the life of Jesus and dwell intently upon it in all its detail, thus embedding the biblical narrative ever more firmly into your mind. In contrast to this, in mindfulness meditation you are emptying consciousness of all discursive thought by focussing on something that has minimal intellectual content, namely, your own current breathing. The aim is thereby to open consciousness to the ever-present transforming spiritual reality beyond our normal awareness. In the teachings of the Buddha this is the second stage of meditation. In this stage one 'enters and abides in the second meditation which is devoid of initial and discursive thought, which is born of concentration' (*Majjhima-Nikaya*, I, 454, Horner 1957, 126), leading on to later stages, eventually (whether in this life or a later one) reaching full enlightenment.

Tibetan Buddhism teaches a rather similar form of mindfulness meditation which (as we saw in Chapter 4) is being studied by neuroscientists. Owen Flanagan of Duke University shows the potential significance of this work:

> We can now hypothesise with some confidence that those apparently happy, calm Buddhist souls one regularly comes across in places such as Dharamsala, India – the Dalai Lama's home – really are happy. Behind those calm exteriors lie persistently frisky left prefrontal lobes. If these findings are widely confirmed, they will be of great importance.
>
> Buddhists are not born happy. It is not reasonable to suppose that Tibetan Buddhists are such a homogeneous biological group that they are, uniquely among humans, born with a 'happiness gene' that

activates the prefrontal cortex. The most reasonable hypothesis is that there is something about conscientious Buddhist practice that results in the kind of happiness we all seek.

What about the effect of Buddhist practice on the amygdala and other subcortical forebrain circuitry? This circuitry, you will recall, is involved in relatively automatic emotional and behavioural responses. Now, thanks to important work by Joseph LeDoux at New York University, we know that a persona can be conditioned – via their amygdala and thalamus – to be scared of things that really aren't worth being scared of. We also know that it is extremely hard to override what the amygdala 'thinks' and 'feels' simply by conscious rational thought.

That said, there is some fascinating early work that suggests Buddhist mindfulness practice might tame the amygdala. Paul Ekman of the University of California San Francisco Medical Center, a renowned researcher on basic Darwinian emotions, is, like Davidson, in the early stages of studying Buddhist practitioners. So far, he has found that experienced meditators don't get nearly as flustered, shocked or surprised as ordinary people by unpredictable sounds, even those as loud as gunshots. And Buddhists often profess to experience less anger than most people.

I believe research like this will eventually allow us to answer the question of whether Buddhist training can change the way the brain responds – most importantly with negative emotions – to certain environmental triggers. Antidepressants are currently the favoured method for alleviating negative emotions, but no antidepressant makes a person happy.[2]

The Dalai Lama is accustomed to emphasise that one does not have to be a Buddhist to reap the benefits of this kind of meditation. One does not have to believe in any kind of greater benign reality which it apparently accesses beyond and within us. So far as the neuroscientist is concerned the experience could be purely self-generated and not connected with any reality beyond the individual ego. The big question, as always, is: Does freely chosen, and persistently practised, meditation cause the heightened activity in the left prefrontal lobes and calm the amygdala, or is it the other way round, and the individual, as part of the total causal system of nature, is caused to engage in meditation with its distinctive effects?

In chapters 6 and 7 I have offered reasons to reject both the identity and the epiphenomenalist theories. If these reasons are accepted, we are committed to affirming some degree of conscious exercise of free will – as contentious a topic as any within the entire subject, and the one to which we shall come in the next chapter. And beyond that we shall (in chapters 11 and 12) come to the crucial question whether such 'numinous' experiences – occurring widely and in a great variety of forms – can rationally be accepted as awareness of a greater reality than appears to normal consciousness, or whether they must on the contrary be classified as hallucinatory.

The alternative possibility, then, to consciousness/brain identity, and also to consciousness as a passive reflection of brain activity with no capacity to initiate thought or action, is that consciousness, plus the unconscious mind, exists as a non-physical reality in continual interaction with the brain.

Is this a return to Cartesian dualism? Not Cartesian, for Descartes held that mind and matter interact in the brain's pineal gland – because all the other organs of the brain occur in duplicate in its two hemispheres, but there is only one pineal gland. He also held that animals have no minds, because for him the mind was the immortal soul and animals cannot be allowed immortality. So what I am proposing is a non-Cartesian dualism.

This requires the reality of consciousness and brain, and also their interactions. But how can mind/brain interaction occur? How can the physical affect the mental, and vice versa? If we have abandoned mind/brain identity we are already committed to there being such interaction, at least in one direction. How does this happen? We can only say that it happens in accordance with natural law. Normally, by the 'laws of nature' we mean the laws of the material universe. But if it is the case that the total universe includes mind as well as matter, and if these interact, at least in the human brain, then the laws of nature must include the laws or regularities in accordance with which they interact.

But whether the interaction is *two*-way will depend on whether consciousness exerts an influence on the brain. This leads us directly to the question of free will.

10
Free Will?

Given the accepted principle that every moment of consciousness has its neural correlates, the crucial question has increasingly clearly become, Which causes which? Does the brain, as part of the closed system of nature, generate conscious states, including those constituting distinctively religious experiences? In the case, for example, of the Buddhist meditators described in chapters 5 and 6, is their apparently free and continually renewed effort to undertake prolonged meditation, with its beneficial results, genuinely free?

Compatibilist and non-compatibilist freedom

Determinism is the doctrine that, given the complete state of the world at any moment, it can only be as it is because its state at the previous moment was as it was. Or, putting it the other way round, in a definition which the philosopher Daniel Dennet[1] uses, 'there is at any instant exactly one physically possible future' (Dennett 2003, 67). This means that what we are at any moment, and in what circumstances, are both predetermined in every detail as part of the total causally determined history of the universe.

This seems to leave no room for free will. But in the philosophical discussions it is common to distinguish between compatibilist freedom, which is a subjective sense of freedom compatible with our being objectively totally determined, and non-compatibilist or libertarian freedom. The term 'compatibilist freedom' is an example of philosophical spin doctoring in the form of a persuasive definition. It sounds as though there are two authentic kinds of freedom of the will, compatibilist and non-compatibilist, or libertarian – which latter sounds rather wild! But the notion of compatibilist freedom is a self-contradiction.

The temptation to adopt it comes mainly from the following consideration. It is obvious that we always do what in the moment of action we, being all that we are at that moment in that situation, do. It is *we* who act, and we who are responsible for our actions. If we had been different, and/or the circumstances had been different, we might well have willed differently and hence acted differently. But nevertheless we act of our own volition. Does this fact make out action free? No. Suppose we have been hypnotised to want to do something. Or suppose an electrical device, operated by someone else by remote control, is able to cause us to will to do this or that. Are our volitions then our own free and responsible volitions? Clearly, not. They are cases of so-called 'compatibilist freedom' but not of genuine free will.

Relating this to the brain, suppose complete determinism obtains. Since every thought and act has its neural correlate this requires the complete physical determination of all the hundreds of millions of neural transactions taking place at each moment. Every intention and action, every thought, speculation and argument, every imagination and fantasy, every moral decision, every physical action is predetermined. But the truism that when we act it is always we, being what we are, who are acting is neither evidence of nor an argument for total determinism.

We can highlight the question that arises in this way: When Shakespeare wrote his plays and sonnets, was every moment of his thinking and feeling, his flow of intelligence and emotion, every phase of every experiment in imagination, every eventual arriving at the perfect phrase, physically determined within a causal chain going back through his life to conception and beyond that to the formation of the earth, of the galaxies, right back to the big bang? And the same question about Beethoven's creation of his symphonies, and every other composer's music? Was Michelangelo's work, and Picasso's, and Einstein's, Mozart's, Kant's, Wittgenstein's, predetermined and theoretically predictable in every minutest detail?

It is not in question that in all our thinking and doing our free will, if we have any, is conditioned and limited by a vast range of enclosing factors: our genetic makeup; our physical structure, including whether the right or left cerebral hemisphere is dominant; our upbringing within a certain society and culture in a particular historical period; all the events of our personal story from pre-birth onwards, including the people we have interacted with, what we have seen and heard and read; and everything else that has gone to make us the unique individual that each of us is. In particular our genetic inheritance provides the ground plan of our character and abilities. In relation to religion, there is some limited evidence, based on a small-scale study of identical twins brought up separately and in different environments, that a religious tendency may be inherited. But while this *may* (the data are too slight to say more than that) be one factor among others, it is certainly not the only one. The question is whether all these contributions to our make-up and development, taken as a totality, determine what we think and do at each next moment, or whether it constitutes the conditions within which we nevertheless exercise a limited freedom. (There is, however, one area in which even such a limited free will is internally constrained, namely, by logic: in so far as we are rational we are not free to reject the tautological proposition that $2 + 2 = 4$ or the conclusion of a valid syllogism – though we may of course reject either of its premises and hence its conclusion.)

The non-compatibilist view is that we sometimes make spontaneous, or creative, decisions to act in a certain way, which are not entirely predictable either by ourselves or others. These occur primarily in two areas. One is in making responsible moral decisions and the other in thinking new thoughts, creating new works of art in music, literature, sculpture, painting, new patterns of sound or colour, which may even surprise ourselves. I do not deny the theoretical possibility that this apparently free creativity may in fact be mechanically determined. But theoretical possibilities do not indicate what is actually the case.

The philosopher Daniel Dennett, one of the strongest proponents of materialistic determinism, derides the idea of non-compatibilist freedom as the absurdity of 'moral levitation' (Dennett 2003, 101), a seeking of 'the false security of a miracle-working Self or Soul' (306). But of course moral levitation or a miracle-working self would only be needed if one presupposes, as he does, the truth of materialism. Given materialism, it would indeed require a miracle to break the causal chain. But in presupposing materialism he is manifestly begging the most basic question.[2]

However, the neuro-systems engineering researcher Igor Aleksander says that 'In living organisms there is plenty of "noise": neurons fire in a probabilistic fashion and inner events synchronise badly with each other and world events... [T]here is sufficient non-determinism in a normally functioning neural system to make the organism "feel" that it can freely take arbitrary decisions' (Aleksander 1999, 194). Many neurophysiologists do not accept the idea that 'neurons fire in a probabilistic fashion'. But this is Aleksander's version of compatibilist free will. According to him, the brain of an organism, such as himself, is in a determined state which causes the body to perform some action, at the same time random conditions within the brain producing the epiphenomenal 'feeling' that it is acting by its own deliberate choice – a process that is going on throughout our waking life. This creates a problem that will assume increasing importance as we proceed. For his account of what is happening when we suppose that we are making free choices must be applied to his own actions, including his thinking out and writing his paper. His brain as a living computer 'feels' as though it is engaging in a free, non-determined, intellectual activity which leads him by insight and reason to develop his theory, although in fact it is not. But computers do not literally feel anything, whether a sense of free will or of anger, depression, euphoria, or any feeling state; and it is not productive to smuggle in compatibilist freedom under a metaphorical cloak.

It is worth emphasising again the significance of the fact that computers can be modelled in their software to simulate human intelligence. A mobile computer can be built that will respond in a pre-programmed way to input from a digital camera so as to navigate its way successfully around obstacles. At a much more complex level a computer can be programmed to play chess, calculating the effect of possible moves by itself and its opponent and aiming at a checkmate, and it can be sufficiently successfully programmed to match a human chess master. The difference is that chess masters can take account of their opponents' strategic style by observing their play in a number of games – but possibly a computer could even have all its opponent's previous games fed into its memory, register a pattern, and be programmed to adapt its own strategy to it. But nevertheless the metal and plastic computer is not conscious, except in a 'so-to-speak' sense. To say that a computer is itself conscious, and is not merely programmed to *simulate* conscious behaviour, is to say that it is not a computer. And the more it can do, and the more evident it becomes that consciousness is not required for intelligent-seeming activity, the more manifestly does the existence of consciousness become a mystery.

Experimental evidence

On the face of it, it seems unlikely that any experimental evidence could be relevant to the free will/determinism debate. However, Benjamin Libet has recently returned to the significance of his earlier experiments (see above pp. 61–2 and 92–3). He notes that he and his colleagues found that while there was that approximately 500 msec. gap between the onset of the readiness potential and the conscious will to act, the latter nevertheless still occurred approximately 150 msec. *before* the muscle was activated to produce the flick of the wrist. 'An interval of 150 msec.', he says, 'would allow enough time in which the conscious function might affect the final outcome of the volitional process' (Libet 1999, 51). He concludes that 'Potentially available to the conscious function is the possibility of stopping or vetoing the final progress of the volitional process, so that no actual muscle action ensues. *Conscious-will could thus affect the outcome* of the volitional process even though the latter was initiated by unconscious cerebral processes' (Ibid., 51–2, his italics). And Libet reports that his subjects did in fact sometimes experience a conscious wish or urge to act which they then consciously suppressed or vetoed (Ibid., 52). He goes on to ask whether the conscious control which vetoes the incipient action may itself be preceded by an unconscious cerebral preparation but thinks not, because 'The conscious veto is a *control* function, different from simply becoming aware of the wish to act . . . [T]here is no experimental evidence against the possibility that the control function may appear without development by prior unconscious processes' (Ibid., 53, his italics). He concludes that we have what might be called a monitoring free will in which the conscious self can override the usually unconscious self-direction of the body by the brain.

This suggests the following hypothesis. The human body, controlled by the brain, functions as an immensely complex organism that acts and reacts in evolutionarily programmed ways, thus far as depicted by the mind/brain identity and epiphenomenalist theories. But it is inhab-ited – that really seems the most appropriate word – by a mental flow consisting of both consciousness and the much greater volume of mental activity occurring below the level of conscious awareness. It is a normal function of the brain to control the body as it negotiates its way from moment to moment within the physical environment, the conscious self simply going along with this as its outcomes emerge continuously into consciousness. It would indeed often be a dangerous distraction for the conscious mind to take control, as in the case of the centipede who

> was happy quite
> until the toad in fun,
> said, 'Pray, which leg goes after which?'
> which worked his mind to such a pitch
> he lay distracted in the ditch
> considering how to run.

William James, one of whose strengths as a psychologist was that he included the evidence of introspection among his data, pointed out that in the small change of daily life the feeling of having chosen often simply endorses decisions taken in the unconscious (James 1981, 1132-5). We do innumerable ordinary things by habit, from much of getting up in the morning, brushing our teeth, much of our eating and drinking, walking around the house and the streets, driving the car on familiar routes, the casual social interchanges of 'Hi', 'How d'you do?', 'All right?', as questions which do not expect an answer, and even much of our casual conversation about nothing significant. Even in what may seem to be very deliberate activities, such as the level of tennis that we see at Wimbledon or any other high-level performance in a sport, very precise judgements are being made all the time without conscious direction, except for overall strategy decisions; and the same is true of other skills in many other spheres.

But if Libet is correct, the monitoring consciousness is able to intervene to veto an action and to make room for a different option to emerge from the unconscious, although in the ordinary routine of life it is only relatively occasionally that such conscious decisions are called for. Thus the voluntary flicking of the wrist or moving of the finger in Libet's experiments was a trivial matter with no reason for consciousness to intervene to veto or change it. The occasions when the conscious self makes deliberate decisions are not concerned with the routine management of the body in its physical environment, or even with much of our habitual interactions with other people in the casual exchanges of daily life. They are concerned rather with more serious conversation, with deliberate moral decisions, and with intellectual effort in thinking through such puzzling issues as, for example, the relation between brain and consciousness and, in creative work, in the arts and in the sciences. Such laboratory experiments as Libet's involve actions measured in milliseconds. But sometimes – for most people not very often – we have to make difficult moral decisions that require what may involve lengthy and perhaps agonising wrestling with a great variety of interacting factors, principles, temptations, obligations, the calculation of likely consequences and so on. Again, in doing work in theoretical physics, or in neuroscience theorising, or philosophical thinking, or in writing a novel, or discussing a political policy, or composing a speech, etc. etc., the conscious self is at work, supported by a vast reservoir of unconscious memory and experience. All this conscious mental effort constitutes action just as truly as moving an arm. And all mental action has its continuous neural correlates. But it is the conscious self that exercises free will, and it is in the exercise of free will that conscious-ness causes, rather than being an effect of, its neural correlates. The two dancing partners still move together in synchrony, but in these moments the conscious self is taking the lead.

So my conclusion is that most of our living is governed by accumu-lated unconscious knowledge and experience, but that we do exercise conscious free will in more significant moments such as our business and professional judgements, when we make carefully considered moral decisions, in creative work in the arts and sciences, in aesthetic discrimi-nations, and when we apply our minds to some interesting and complex or debateable issue. I believe, for example, that in my writing and your present reading of this discussion we are both exercising intellectual freedom.

Even here, however, our freedom is of course exercised within the parameters of genetics, environment, life history, availability of informa-tion, etc. etc. As Hans Küng says,

> I know that I am both conditioned by the environment and pre-programmed by heredity. And at the same time I know that I am not totally conditioned by either of these. Within the limits of what is conditioned and what is innate I am free, and therefore not simply predictable. I am not an animal and I am not a robot. (Küng 2003, 17)

Or, as Steven Rose (despite being a materialist) puts it, 'living as we do at the interface of multiple determinisms we become free to construct our own futures, though in circumstances not of our own choosing' (Rose 2005, 301). Otherwise, why would he write at length – and very helpfully – about the ethical decisions presented to us by the rapid development today of neurotechnology?

Quantum indeterminacy

I am arguing for a degree of conscious free will as opposed to complete physical determinism. But let us at this point note, in order to set aside, the question whether quantum mechanics and the element of indeterminacy, or it may be of unpredictability, at the sub-microscopic level, is relevant. Those of us who are not physicists but who listen to what the physicists say, hear two opposite theories. One is that there is genuine randomness at the quantum level; and some philosophers of mind extrapolate this to the macro level of the brain. (But that extrapolation ignores the fact that randomness in the behaviour of the individual quanta would cancel out in the vast statistical magnification to the macro level.) The contrary school of thought holds that the apparent quantum randomness is really unpredictability – unpredictability by us, but not by a hypothetical omniscient observer – rather than an objective randomness. There has accordingly been much discussion about whether quantum mechanics can throw light on the mind/body problem, some (e.g. Stapp 1995) arguing that it can and others (e.g. Ludwig 1995) that it cannot. But rather than following the debate through its technical intricacies it is sufficient for our present purpose to see that if macro events on the scale of the activities in the human brain happened at random this would no more result in free will than would complete determinism. Free action, if it exists, including the intellectual activity of pondering these matters, can be neither random nor determined. But the central question remains whether consciousness can not only be affected by, but can also affect, neural activity.

The problem of self-reference

Those who believe that our thoughts and actions are either randomly caused or rigidly determined by neural events must accept that their theory applies to their own thought processes in arriving at and advocating that theory. Rita Carter, expounding what she takes to be the outcome of the neurophysiologists' work, says,

> some illusions are programmed so firmly into our brains that the mere knowledge that they are false does not stop us from seeing them. Free will is one such illusion. We may accept rationally that we are machines, but we will continue to feel and act as though the essential part of us is free of mechanistic imperatives. But future generations will take for granted that we are programmable machines just as we take for granted the fact that the earth is round. (Carter 1998, 206–7)

Who are the 'us' who know that free will is an illusion by which we cannot help being deluded? Who are the 'we' who can accept rationally that the thoughts that we take to be rational are in fact mechanically determined? If this 'we' is indeed deluded, how can it know that it is being deluded? If we are machines how can we accept *rationally*, rather than just being mechanically caused to think, that we are machines? Carter inadvertently excludes herself from the domain of her statement – as do many other writers in this field. A computer could be programmed, that is causally determined, to 'believe' (in a so-to-speak sense) that it is a machine, and to 'believe' that it has come to this conclusion by a rational process of thought. But it could equally well be programmed to 'believe' the opposite. As Epicurus said, some twenty-three centuries ago, 'He who says that all things happen of necessity cannot criticize another who says that not all things happen of necessity. For he has to admit that the assertion also happens of necessity'.[3] Or as the biologist J. B. S. Haldane succinctly put it, 'If my mental processes are determined wholly by the motions of atoms in my brain, I have no reason to suppose that my beliefs are true' (Haldane 1927, 209). Indeed, if my mental processes are totally determined there is no 'I' who could rationally believe anything. A number of others have also made this point. The philosopher of science, Karl Popper, also has a formulation of the argument (Popper and Eccles 1977, 76f.), although his seems to me unnecessarily complex. So let me put it in my own way.[4]

Let us suppose that the physical world is completely determined, at least at the macro level of our bodies, including of course our brains. And suppose, as will then be the case, that some of us are causally determined in such a way that they believe that complete determinism obtains while others are causally determined to believe the contrary. The question is whether those who are right in believing that they are totally determined can properly be said to *know* or *rationally believe* that they are right, or whether on the contrary if they are right they can never properly be said to know or rationally believe this?

Suppose there is a non-determined observer watching our totally determined world from outside it. This observer is able to think freely, to direct her attention at will, to weigh up evidence and consider reasons, and out of all this to form her own judgements. She can see that our world is a completely determined system and that everyone in it is completely determined in all their actions, thoughts, imaginings, feelings, emotions, day dreamings, visualisings, and all their reasoning, judging and believing. But while this undetermined observer knows that we earthlings are all completely determined *she* knows it in a sense of 'know' in which even those earthlings who correctly believe it nevertheless do not know it. I am not here invoking an ideal sense of 'know' in which it turns out that we can only be said to know tautologies and the immediate content of our own present consciousness, but in the everyday sense of knowledge as well-based rational belief. Thus if there is or could be free will, including non-determined intellectual volition, a free being can come rationally to hold beliefs in a sense in which a totally determined being never can. Let us call the free being's knowledge A and the determined being's knowledge B, and of their functioning respectively in mode A and mode B.

Given this terminology, I suggest that those among us who believe that a total determinism obtains, and who of course believe that they are right in so believing, are in the impossible position of implicitly professing to function in mode A when, if they are right, they can in fact only be functioning in mode B, the determined mode. This, I suggest, is a self-refuting position in the existential or performative sense incurred, for example, by someone who says, 'I do not exist'; for in order for anyone to assert that they do not exist, what they assert must be false. Likewise, to assert in mode A – that is, as a self-critical evidence and reason-based judgement – that all judgements including this one can only be made in the physically determined mode B is to be in a state of performative self-contradiction.

In other words, the argument between the determinist and the non-determinist can only take place in what both assume to be mode A. But whereas the non-determinist believes that what they are both assuming is true, the determinist believes that it is false, and is thus claiming in mode A to know that there is no mode A!

Alternatively, however, cannot a computer be programmed to go through a deductive process and reach the correct conclusion? And what could be more rational than the logical process pursued by a computer? May not our brains be biological computers able to function in this way? This is in effect what the determinist believes to be the case. We are totally determined, but the determinist may nevertheless be determined in such a way that he arrives at a true conclusion, just as a computer may.

It is true that we *may* be totally determined, in which case the determinist is determined in such a way that what he believes is true. But, if so, none of us can ever know or rationally believe this to be the case. Two people debating the question would be like two computers purring away in accordance with their different programmes, with only an outside observer operating in mode A being able to tell which is and which is not programmed to arrive at the truth. In the case of computers, the mode A outside observer is the programmer, who has to know what sound reasoning and correct premises are in order to programme the computer to reach the truth. Or, of course, if the computer is built and programmed by a prior computer, the mode A observer is the non-determined programmer of that computer; and so on in as long a regress as you like. And likewise with ourselves considered as fully determined computers. If anyone is to know what is true and what is false among the conclusions which differently programmed human computers reach, that cannot be any of us in mode B, but could only be a non-determined mode A programmer.

But perhaps, to try another possibility, the ultimate programmer is nature itself, for true beliefs aid survival. May not the evolutionary pressures of the environment gradually eliminate wrongly programmed brains while rewarding correctly programmed ones, thus moving the whole development in a truth-finding direction? Perhaps there is no mode A consciousness, but nevertheless the whole process whereby our brains have become as efficient as they are is a purely natural phenomenon.

But this suggestion is also beset by problems. One is the original one that if this theory is true, including what is then the case, namely, that our brains are causally determined, we could never know or believe this in mode A, since all believing would be in mode B. But further, why would a truth-seeking machine arrive at the species-wide delusion that it is not determined? Presumably because the delusion has some form of survival value. But how could it possibly have survival value if we are simply totally determined computers? Being determined, we do what we are caused to do, and consciousness, whether deluded or not, adds nothing.

However, it is true that biological evolution, in its continual experimentation, has sometimes produced non-functional by-products, and perhaps consciousness is one of these. Perhaps it is like the spandrels referred to in Chapter 8 (pp. 101–2). But this 'perhaps' is dwarfed by a massive 'perhaps not', because generally the evolutionary process has aided efficient function and, unless there are positive reasons to the contrary, the presumption must be that consciousness has some positive function.

It is clear that we must and do *assume* that we are free. We assume this not only as we proceed from moment to moment in daily life but also in our moral life, making ethical judgements between right and wrong – as Kant pointed out (Kant 1947, 116). Whether or not determinism undermines the moral life has been endlessly debated. On the one hand, if the universe is a totally determined system, this includes our using moral language and (epiphenomenally) thinking ethical thoughts. But, on the other hand, bearing in mind the distinction above between mode A and mode B thinking, what we normally mean by ethical right and wrong, good and evil, moral responsibility, liability to praise and blame, justice, reward and punishment, presuppose a mode A point of view, which if determinism is true does not exist. In this sense, determinism does undermine morality.

My conclusion is that we have to reject total physical determinism and allow for free rational judgements, genuine moral choices and the existence of non-physical as well as physical reality. This opens up enormous further possibilities. If our mental life is not purely electro-chemical neural activity, nor an epiphenomenal reflection of what is going on in a physically determined brain, it follows that there is non-physical reality as well as the physical universe. The human person is more than a physical organism, and it cannot be excluded a priori that there may be a non-physical supra-natural reality, perhaps of the limitless significance that the religions claim, and also an answering non-physical aspect of our own nature.

Part III

11
The Epistemological Problem

Our epistemic situation

We all believe that there is a surrounding world which impinges from moment to moment on our senses, so that through the continuous operation of enormously complex neural circuitry we have a generally reliable awareness of that world as it appears to animals with our perceptual equipment, and are thus able to act appropriately within it. We all believe that it exists, and yet we cannot provide any logical argument to back up this belief, because any argument will appeal to the evidence of the senses, thus begging the question by assuming what it is trying to prove.

This anomalous epistemological situation was progressively clarified in the developing British empiricist tradition. I must summarise with a brevity which cannot do justice to the originality and power of these thinkers.

John Locke (1632–1704) adopted and formulated the distinction between what he called primary and secondary qualities. The primary qualities of solidity, extension (i.e. size), figure (i.e. shape) and movement belong to the collections of particles of which the world consists, while the secondary qualities of colour, sound, warmth, smell are effects in consciousness of the impact upon us of those primary qualities. Although atoms have now dissolved into protons, neutrons, molecules, and all perhaps ultimately into 'strings', and classical has now given way to quantum physics based on highly mobile quanta of energy, all this corresponds to Locke's primary qualities. For we do not perceive any of this but only its effects in our consciousness. In the macro world, sound as something heard is not a property of the sound waves which cause the experience of hearing; colour as seen is not a property of the light waves that cause it; likewise taste as experienced does not exist in the particles that excite our taste buds; nor do smells as experienced exist in the airborne chemicals which cause them. If there were no conscious beings there would be no colours, sounds, smells, or tastes, but only their potential physical causes.

However, a generation later George Berkeley (1685–1753) pointed out that the world of primary qualities is also an unprovable assumption. We only *know* with certainty the contents of our own consciousness. Why then assume that there is a physical world out there producing these mental images within us? All that we know to exist is what we perceive. So for us 'to exist is to be perceived', and the world around us, including the other people with whom we interact, exists only in our own minds. This would be solipsism – 'oneself-only-ism' – had not Berkeley rescued himself from this by attributing the continuity and coherence of our perceptions to the work of God. He spoke of 'this consistent, uniform working which so evidently displays the goodness and wisdom of the governing spirit whose will constitutes the laws of nature' (*The Principles of Human Knowledge*, 1710, para. 32. Jessop 1945, 44–5).

Although this Berkeleyian idealism is logically possible, and cannot be disproved, no one seriously believes it in its solipsist form – except the lady who wrote to Bertrand Russell saying that she was a solipsist and was surprised that there were no others (Russell 1948, 180). It is nevertheless conceivable that only my own consciousness exists – the idea can only be stated in the first person – and that everything and everyone of which I am aware exists only in my mind. The only exception for Berkeley, as we saw, is God. But why make this exception? Omitting God from the scene, David Hume (1711–76) radically changed the terms of the discussion by claiming that we believe in the reality of the external world simply because it is our nature to do so and not as a result of, or justified by, philosophical arguments – none of which are in fact sufficient. In his *Treatise of Human Nature* (1739), discussing 'the existence of body [i.e. matter]', he says,

> Nature has not left this to [our] choice, and has doubtless esteem'd it an affair of too great importance to be trusted to our uncertain reasonings and speculations. We may well ask, What causes induce us to believe in the existence of body? but 'tis vain to ask, Whether there be body or not? That is a point, which we must take for granted in all our reasonings. (Bk I, section ii. Selby-Bigge (ed.) 1896, 187)

The mind simply acknowledges what is forced upon it, namely, that most of its perceptions come with a distinctive and irresistible force and form a single ordered system which we call 'reality' or 'the world'. From our point of view, we perceive a world in which we live and no amount of philosophical reasoning can either establish or refute this. To trust our senses is a matter of what can be called natural belief, or pre-philosophical common sense. And this natural belief is a pragmatic necessity: if we did not act on it we would soon perish.

G. E. Moore (1873–1958), one of the most important philosophers of the first half of the twentieth century, at this point supporting Hume, insisted that we *know* many things that we cannot *prove*. In his famous essay 'A Defence of Common Sense' he says, 'I *know*, with certainty . . . [that] There exists at present a living human body, which is *my* body. This body was born at a certain time in the past, and has existed continuously ever since, though not without undergoing changes . . . [T]he earth has existed also for many years before my body was born . . . '(Moore 1925, 193–4), and so on in a list of common-place things such as the existence of the bookcase and mantelpiece in his study. And everyone else has an equivalent body of knowledge. Moore is insisting, as also did his contemporary Ludwig Wittgenstein in an extraordinarily creative period of twentieth-century Western philosophy, that the ordinary knowledge that we all share, and express in the ordinary language that we have in common, neither needs nor is able to be backed up by philosophical arguments.

The fact is that in the ideal (or Platonic) sense of 'know' as a direct vision of truth, or being in a state of mind such that it is logically impossible to be mistaken, we only know the immediate content of our present consciousness, and (subject to the logical possibility of Descartes's 'malicious demon' who manipulates our minds) analytic, or tautological, truths. This ideal sense would, by contrast, reduce our ordinary use of 'know' to 'believe' and thus rule out our ordinary use of 'know'. It is therefore preferable in practice to mean by it well-justified, or warranted, belief, even though this never amounts to the Platonic ideal of knowledge. This is the basis on which I am proceeding here.

The principle of critical trust

Hume, standing on the shoulders of Locke and Berkeley, and supported by the common sense and ordinary language philosophers of the twentieth century, enables us to formulate the implicit principle by which we live all the time. This is that we accept what appears to be there as being there, except when we have reason to doubt it. Thus it seems to me at the present time that there is a computer screen in front of me, and that I am making words appear on it by means of a technology which I can use but do not profess to understand, and such 'seeming' is as much as we have or need. We normally trust our experience, and could not live for a day, or even an hour, if we did not.

This is not, however, a blind but a critical trust, always in principle open to revision.[1] If I suddenly woke up in bed and realised that I had been dreaming that I was in my study and working on the computer I would then, retrospectively, reclassify that experience as delusory – in the special sense in which dreams are delusory. In saying this I am using the larger mass of my experience in the course of which I have become familiar with sleeping and dreaming and have become able to distinguish between dreams and waking life. But there are also waking situations in which I have reason afterwards to distrust what appears to be the case. We know about mirages in the desert, and distorted figures in concave and convex mirrors, and thinking for a moment that a bit of branch or a leaf is a bird sitting in the tree, or hearing what at first seems to be a car coming up the drive but which we quickly realise is the sound of a lawnmower next door, etc., etc.

There is a difference between illusions and delusions. As an example of the former, I may for a few moments believe I see someone standing in the shadows in the corner of the room but then realise that this was an illusion. My mind, which is all the time unconsciously interpreting a mass of sensory signals, had misinterpreted the shape of the shadow. A delusion, in contrast, as I am using the term, is not a misinterpretation of externally presented data but pure projection, usually caused by some mental or neural malfunction; and it is sometimes not the deluded individual but others who recognise it for what it is.

The implicit principle by which we all live, then, is critical trust. We could not live on any other basis. If I did not trust my perception of the solid wall in front of me I would walk into it and injure myself. If I did not trust my perception of cars moving along the road I would be run over. If I did not trust my perception of the telephone I would not use it. If I did not trust my perception of the visitors who have come to lunch I would not prepare any food for them. We live all the time by a trust which is the most basic kind of faith. And we do not feel any need to justify it – which, as we have seen, is in any case not possible. Critical trust, then, is part of our working definition of sanity. We would count as insane someone who lacks it.

Critical trust and religious experience

Why, then, should not this principle of critical trust apply to apparently cognitive experience generally, including religious experience? *Prima facie*, it should, for religious experience is as genuinely experience as sense perception. The naturalistic thinker, whose philosophy has no room for a transcendent divine reality, need not hesitate to accept this, for, according to our principle, it is rational to trust our experience *except* when we have a reason not to. This holds even if he or she has personally experienced a moment of religious awareness – she may on reflection dismiss it as illusory, for in the case of religious experience there are, from a naturalistic point of view, good reasons not to trust it.

These 'good reasons' lie in the differences between sensory and religious experience. These seem so great and so fundamental that the same principle cannot properly be used to cover them both. What are these differences?

First, sense experience is universal. All human beings, and indeed all animal species, perceive the world in which they live. True, there are many variations. The dominant sense in humans is normally sight, in elephants it is smell, in bats it is a kind of radar. Again the different senses are often not equally acute: they tend to decline with age, and some people are colour blind or tone deaf. Some lack one sense altogether, being blind, or two senses, being both blind and deaf. So there are innumerable differences in the ways that we perceive our environment. But nevertheless we do all perceive, however incompletely, what is recognisably the same world.

In contrast to this, religious experience, in the sense of a putative experiential awareness of the Transcendent, is not universal. The earliest surviving evidences of human life do indeed include some kind of religious dimension, suggesting an innate tendency to experience the natural in terms of the supranatural. This was probably a pervasive feature of tribal and national societies of the pre-axial ages. But with the individualising of religion (as described in Chapter 1) religious experience gradually became personal as well as communal, a voluntary participation in a process of spiritual/moral transformation. In this new situation, only very few outstanding individuals experience their lives religiously all the time, and the proportion of the general population who do so sometimes, whether in acts of worship of some kind or in their daily lives, varies greatly within different cultural contexts. In our contemporary Western secular societies such evidence as we have (as noted in Chapter 2) indicates that approximately one-third of people experience at least once in their lives, and often more than once, a moment or period of apparent consciousness of an overwhelmingly significant reality beyond themselves and their fellow humans. And even when we add that the impact of transcendent reality may typically be experienced within our modern naturalistic culture in terms of ethical rather than religious concepts, it is still true that unselfish response to an inner call to serve others in need, although happily not rare, is also far from universal.

This is correlated with the fact that awareness of the Transcendent is not compulsory. We cannot help perceiving the physical world: it continuously forces itself upon us. But while sense experience is compulsory, religious experience is not.

Second, sense experience is very largely uniform throughout the world and throughout the centuries. It is not totally so, because of the physiological differences mentioned above, and also because of cultural variations arising from geographical and climatic factors that can affect the emotional dimension of our awareness of our environment – the jungle that is experienced as terrifying to a stranger is a familiar home to its inhabitants. But it remains a jungle to both, and because we all live in the same world we are all compelled to experience it in basically the same way. In contrast to this, religious experience, in the sense of experience structured in terms of religious concepts, takes an enormous variety of different forms within different religious cultures, both around the world and through the ages. As we saw in Chapter 2, it includes the sublime, the ridiculous, the peculiar and the positively evil. It includes the sense of being part of a much greater reality which is friendly, or benign; feeling called by an avenging God to commit murder or even genocide; a sense of the presence of an all-loving God; being uplifted within the beauty and solemnity of an ornate church service, or within the expectant silence of Quaker worship; being terrified by the thought of hell; encountering the 'being of light' in a near-death experience; release from fear and anxiety into an openness to others in meditation; seeing the world as suffused with the divine in a way that engenders love and compassion. And so on, almost indefinitely.

How can this be at all comparable with sense experience? The object of human sense experience through the ages and around the globe is the same physical world. But the object of human religious experience through the ages and around the globe is not the same supposed sacred or divine reality. (The word 'supposed' or 'putative' applies to each of the following examples, although it would be clumsy to add it every time). On the contrary, it is a mass of mutually conflicting reports such that if one experience is authentically cognitive of transcendent reality then it seems that all, or most, of the others must be inauthentic. If the Transcendent is a divine Person who has created everything other than him/herself, how can it also be the transpersonal Brahman or

Dharmakaya? How can the theistic experience of being in God's presence be genuine if the non-theistic Buddhist experience is genuine? If God is strictly unitary, as Judaism and Islam proclaim, how can God be a Trinity as Christianity proclaims, and so how can their respective forms of religious experience all be valid?

Differences and contradictions

Even within the same religion, both at different times and at the same time, there are differences some of which amount to contradictions.

Within Christianity, there is the division between the Roman Catholic, Reformed or Protestant, and Orthodox churches. But as a more fundamental example, God was thought of and experienced in the early medieval period in Europe as a terrible threatening power, with unending torment in hell believed to be the fate not only of all unbaptized people but also, within Christendom, of sinners who had not made their confession and been absolved by the Church. And because there was so much suffering from diseases, plagues, droughts, floods, warfare and pillage it seemed that God must be very angry with his people. For mercy one prayed, not to God, or to Christ, whom one would face as the stern judge on the Last Day, but to the Virgin Mary or a local saint.[2] It was only in the thirteenth and fourteenth centuries that the thought of God as love, and of Jesus as love incarnate, was widely rediscovered. The dreadful hell-threatening God of Church-engendered religious experience of the tenth century was quite different from the joyful experience of divine love by such mystics as Julian of Norwich (1342–14??) to whom (as we saw in Chapter 3) the meaning of her vivid visions and auditions was revealed as love. 'What, do you wish to know your Lord's meaning in this thing? Know it well, love was his meaning. Who reveals it to you? Love. What did he reveal to you? Love. Why does he reveal it to you? For love' (Julian of Norwich 1978, 342. Long text, ch. 86). But still today there is a strong stream of fundamentalist 'hellfire' Christianity alongside and in tension with 'God is love' Christianity.

Within Judaism there are today divisions between its Orthodox and Reformed branches. And, going back to the scriptures, there is a significant development in the Jewish concept of God. According to the Torah, God as a violent tribal god ordered the Israelites, 'Now go and smite Amalek, and utterly destroy all that they have: do not spare them, but kill both man and woman, infant and suckling, ox and sheep, camel and ass' (1 Samuel 15:3), and on another occasion caused the sun to stand still for a day so that they could have more time to slaughter the Amorites (Joshua 10:12–14). The kind of religious experience behind such stories is very different from that of the psalmist who speaks of God as 'merciful and gracious, slow to anger and abounding in steadfast love' (Psalm 103:8), so that 'As a father pities his children, so the Lord pities those who fear him. For he knows our frame: he remembers that we are dust' (Psalm 103:12–13). And there are numerous other texts in both categories. Post-biblical rabbinic Judaism has very largely followed the more humane tradition. The Hebrews' religiously experienced awareness of their history must have been very different within different individuals and at different points in that history.

Within Islam there is the division between the Sunni and Shia branches, and within the Qur'an between, on the one hand, verses which speak of God intervening to aid the Muslims in battle: 'Indeed God has helped you on many occasions, even during the battle of Hunain ... and sent down troops invisible to punish the infidels. This is the recompense of those who do not believe' (Qur'an 9:25–6), and on the other hand verses which treat non-Muslims with an equal respect, such as

> To each of you We have given a way and pattern of life. If God had pleased He could surely have made you one people (professing one faith). But He wished to try and test you by that which He gave you. So try to excel in good deeds. To Him you will all return in the end, when He will tell you of what you were at variance. (5:48)

There are numerous other verses of both kinds, both expressing and evoking different forms of religious experience.

There is also a distinction, amounting in some Muslim cultures to a contradiction, between 'mainstream' Islam, focussed on the absolute transcendence of God and expressed in the ritual observances and obedience to the Shari'a laws, with a powerful sense of the reality of both paradise and hell, and the more mystical, Sufi, focus upon the immanence (as well as transcendence) of God, for 'We created man ... We are closer to him than his jugular vein' (Qur'an 50:16). Within this form of Islam God is 'immanent both in human souls (*anfus*) and in the spatio-temporal order (*afaq*)' (Yaran 2004, 5), and there is a greater emphasis on God's love for humanity and the answering human love of God. This lies behind the famous words of the female mystic Rabi'a (eighth century CE), 'O God! if I worship

Thee in fear of Hell, burn me in Hell; and if I worship Thee in hope of Paradise, exclude me from Paradise; but if I worship Thee for Thine own sake, withhold not Thine everlasting Beauty' (Nicholson 1979, 115).

We have already looked (in Chapter 2) at the mystical unity sought by the Sufi masters and I shall not repeat that here. But this is probably as rare as the unitive experience within the other monotheisms, and in order not to exaggerate the difference between the mystical and the more 'ordinary' forms of Muslim religious experience – for the Sufi influence is widespread today in varying degrees, though not dominant, in India, Pakistan, Bangladesh, Malaysia, Turkey, North Africa, sub-Saharan Africa and Persia (Greaves 2001, 15–17) – we should note the sense of God's presence, experienced by different Muslims at different times and in different degrees during the daily prayers, particularly the noon prayers in a mosque, in wonder at the regularities and complexities of nature, and in a sense in moments of good fortune or healing that this was God's work, and in what many report to be the profound spiritual experience of the pilgrimage to Mecca. And so while Muslims do not normally speak of 'religious experiences' they do enjoy their own forms of this, and these are of much the same nature as Christian religious experience. But in all this we have been seeing yet more examples of the variability which distinguishes religious from sense experience.

This continues when we turn to what the West has labelled Hinduism, consisting in the many diverse streams of the religious life of India and embracing widely different forms of religious experience from the village worship of a local deity to this combined with the more overarching worship of Vishnu or Shiva, to the unitive experience of advaitic mystics. However, the worshippers of the male Shiva or Vishnu, and of the great goddess Devi of whom other female gods, such as Kali and Durga are expressions, do not argue about which is the true God, because they all are, as different manifestations of the 'formless' or ineffable ultimate reality of Brahman. There is thus as much variety, but less internal contradiction, within Hinduism than within the 'Western' religion.

Within Buddhism there is the division between the Mahayana and the Theravada. But while the methods of meditation vary between the Tibetan, Zen and Theravadin traditions, the experiential outcome is essentially the same and does not create the same problem that we found within the monotheisms. Again the internal tensions and contradictions are much less than in the 'Western' monotheisms.

But taking religion globally, the problem of diversity is real. And so the fact that sense experience is compulsory, hence universal and globally uniform, whereas religious experience is neither compulsory nor universal nor uniform constitutes a strong argument for the conclusion that the critical trust principle cannot be applied to both.

Or can it? This is the question to be pursued in the next chapter.

12
The Epistemological Solution

Experiencing as interpreting

Epistemologists distinguish three main positions (with various versions within each) concerning the relation between our conscious experience of the world and the world of which we are conscious.

One is naive realism, our natural everyday assumption that the world around us is just as it seems to us to be. For all practical purposes this serves us perfectly well. For as we have evolved our senses have been continuously tuned to detect only those aspects of the total environment that we need to be aware of in order to survive and flourish. But the world as we experience it is in fact a minute selection of the totality discovered by the sciences. We hear only a small part of the sound scale – some other animals can hear sounds too high for us to hear. There is an electromagnetic spectrum from cosmic rays as short as four ten-thousand-millionths of an inch to radio waves as long as eighteen miles; but our human senses respond only to those between about sixteen and thirty-two millionths of an inch. Nor do we detect most of the chemical differences in our environment. We experience the wooden table as a solid three-dimensional, heavy, extended, static, coloured object with its own distinctive feel and smell. But for the physicist it is mostly empty space with hundreds of millions of molecules in constant rapid motion, none of them having weight, colour, sound, smell, or even fixed position. But if we perceived it at that micro level we would be unable to act and react in relation to it. We are conscious of it in the form that answers to our needs as the organisms that we are, formed for and by our inherited niche in the macro-micro scale.

As the extreme opposite of naive realism is the 'idealism' which holds that the perceived world exists only in our consciousness, or rather in *my* consciousness since the other people with whom I interact are also part of my perceived world. We met this in the last chapter as it was presented by George Berkeley, except that he avoided this solipsistic conclusion by affirming the independent existence of God who feeds our perceptions to us in the regular way that we call the order of nature. Without that, solipsism would be as irrefutable as it is also unbelievable.

The third, middle, position is critical realism. Its basic principle goes back beyond Immanuel Kant (1724–1804), the most influential philosopher of the modern period. There are many earlier intimations of it, but it was he who worked out its implications in a systematic way. His philosophy is immensely complex, though for the most part with an architectonic unity, and is open at several points to varying interpretations. But he affirmed a reality beyond us and existing independently of us, but argued that we are not aware of it as it is in itself, unobserved, but only as the innate structure of the human mind is able to bring the impacts of that reality to consciousness as the phenomenal world. Thus we are aware of the world as it appears to us, with our particular cognitive equipment and forms and categories of consciousness. As one philosopher puts it,

> If we think in terms of the metaphor of catching things in the network of experience, [the categories of thought] are the meshes of our net. Only what can be caught in them is available to us. Anything that passes through them untouched will not be picked up by us, and neither will whatever falls outside our nets altogether. (Magee 1997, 182)

The term 'critical realism' was coined by American philosophers in the twentieth century to signify a realist affirmation of a world existing independently of us while recognising the creative contribution of the mind to our awareness of that world. This has been amply confirmed since and has become long established in cognitive psychology and the sociology of knowledge.[1]

In speaking, then, of experiencing as interpreting I am not using 'interpreting' in the sense in which we may interpret a text, as in biblical interpretation (or in the jargon of the biblical scholars, hermeneutics), but in the sense in which we are all the time interpreting the impacts of our environment upon our senses. And I am using 'meaning' to mean (among it's many meanings) the character of a state of affairs in virtue of which we can act and react purposefully within it. What

William James called a blooming buzzing confusion would have no meaning for us, but the world as we consciously experience it does; and we both find and impose this meaning by integrating those fragmentary aspects of the environment selected by our senses. The basic structure of meaning (which Kant identified as the forms of space and time and such categories as substance, or thinghood, and causality) is integral to our human nature as part of the world; but the further and 'higher' levels of meaning are created by our culturally formed creative imagination.

This is well illustrated by what Ludwig Wittgenstein (1889–1951) called 'seeing as'. He introduced this through puzzle pictures, such as Jastrow's duck-rabbit – you can see the same lines on paper as representing the head of a duck facing left or the head of a rabbit facing right, and consciousness tends to alternate between them. There are also much more complex puzzle pictures, for example, a page of what are apparently a dense but random spattering of dots in which you may suddenly see the outline of a human face. As Wittgenstein says, we '*see* it as we *interpret* it' (Wittgenstein 1953, 193). We can readily expand 'seeing as' into 'experiencing as', using all the senses in concert, as we do all the time in daily life. Wittgenstein, sticking strictly to our ordinary everyday ways of speaking, did not take this further step. He points out that while it makes sense to say 'Now he is seeing Jastrow's figure as a duck', we would not on seeing a knife and fork on the table naturally say 'Now I am seeing this as a knife and fork', because that is the only way we can see them. As he says, 'One doesn't "*take*" what one knows as the cutlery at a meal *for* cutlery' (Ibid., 195). But I think that he was mistaken at this point. It is true that in our culture this is the only way we have learned to see a knife and fork on a dinner table. But if a time machine could bring some stone-age persons into the room they would not see what are to us the knife and fork as a knife and fork. They would not have those concepts, which are integral to a wider cultural context that includes tables and chairs, plates and drinking glasses, kitchens and dining rooms, houses and streets, factories and shops, etc., etc. They might see the objects on the table as sacred shining objects, full of *mana* and not to be touched, or as small weapons, or as gods to be worshipped or placated, or perhaps in yet other ways of which we have no conception. But they would not see them as what we mean by knives and forks.

Experiencing-as, then, is recognising something as having meaning in the sense that we can behave appropriately in relation to it – in this case by using the knife and fork as aids to eating. And experiencing a situation as being this or that particular kind of situation is to recognise it as having meaning, or significance, such that we can behave within it in (what we think is) an appropriate way.

Not only seeing knives and forks, etc., then, but *all* our conscious experience is experiencing-as, using our conceptual resources to find meaning in the world as it presents itself to us. Some of our concepts, such as mountain, rain, tree, earth... are almost universal among humans, available to stone-age persons as much as to ourselves today, but very many others arise out of, and are part of, the development of human cultures. And because there are different ways of being human, which are the great cultural streams that have formed through the centuries, there are culture-specific concepts as well as the globally operative ones that Kant identified.

Levels of meaning

Seeing the objects on the table as a knife and fork to be used in eating is for us an example of empirical or natural meaning. They are particular discrete objects, but along with other discrete objects they are usually experienced as elements in a larger situation – the meal, which is itself part of a yet larger situation. We normally live on the situational level of meaning. My present use of the computer in front of me involves aware-ness of being engaged in writing a book, which in turn involves aware-ness of being part of a society that includes books, printing, publishers, readers, libraries, etc. We live in expanding circles of meaning which exhibit stability and yet also continuous change.

Within this continuously changing world we are aware of different layers or levels – using the two terms synonymously – of meaning. An empirical situation may also have the higher level of meaning in which we are conscious of its moral significance. For example, I see someone ahead of me staggering and falling to the ground. She may have had a heart attack or a stroke or been let down by a trapped nerve in the leg or spine. The purely natural meaning of the situation is just the bare fact of this body on the ground. But we feel called upon to help her if we can. Whether or not we act on it, we feel some degree of moral obligation arising from our common humanity. For ethical meaning is essentially social, concerned with our relationships with other people as people. This is a further layer of meaning that we find in many empirical situations. And it is a 'higher' level of meaning in the sense that it presupposes empirical meaning. For there would be no ethical meaning without empirical situations to be experienced as having this further kind of significance. (There seem, however, to be some individuals who are totally a-moral, for some reason defective in that they are completely unaware of the moral significance of the situations in which they find themselves. But they are, happily, the rare exceptions.)

According to the religions there is yet another level of meaning which supervenes upon empirical situations, both those that do and those that do not have ethical significance, though the two generally merge into one in the experient's life. It will be sufficient, after the fuller treatment in Chapter 2, to mention here only one form, nature mysticism, in which the physical situation is experienced as having religious meaning. For example,

> I was standing on the edge of a low cliff overlooking a small valley leading to the sea. It was late afternoon or early evening and there were birds swooping in the sky – possibly swallows. Suddenly my mind 'felt' as though it had changed gear or switched into another view of things. I still saw the birds and everything around me but instead of standing looking at them, I *was* them and they were me. I was also the sea and the sound of the sea and the grass and sky. Everything and I were the same, all one. It was the most peaceful and 'right' feeling imaginable and I knew without any smallest doubt that everything happened for a reason, a good reason, and fitted into everything else, like an arch with all the bricks supporting each other and their cornerstone without cement, just by their being there. Everything was RIGHT. (Maxwell and Tschudin 1990, 47)

The experient (a woman in her thirties) was of course conscious of the presence of the land and sea and birds, but at the same time of a further dimension of meaning consisting in a sense of continuity with the surrounding world, and of the purpose and 'rightness' of everything. If translated into theistic language this would be a sense of an overarching divine presence and purpose. If translated into Buddhist language it would be a sense of the reality of the universal Buddha nature which is the ultimate nature of everything, including ourselves. In itself, as an isolated moment, this experience had no ethical meaning, although in so far as it affected her basic dispositional state it will have influenced the woman towards a loving and compassionate attitude to others as all parts of the same universe and sharing in its 'rightness'.

The religious meaning of empirical situations is a further 'layer', often superimposed on their moral significance. But the two layers merge when someone is conscious either of the religious meaning of particular social events or of a wider history as it is unfolding around them, or of an imperative to behave in a certain way within a situation which already has it's own moral character. For example, the abolition of slavery in the British empire was initiated on religious grounds by the Pennsylvania Quakers who condemned slavery in 1688. Again, those Church leaders in South Africa, led by bishop (later archbishop) Desmond Tutu, who opposed apartheid were conscious of a religious call to oppose an evil regime that was totally contrary to all Christian values. In each case the religious imperative was not an alternative to the purely moral imperative (which was equally felt in apartheid South Africa by atheist communists), but a further dimension of meaning. This further dimension is, for those who experience it, the ultimate horizon in the expanding circles of meaning.

Cognitive freedom

This hierarchy of levels of meaning is correlated with a hierarchy of degrees of cognitive freedom. As we have already seen, we have minimal freedom in our awareness of our physical environment. It forces itself upon us, and if we could – though fortunately we can't – completely ignore it, it would soon exterminate us.

But we have a greater degree of freedom in our awareness of the ethical significance of situations. To be human is to have developed the capacity to see in many of life's situations that we are subject to a moral claim upon us to act in one kind of way rather than another – basically, not wantonly to injure others, but to treat them as fellow human beings of the same basic value as ourselves. Usually, it is easier to see what we ought *not* to do than what we ought to do. But we also have a distinctively human capacity to evade the dawning awareness of a moral obligation. We are uncomfortably aware, or conscious that we are in danger of becoming uncomfortably aware, that we have a responsibility to help this person, or to right this wrong, or to refrain from some course of action that is to our advantage but is unfair and damaging to others. But we rethink the situation, we look at it in a different light, we focus on one aspect while losing sight of another, or in some other way we convince ourselves that we are not really morally involved in the situation, or that it is all someone else's fault and there's nothing that we can do about it. In thus reconceptualising a situation we often rename it. This is most blatantly evident in the language of war. Instead of asking how many young men were killed in the battle, the generals ask what was the body count; when innocent civilians are killed this is collateral damage;

when you accidentally bomb or shoot at your own side, or an ally, this is friendly fire; and so on. In short in the exercise of our moral freedom we have a remarkable capacity for individual and collective self-deceit.

We have an even greater degree of cognitive freedom in religion. It is the teaching of each of the world faiths that the divine reality does not force itself upon us, but leaves space for an uncompelled response on our part. On the one hand, there is an aspect or dimension of our nature that is inherently capable of responding. This is in Christian terms the image of God within us, 'that of God in everyone'; or in Rabbinic terms God's immanence in the 'implanting of the Divine life within the human soul' (Jacobs 1973, 63); or in Islamic terms the fact that 'We [God] are closer to him [mankind] than his jugular vein' (Qur'an 50:16); in Hindu terms, the *atman* which we all are in the depths of our being; and in Buddhist terms the universal Buddha nature. But, on the other hand, the Transcendent is only apprehended through an uncompelled exercise of this capacity. For the Ultimate exists at an epistemic distance from us which makes possible the (limited) human autonomy in virtue of which we exist as responsible individual persons.

Consider this first in the case of the monotheisms.[2] If we are freely to come to God, God must be initially at a distance from us – not a spatial distance but a distance in the dimension of awareness. If in becoming conscious we found ourselves in the immediate presence of a God of infinite knowledge and power, infinite goodness and love, but also of justice and righteousness, knowing us through and through so that no act or thought or emotion or imagination or fantasy of ours is hidden from him/her, we would have no real moral freedom in relation to the deity. In order to give us that freedom God must 'stand back' as, in Martin Luther's famous phrase, *deus absconditus*, the hidden God. Many Christian thinkers have been well aware of this. Pascal (1631–63) puts it particularly eloquently:

> It was not the right that He should appear in a manner manifestly divine, and completely capable of convincing all men; but it was also not right that He should come in so hidden a manner that He could not be known by those who should sincerely seek Him. He has thus willed to make Himself quite recognizable by those; and thus, willing to appear openly to those who seek Him with all their hearts, He so regulates the knowledge of Himself that He has given signs of Himself, visible to those who seek Him, and not to those who seek Him not. There is enough light for those who only desire

to seek Him, and enough obscurity for those who have a contrary disposition. (Pascal 1947, 119. *Pensees* no. 430)

As Pascal puts it here, and also according to many in the high Calvinist tradition, it is sin that blinds so many to the presence of God. But there is also a more humane understanding of the situation. The twelfth-century Hugh of St Victor wrote,

> [I]t was necessary that God should show Himself, though hidden, lest He be entirely concealed and entirely unknown; and again, it was necessary that He should conceal Himself, though shown and known to some degree, lest He be entirely manifest, so that there might be something which through being known would nourish the heart of man, and again something which through being hidden would stimulate it. (Hugh of St Victor, 1951, 42)

Or as the thirteenth-century Sufi Ibn 'Ata' Illah said, 'Only because of the intensity of His manifestation is He veiled, and only because of the sublimity of His light is He hidden from view' ('Ata' Illah 1978, 88). Again the twentieth-century theologian John Oman expresses it well, 'The peculiarity of the supernatural environment is that we cannot enter it except as we see and choose it as our own' (Oman 1931, 309).

Oman's formulation of the idea of epistemic distance (not his phrase) bridges the gap between the theistic and non-theistic religions in that the same principle applies to both equally. For if the ultimate reality is not an infinite person – or three infinite persons in one – but the 'formless' or ineffable Brahman, or the Dharmakaya/Nirvana/Buddha nature, or the Tao, we have deliberately to open ourselves to the universal presence of that reality in order to become conscious of it. The Hindu must follow one or other of the paths (*yogas*) of action (*karman*), knowledge (*jnana*), or devotion (*bhakti*). The Buddhist must follow the Noble Eightfold Path, described in Chapter 4, which includes right ethical conduct, right mental discipline, eliminating such negative emotions as hatred, jealousy, intolerance, and the attainment of the positive attitudes of *metta*, love and *karuna*, compassion. And the Taoist must (in so far as this can be inadequately expressed in a sentence) become conscious of the 'flow' of the universe, with its complementary currents, and learn to respect differences, acting by an inaction which nevertheless produces harmony.

Thus within each of the great non-theistic traditions, as within the monotheisms, deliberate effort (or in the case of Taoism what can be called, paradoxically, effortless effort) is required. The supra-natural – a more acceptable term today than Oman's 'supernatural' – environment, whether experienced as a personal God or a transpersonal Reality, is always and everywhere there to be accessed, but is not forced upon our consciousness.

This is why, from a religious point of view, experience of the Transcendent is neither universal nor uniform. It is not universal, at any given time, because it is not forced, or does not force itself, upon anyone; and it is not uniform around the world because the human contribution to the forms of authentic religious experience varies within the different cultures and traditions of the earth.

My conclusion, then, is that the obvious differences between sensory and religious experience do not constitute a valid reason to rule out the latter as delusory. It is entirely reasonable, rational, sane, for those who participate in what is apparently an awareness of the Transcendent to believe, and to base their lives on the belief, that in living as physical beings within the natural world we are at the same time living in relation to a transcendent-and-immanent reality whose presence changes the meaning for us of everything that we do and that happens to us.

13
Any Particular Religion?

Which religion?

In some 98 per cent or more of cases the religion to which anyone adheres (or against which they rebel) depends upon where they were born. Someone born into a Christian family in the United States, Britain, Uganda, Brazil, or anywhere else is very likely to become a Christian (practising or nominal) rather than a Muslim, Hindu, etc. Someone born into a Muslim family in Egypt, Indonesia, Pakistan, Iran, Turkey, or anywhere else is very likely to become a Muslim (again, practising or nominal) rather than a Hindu, Buddhist, Christian, etc. Someone born into a Buddhist or a Sikh family is very likely to become a Buddhist or a Sikh, and so on round the world.

There are of course voluntary conversions from one religion to another because of the individual's dissatisfaction with his/her inherited faith and attraction to another. These happen in all directions, and when they happen we can only assume that the move is a right one. But these are statistically insignificant compared with the massive transmission of faith from generation to generation within the same tradition.

There have also been mass conversions in the age when the ruler determined the religion of his population, as was often the case after Christianity became the official religion of the Roman Empire, or again after the Reformation of the sixteenth century – when the ruler opted for either the Catholic or the Protestant cause his people were automatically included. In the twentieth century the leader of the Outcastes, Untouchables, Depressed Classes or, Gandhi's name for them, Harijans (children of God), now Dalits, in Hindu India, were led by Dr B. R. Ambedkar, who took part in drafting India's Constitution, including the banning of caste discrimination, and became the

Law Minister in the Nehru government. But in 1954, dissatisfied with the law's implementation, 'in reaction to the centuries' long oppression of the so-called Untouchables by caste Hindus . . . [Ambedkar] rose like a Joshua from [the Untouchables'] ranks, insisting that they had waited in vain for justice, and it was time to renounce Hinduism altogether and embrace a more egalitarian religion, Buddhism' (Chatterjee 2005, 188), though Ambedkar had his own selective understanding of Buddhism. He led some 200,000 to leave Hinduism and become Buddhists, and today there are said to be some eight million Buddhists in India. Ambedkar chose Buddhism, after a careful study of the world religions, because it was a religion of Indian origin that had always rejected the caste system, whereas Christianity was a foreign religion and caste distinctions continued undiminished among Indian Christians, as also among Muslims.

Such rare cases apart, we normally inherit our religion along with our culture and our language. Indeed we usually inherit at the same time membership of some particular branch of that religion. But today, in the case of Christianity, there is also another dividing line, crossing the denominational boundaries, between what can broadly be called conservatives, including evangelicals, many of whom are biblical fundamentalists, and liberals or progressives. Liberal-minded Catholics in many ways have more in common with liberal-minded Protestants than with their own conservative hierarchy. Conservative-minded Episcopalians often have more in common, in outlook and social attitudes, with Catholics than with their own liberals and 'radicals'. In this matter of conservative or liberal outlook there is, as these cases indicate, much more scope for individual inclination and choice than in organisational membership.

These are examples from within Christianity of the fact that we are, generally, not only born into one religion rather than another, but also into one branch of it rather than another. Or of course increasingly, in Western Europe, into a consciously non-religious, secularist or atheist environment, whose outlook we may well inherit. In Chapter 11 I outlined the comparable divisions within Islam, Hinduism and Buddhism, and need not repeat that here.

What does this imply for the question, Which religion? For many people, it means that they must show, or at least believe, that the religion into which they happen to have been born is the truest and best, or even the one and only true and 'salvific' faith. The world-view which is part of our cultural environment and of the intellectual air that we breathe, normally seems to us to be obviously true, and anything importantly different as therefore obviously mistaken. For we have been formed by it, it has made us in its own image, so that it fits us and we fit it as usually no other can. For that reason it is generally best to remain within one's inherited religion, trying both to live it out fully and yet at the same time to take part in its continual development and reformation.

However, today more people than in the past are acutely aware of the reality of faiths other than their own. Indeed many have always been aware of them because another faith means their fellow citizens, sometimes their neighbours. Particularly in Europe and the USA, millions of Muslims, Hindus and Sikhs have become part of the new multi-faith Western societies – to which the Jews have also long belonged, though often persecuted and, in the twentieth century, subjected to the appalling mass murder of the Holocaust. Socially, the presence of the new religious communities produces both enrichment and friction; religiously it compels the churches to think harder than they have in the past about the relationship between Christianity and other world religions, a task which they still do not seem ready to pursue beyond the point of friendly co-existence. For our upbringing makes us vulnerable to misleading stereotypes of an alien faith, as today between Christianity and Islam, each perceiving the other as a threat and reacting to it as a threat, thereby creating conflict.

In this complex, mixed-up, unstable world situation, there are thus millions who do not need to ask Which religion? because they think that they know the answer already. But, for those for whom it is a genuine question, how can it be answered? If given an open choice, which multi-faith religious education makes more possible than in the past, it is a matter of temperament and preference – cultural, aesthetic and philosophical as well as spiritual. But undergirding this is the criterion of the faiths themselves, their fruits in human life, individual and corporate. The direct fruit is in personal attitudes and outlook, the practice of love and compassion. The Golden Rule of treating others as you would wish to be treated (or, perhaps better, not treating others as you would not wish them to treat you) is found within each of the world faiths.[1] The question is to what extent the basic universal principle of love (in one of that word's many meanings) or compassion, feeling with and for others, is acted upon.

Trying to look objectively at the world religions as historical entities, is it possible to rank them in terms of their beneficial or harmful effects on the human community? I believe (as argued in Chapter 1) that the factors involved are so complex, and often incommensurable, that no overall ranking is realistically possible. We can identity particular respects in which at a particular point in history one tradition is at some point manifestly causing more harm or doing more good than some other, either to its own adherents or to the wider world. But the world religions are long-lived phenomena, spanning centuries and going through periods of growth and of decline, of social and cultural flourishing and of stagnation and weakness. Taking them as historical totalities, at any given time they may be at different stages of their development.[2] And when we try to look more specifically at a faith's production of human goodness in ordinary people, and also of outstanding saintly individuals, it would be hazardous in the extreme for any of the great faiths to claim that its adherents are, morally and spiritually, better human beings than the rest of the human race.[3] We have no statistics here, but certainly the onus of proof, or of argument, lies upon anyone who ventures to make such a claim.

From the point of view, then, of our present inquiry we are left with the original problem. If religious experience is (when winnowed by the 'fruits' criterion) accepted as a genuine awareness of reality beyond as well as within us, we have to face the fact that it reports different and incompatible transcendent realities, giving rise to different and incompatible belief-systems. One major incompatibility is that between belief-systems in which the Transcendent is an infinite Person and those in which it is a transcategorial (or ineffable) Reality beyond the distinction between the personal and the impersonal. And among the reported deities the strictly unitary God of Judaism and Islam is not the divine Trinity of Christianity or the Vishnu or Shiva of theistic Hinduism. Nor, among the non-theistic faiths, is the Tao the same as Brahman or the Dharmakaya.

It seems, then, that one at most of the incompatible reports can be correct and the rest deluded, producing false beliefs. But if only one of the many belief-systems, originally and still essentially based on religious experience, can be true, it follows that religious experience generally produces *false* beliefs – with the single exception of one's own – and is thus a generally *unreliable* basis for belief-formation! This is the opposite of the principle that I want to establish. Can this challenge be met?

Salvation

Salvation will emerge as it is a key concept. However, because 'salvation' (and 'salvific') are distinctively Christian terms, we must pause over them. I shall be using them in a generic sense arising from the fact that each of the great world faiths shows the same basic pattern. It begins with an acute awareness of the human condition as radically defective, imperfect, unsatisfying. Judaism and Christianity have the myth of the fall of Adam and Eve in the Garden of Eden, and the Western Church has developed this into the doctrine of original sin: we have inherited a primal fall from grace – traditionally a historical fall, but understood by many modern Christians as an 'as if having fallen' state – which can only be reversed by Christ's saving work. This is understood today in various ways, from an atoning sacrificial death to a revelation of God as our co-sufferer. For Islam we are made out of the dust of the earth and are frail and fallible creatures, subject both to the judgement and the infinite mercy of God, to whom we must submit our entire lives, hoping to receive a place in paradise. For Hinduism we live in a state of *maya*, delusion, which produces all the problems of the world but from which we can escape by attaining *moksha*, the realisation of our innate oneness with the ultimate reality of Brahman. For Buddhism likewise we live in a state of *dukkha* (suffering, unsatisfactoriness) from which, however, we can be delivered by attaining enlightenment, nirvana, for which the Buddha taught his Noble Eightfold Path.

Thus each of the post-axial religions acknowledges, indeed stresses, our human finitude, suffering, mortality, and our inveterate tendency to injure one another both individually and collectively; and each affirms the real possibility and availability of a limitlessly better existence, to which it shows the way. In the generic sense of the word that I am using, each offers salvation. It is sometimes said that each faith is an answer to a different question. But this is misleading. The concepts and the paths are different, but for each the basic question is, in the generic sense of 'salvation' that I have indicated, What must I/we do to be saved?

Responses to religious diversity

In the current active and widespread discussions about the relationship between religions there are three main contenders, each with its subdivisions.

Exclusivism

Exclusivism is the view that there is one and only one true and salvific faith. For the sake of exposition let us suppose, hypothetically, that this is the case and, again for the sake of exposition, let us suppose that this is Christianity. Christian exclusivism, then, is the claim that only Christians are saved. In traditional Catholic terms this is the *Extra ecclesiam nulla salus* (outside the Church, no salvation) doctrine, gradually modified in the nineteenth century and finally superseded in some of the statements of the Second Vatican Council in the 1960s and since. This exclusivism was also the motive behind the Protestant churches' huge missionary activity in the seventeenth, eighteenth and nineteenth centuries, working in tandem with British imperial and economic expansion. David Livingstone told a British audience, 'I go back to Africa to make an open path for commerce and Christianity' (Morris 1973, 393). In 2005 there are approximately 440,000 Christian missionaries working in countries other than their own,[4] 80 per cent being Western, mainly from the USA, and 20 per cent but growing from non-Western, mainly South Korea.[5] There are uncertainties about all such statistics – for example, counting husband and wife as two missionary units. It is also not clear what proportion are evangelical converting missionaries and what proportion (generally from the 'mainline' churches) are doing educational, medical and agricultural support work. Of the converting Christian missions it seems that some 60 per cent target non-Christians, while others target Christians of the mainline churches. Islam is also a missionary faith, with some 70 per cent of Muslim missions addressed mainly to other Muslims. Buddhism, again, is a missionary faith which spread from India north into China, Tibet, Korea, Japan, south into Sri Lanka, east into Thailand, Burma, Vietnam, Cambodia, Laos, and west into Kashmir, Afghanistan, Turkistan, Mongolia, Persia. This never involved forced conversion, and in the West today, Europe and north America, it is making an increasing appeal by its own inherent attraction.

The familiar criticism of Christian exclusivism is that it seems to others to be a sheer absurdity, fuelled by fundamentalist theology and ignorance of other faiths, and arising from the unthinking assumption that the religion into which one happens to have been born is the one and only true faith. A new sensitivity to this has now led many US exclusivists to rename themselves particularists! Clearly, the same critique of Christian exclusivism also applies to all other religions. Among the other monotheisms it does not affect Judaism, which is explicitly a covenantal relationship specifically with the Jewish people. Within Islam exclusivism continues as an unquestioned assumption among many who live in more traditional areas and who do not have the time or inclination to indulge in theological reflection, although the move away from an established exclusivism is growing among the minority of 'progressive' or 'reformist' Muslim scholars.

Inclusivism

Returning to Christianity, the fundamentalist/evangelical movement may well today amount to the majority of the Christian world, and here exclusivism continues in varying degrees of dogmatic certainty. But among the mainline churches the great majority of theologians and church leaders have moved on in the course of the twentieth century from exclusivism to inclusivism. This, in Christian terms, is the view that salvation for anyone is brought about solely by the atoning death of Jesus, but is nevertheless not confined to Christians but is available, in principle, to all humanity. Non-Christians may be (in the Catholic theologian Karl Rahner's famous phrase) anonymous Christians, being in a spiritual state such that they *would* respond to the Christian gospel if it was properly presented to them; or, as a more recent development, they will encounter Christ in the moment of death, or after death, and be able to accept him then as their Lord and Saviour.

There is a partial Muslim equivalent in the idea of the People of the Book, which includes Jews and Christians, and an extension of this among some reformist Muslim thinkers in the recognition of the Buddha, Lao-Tzu, Zoroaster and others as being among the long succession of earlier prophets, but with Muhammad remaining as the final prophet. In the Qur'an we read, 'Say "We believe in God and what has been sent down to us, and what has been revealed to Abraham and Ishmael and Isaac and Joseph and their progeny, and that which was given to Moses and Christ, and to all other prophets by the Lord. We make no distinction among them, and we submit to Him"' (2:136). But in the monotheisms with hundreds of millions of adherents, Christianity and Islam, each retains the belief in its own central and normative position. This is the essence of inclusivism.

The basic criticism is that, when judged by their fruits in human life, it is impossible to maintain that one's own religion, whichever it may be, is morally and spiritually superior to all others. Observation and experience of the ordinary members of the different faiths does not indicate that any one group consists of morally and spiritually better human beings than the rest of the human race, or produces more saints/mahatmas per capita than other religions. (On their social/political fruits, see Chapter 4). But surely 'the only true religion' *ought* to produce more saints and, generally, better human beings.

Despite this, in the case of Christianity, the majority remain today within the intellectual horizons of either exclusivism or inclusivism.

Pluralism

Put negatively, religious pluralism is the view that there is no one-and-only true and salvific faith. Subject to the 'fruits' criterion, which rules out violent fanatical sects (including those within the world religions themselves), pluralism regards all the 'great world faiths' as equally authentic and salvific. In the poetic words of the Persian Sufi, Rumi, 'The lamps are different, but the Light is the same; it comes from Beyond' (Rumi 1978, 166). Clearly, this needs to be worked out much further philosophically, and there is a variety of ways in which this is being attempted, some of the most prominent of which I shall discuss in the following two chapters.

14
Responses to Religious Diversity

I have argued that both exclusivism and inclusivism are manifestly inadequate. The basic reason for this is, in a nutshell, that equally intelligent, informed, genuinely religious, and morally and spiritually advanced people belong to different faith traditions. This fact alone is enough to lead us to religious pluralism, because it is incompatible with both exclusivism and inclusivism – at any rate, in the latter case, without complex epicycles of additional theory. But there are many forms of religious pluralism, with the number still growing. It is not possible to discuss them all here and I must restrict myself to some of the currently most influential.

Multiple aspect pluralism

This has been developed by several writers. I shall focus on Peter Byrne's version of it. In briefest summary, he proposes that there is an ultimate transcendent reality with multiple aspects, both personal and non-personal. Each of the great religions is based on an awareness of one or another facet of the many aspects of this reality. His approach is philosophical, and he suggests that the reality itself can be thought of as a 'kind': thus

> the properties manifested in typical circumstances by a kind like gold are not final determinants of the meaning of the word 'gold'. Gold can manifest quite different properties in non-typical circumstances (for example, in molten, fluid form). Rather we use 'gold' to refer to an underlying substantial nature which agreed samples of gold are presumed to share. The real essence of natural kinds of this sort lies beneath their manifest nominal qualities and in

the case of many kinds may be quite unknown. So, by parallel reasoning, one can postulate that transcendence, divinity is a supernatural kind. Its real essence is something that underlies its typical manifestations. On this view the sacred as personal Lord and as unlimited ocean of being or unbounded, numinous wholly other are manifestations of a real essence of transcendence which lies behind them...Just as gold, at normal temperatures, really is yellow, lustrous and hard, so the transcendent reality is personal Lord and impersonal ground of being in appropriate manifestations of its real essence. Yet, just as the nominal essence of gold does not exhaust its nature but points beyond itself to its real essence, so the nominal essence of the transcendent does not exhaust itself but points beyond itself to its real essence. (Byrne 1995, 159–60)

Transcendence is not, however, he says, one kind among others; it is unique and ultimate. Thus the different religions have a genuine knowledge of the transcendent, but each of a different aspect of it. Further, all our human expressions of these different aspects are metaphorical: 'the sacred is beyond the categories of personality and impersonality when its real essence is considered' (161). Again, 'the real essence of transcendence is beyond positive, literal description and categories and...the relationship between the real essence of the transcendent and its manifestations is not intelligible in the manner of natural kinds and their outward properties' (162).

The practical outcome, in terms of interfaith dialogue, is that 'different religions have complementary insights into the one reality and thus that a fuller account of that reality can be provided if these insights are set alongside each other' (165). This suggests the possibility of a global theology incorporating all these complementary insights, since 'pluralism sees individual traditions as aspects of an overlapping encounter with the one reality' (200). However, Byrne resists this conclusion. He endorses 'the emphasis on modes of experience as the characteristic evidence of the human claim to have contact with the transcendent...This of course implies that only within forms of practice that constitute living in harmony with ultimate reality – that is, in religions – can any worthwhile relationship with the sacred be achieved ' (197), although he does welcome the fact that 'as traditions they may well profit from sharing insights, spiritualities and the like' (200). He does not, however, allow, as I want to do, for authentic responses to the Transcendent not structured in terms of religious concepts.

The idea of multiple modes of experience of the one ultimate reality is quite close to, although still different from, the philosophy of religious pluralism to be offered in the next chapter. I welcome Byrne's important contribution. I do not, however, accept his criticism of my own theory, to be developed in the next chapter. He believes that it 'threatens the realist perspective on realist discourse' (viii) because of its Kantian-like distinction between the inaccessible (to us) noumenal Reality in itself and its phenomenal manifestations to human consciousness, this latter taking different forms according to the different conceptualities and modes of experience developed within the different traditions. He sees this as non-realist because it is an application of critical realism (as discussed in Chapter 12): the Real is *real* but, as in the case of all our other awareness, is knowable by us only in the ways that our cognitive equipment makes possible. But in my view this is a form of realism not of non- or anti-realism – indeed it is the only realistic form!

Polycentric pluralism

The most extreme possible form of polycentic pluralism[1] would hold that the religions are completely distinct and unrelated, each worshipping or otherwise responding to its own Ultimate, and with its own path to its own expected end. This would be a religious version of the multiverse theory in scientific cosmology.[2] It would involve a plurality of separate and unrelated universes (because monotheism holds that God is the sole creator and lord of the entire universe) presided over by different deities or constituted by different non-theistic realities. This is logically possible. But it would do nothing to illuminate the relation between the religions of this world. For these all exist within the same universe, and the fact – if it is a fact – that there are other universes of which we know nothing cannot throw any light on our own situation.

But more relevant forms of polycentric pluralism have been developed quite recently by several writers, one being Stephen Kaplan (Kaplan 2002, to which the page references following refer). His book is 'an attempt to envision how more than one religious tradition can be ultimately true, not penultimately true. It is an attempt to conceptualise the logical framework in which ultimate reality, in an ontological sense not an epistemological sense, may be conceived of as plural, not singular' (ix–x). He distinguishes between, on the one hand, an ultimate reality, which he defines as 'that ontological nature that provides individuals with a soteriological conclusion to existence – with a form of salvation of liberation' (24), and, on the other hand, a metaphysical system, which is 'a theory about all reality', and his aim is to 'show that there may be more than one type of ontological structure or nature within the one metaphysical system and, therefore, more than one ultimate reality' (24). He is here creating his own stipulative definition of 'ultimate reality' designed to make it possible for there to be many such. As the term is normally used this is not possible – there can only be one *ultimate* reality.

Kaplan proposes a metaphysical system (or, as I would say, a conception of ultimate reality) analogous to, but not dependent on the truth of, David Bohm's suggested holographic model in physics. In holography an object is photographed by laser film which does not record a two-dimensional image of it, as in ordinary photography, but the information necessary to produce an image which when projected appears as a three-dimensional object. The hologram itself consists in the stored information. Its projection can then be viewed, like a solid object, from different perspectives and distances, presenting different appearances to different observers. In its application to religion these are the different God figures – Jahweh, Holy Trinity, Allah, Vishnu, Shiva, etc.

But the holographic model is also intended to account for the non-theistic religions. Following Bohm, Kaplan distinguishes between the 'implicate' and 'explicate' domains or orders. 'The implicate order refers to the film. Specifically, it refers to the unusual manner in which the information is recorded on the film. The explicate order refers to the object that is filmed and the reproduced image of that object' (102). The latter consists of different parts of the object, while the former is a unity. Thus the implicate order is an undivided wholeness, whereas the explicate order is multiform.

Kaplan then transfers this scheme to the 'ontological possibilities' (117) described by the different religions (although he does not profess to know whether all or even any of them are in fact real). But in his hypothesis the implicate order corresponds to the non-dual One of Advaita Vedanta in which all apparent duality and difference is enfolded in the undivided wholeness of Brahman. The explicate order corresponds both to the various Gods in the theistic traditions and also the Buddhist conception of ultimate reality as an ever-changing flow of interrelated events. Kaplan asks the reader 'to assume that the implicate and the explicate domains logically demand each other' (124), and mutually interpenetrate, and therefore exist simultaneously. 'This scenario', he says, 'allows us to envision how different ultimate realities can be simultaneously existent and equal' (126).

Despite his pluralistic intention Kaplan is proposing one unitary system, which he chooses not to call what it clearly is in ordinary usage, namely, a conception of a single ultimate reality as having different aspects, implicate and explicate, the latter fragmented into the different deities. His denial of this depends entirely on his own redefinition of 'ultimate reality', tailored to fit his theory.

There are further problems in Kaplan's theory. It is integral to it, as we have seen, that all the ultimate realities have an equal status: 'each of the faiths reviewed [i.e. the major world faiths] offers a distinct, yet equal, soteriological conclusion to human existence' (47). But in what sense are they all equal? Kaplan's answer seems to be: in their ontological status – that is, they are all equally real. He does not raise the question whether they are all qualitatively equal, because each 'nature', or 'ultimate reality', is 'as soteriologically effective as any other nature' (159). That is, it produces the end-state which it has promised and which the individual has chosen. Whether the different end-states are deemed by anyone to be equally desirable is immaterial for, as Kaplan says, 'This model calls for individuals to choose . . . Choice is necessary' (161). His scenario is one in which each person chooses what is for him or her the most desirable soteriological conclusion, so that everyone is eventually able to enjoy the end-state that they most value. For some that is an eternal relationship with a loving God, for some absorption into the ultimate One which we all are beneath the illusion of individuality, and, for some, realisation of the ultimate Emptiness of all distinctions.

Kaplan sees it as a major attraction of his theory that this is a form of

> metaphysical democracy. Democracy, understood here as the ability and freedom to choose, is enshrined in the ontological structure of the universe . . . In this model [the three basic options of] oneness [in advaita Vedanta], emptiness [i.e. the *sunyata* of Mahayana Buddhism], and individuality [in the theisms] are ways of 'being' that one chooses; they are not metaphysical impositions from a monolithically structured universe. (161–2)

So, presumably, some people live beyond this life in a heaven, some are absorbed into the one reality of Brahman, and some transcend all distinctions including that between self and other. Thus 'in this model we need not tell a religious tradition that that which it has experienced as ultimate reality is not ultimate reality' (160–1), because each experiences its own separate ultimate reality. And all three options are ontologically real, though only for their own adherents.

The most striking feature of Kaplan's theory is its extreme abstractness and remoteness from the historical reality of religion. It depends, as he emphasises, on everyone choosing their own preferred ultimate reality. However, at ground level this is completely unrealistic. The reality is that the vast majority of men and women do not have before them a range of alternative religious possibilities which they can compare and among which they can then make their choice. In the vast majority of cases, people are born into and live within one particular religious tradition and usually know little, often virtually nothing or only some distorted caricature, of the others, certainly not enough to make an informed choice. Given a genuine choice, many might *not* prefer the end-state provided by the religion into which they happen to have been born. And what is the fate of those many in the modern secular West who share the prevailing naturalistic assumption – explicit and implicit humanists and atheists – who do not believe in any religion? Presumably they simply cease to exist. (This might well apply to Kaplan himself, for he stresses that 'The truth or falsity of any religious tradition is beyond the knowledge of this author' [117].) And what of the many others who do not accept a naturalistic materialism and believe, or half-believe, in some kind of survival of bodily death, but without having any idea of what form it will take? Do they survive in some kind of amorphous fog? Or what?

When we take account of ground-level reality we see how detached Kaplan's theory is from it. Consider the Christian tradition in its two thousand years' history. Kaplan says that for Christianity each individual has an immortal soul and 'It is a loving, gracious God who guarantees the individual's existence' (144). But (as I mentioned in the previous chapter) most ordinary medieval Christians were born into a belief-system which guaranteed eternal torment in hell for that large majority of the human race who lived outside the Catholic Church; and they dreaded it for themselves if they should die before receiving absolution for their sins. This was a genuine terror which it is difficult for us to imagine today. In this period it was the minority of mystics and those whom they influenced who believed in a loving, gracious and forgiving God. Kaplan is picturing the Christian tradition in a greatly oversimplified way.

Other comparable situations are readily found within other traditions. For example, in the early Torah tradition Jahweh is the violent tribal God of ancient Israel; and the expected end-state was the gloomy shadowy half-existence of Sheol. Here the tribal warrior deity was the ultimate reality. The same would apply to the God of the Aztecs, an important part of whose religious practice 'was human sacrifice, usually carried out for the purpose of nourishing or renewing the Sun or other deity (or to otherwise appease it), thus ensuring the stability of the universe... For example, women and masses of captive warriors were sacrificed in front of the shrine of Huitzilopochtli atop the Templo Mayor...' (Carrasco 1987, 28). For the Aztecs this literally blood-thirsty deity was the ultimate reality.

In short, I find Kaplan's theory intriguing as an ingenious theoretical exercise, of the kind in which many philosophers today indulge, but not in the least helpful in trying to understand the relationship between the religions of this world.

Another kind of poly-centric pluralism also includes the different eschatologies of the different religions. This has been provided by S. Mark Heim (Heim 2001, with a preliminary hint in Heim 1995). He says, in summary, that the different world religions are distinct entities, constituting paths to different and mutually exclusive ends, both within this life and beyond it. He proposes not only that the different major religions have their own different conceptions of the Ultimate, some theistic and others not, and their correspondingly appropriate spiritual paths, each leading to its own expected fulfilment, but also that this fulfilment includes its own expected post-mortem state – the Christian heaven, the Islamic paradise, *nirvana*, union with Brahman, and so on. Thus all these eschatological situations are ontologically real – they actually exist. In Heim's own case, this is not a genuine religious pluralism as I defined it above because he explicitly affirms the unique superiority of the Christian end both now and in eternity. People of other faiths achieve their own inferior goals, but, according to Heim, the whole ensemble of different ends forms a rich and valuable tapestry in the sight of God. Within this picture the fullness of God's riches is available only to Christians, others having access to ends that are good but much less good than that which Christians receive. However, he argues, this dispensation is fair and just because all can attain the goal that they have themselves chosen – he thinks of people around the world as all having chosen their own preferred religious end.

Like Kaplan's theory, this too is totally unrealistic at ground level. In practice Heim's theory means that those who have the good fortune to be born in Christian countries may receive the supreme good, but those with the misfortune to be born in Muslim or Hindu or Buddhist etc. societies will, unless they convert, only receive varyingly lesser goods. This is a new form of Christian inclusivism, one that is better for non-Christians than the older exclusivism, which consigned them all to hell, but worse than the currently popular inclusivism, taught by the Catholic Church and the majority of non-fundamentalist Protestants, which extends the full benefits of Christian salvation eventually to all, if only beyond this life. Heim's view also involves a horrific conception of God; for what kind of God would so dispose his creation that the large majority of human beings have no chance of receiving the supreme good – this being restricted to his chosen people, the Christians?

But with or without Heim's hierarchy of eschatological ends, the scheme is unsustainable. For each religious package of beliefs and practices includes a belief about the nature of what Heim calls the religious ultimate (Heim 2001, 35 etc.). And we cannot have an eschatological religious end without the divine power or the cosmic process or structure that undergirds and sustains it. We cannot, for example, have the Christian cosmology of divine judgement and heaven and hell (and perhaps purgatory) without the omnipotent God who judges and is able to dispose as he wills of all human beings, Christian and other. And there can by definition be only one such Being. But within the same universe of religions there are other supposedly omnipotent creators and lords of the whole earth who form part of the different totalities of Judaism and Islam and Sikhism and some forms of Hinduism and indeed, going beyond the great world faiths, many other smaller theistic traditions. Again, according to Buddhism there is no divine creator, and the karmic process does not involve a divine judgement; while according to some strands of Hindu thought the universe is an uncreated beginningless and endless process – though with each individual eventually graduating out of it into unity with Brahman. So while these different cosmic situations can co-exist as human belief systems they cannot co-exist ontologically, or in reality. There cannot be the different ends of which Heim speaks if these are integral to ontological realities which cannot co-exist in the same universe.

Again then, like Kaplan's religiously neutral hypothesis, Heim's distinctively Christian and trinitarian theory does not help us to find any comprehensive understanding of the relationship between the existing religions. I shall suggest in the next chapter what I believe to be a more adequate hypothesis.

15
A Philosophy of Religious Pluralism

The Transcendent

It is necessary first to establish some terminology. In the 'Western' monotheisms (though all in fact originated in the middle east) we think of the ultimate reality as an infinite, eternal, all-powerful, all-good personal being. A personal being is a person: the distinction which some theologians have tried to draw between God as personal and God as a person is meaningless – what could a personal non-person be? God, then, is thought of as the infinite person or, in the case of Christianity, as a trinity of persons who are three in one and one in three. It would be possible to stretch the familiar term 'God' to refer to the Ultimate without specifying whether that reality is personal, impersonal or beyond the personal/impersonal distinction. But the word carries for us in the West so strongly personal a connotation that it is wiser at present to avoid it when intending the more open or generic meaning, as I mentioned earlier (p. 36). Terms commonly used are Ultimate Reality, the Ultimate, the Transcendent and, less commonly, the word that I have myself introduced, the Real. Since none of these has a privileged status I shall use them all, taking advantage of the stylistic flexibility this allows, though most often speaking of the Transcendent, with or without a capital T.

The premises

The philosophy of religious pluralism that I shall offer depends upon certain premises, for which I have argued earlier in this book. One is that it is reasonable to believe that religious experience in its different forms around the world is not purely human projection but is at the same time a response to the universal presence of transcendent reality (ch. 12). This is not true of everything that comes under the broad heading of religious experience, which as we saw extends from the sublime to the ridiculous and to the positively dangerous. But the religions have as their common criterion the moral and spiritual fruits of the experience in human life (ch. 4). Another premise is that the world faiths are, so far as we can tell, on a par in respect of these fruits (ch. 14).

The basic distinction

The hypothesis that I want to offer depends upon a fundamental distinction. On the one hand we need to recognise that the Transcendent in 'its' inner nature is beyond human description or comprehension. In traditional theological language it is ineffable or, as I would rather say, transcategorial, beyond the scope of our human concepts. It is to this ultimate transcategorial reality that the religions are oriented and to which they are human responses. The other half of the distinction consists of the specific forms in which we humans are aware of that transcendent reality within, but not only within, the historical religions.

My suggestion, constituting the 'pluralist hypothesis' that I have presented,[1] uses Kant's distinction between the things-in-themselves and their phenomenal appearance, which I outlined earlier (p. 138). Kant himself was discussing sense perception and did not apply the distinction to religion – his own philosophy of religion was quite different and he presumably would not have approved of the current twentieth- and twenty-first-century religious pluralist use of it. The distinction between the reality in itself and that same reality as object of human awareness, with the indispensable contribution which the activity of observation makes, is the only aspect of his philosophy that I want to borrow. I do not need (or want) his entire complex architectonic system of forms and categories. The distinction that I am using was not entirely new with him; but he was nevertheless the most original as well as the most influential philosopher of the modern period, and it would be unjust not to acknowledge his massive contribution in making it definitively clear that the mind is not passive, but constantly active, in its awareness of the world. This has since been confirmed by cognitive psychology and the sociology of knowledge, and is also recognised in quantum physics.[2] But the basic idea was expressed centuries earlier by Thomas Aquinas in his brilliant statement, 'The thing known is in the knower according to the mode of the knower'.[3]

Applied to religion, the distinction is between, on the one hand, the Transcendent in itself, which is transcategorial, outside the field of our conceptual repertoire, and, on the other, the various forms in which this is humanly thought and experienced and responded to within the different religions. (I shall come in the next chapter to awareness of the Transcendent outside the organised religions). This does not mean that the Real is an agent *causing* the many different human images of it that the history of religions records. It means that there is an inbuilt human capacity to be aware of the universal presence of the Transcendent, in virtue of its immanence within our own nature – indeed according to some traditions an inner unity with the Transcendent – which is, however, always manifested in particular culturally and historically conditioned ways. (This application of Kant's distinction to religion avoids a problem that beset his own use of it, namely, that in his system the thing in itself causes its own phenomenal appearances, although causality, according to him, is one of the categories in terms of which we form that phenomenal world.)

The Transcendent as beyond human description

All the great world faiths affirm, in their different ways, the indescribable nature of the ultimate.

Beginning in the East, the usual term corresponding to the English ineffable or transcategorial is 'formless'. Hindu advaitic philosophy distinguishes between *nirguna* Brahman, Brahman without attributes, devoid of name-and-form, the transcategorial nature of which is famously expressed in the phrase *neti, neti*, not this not this,[4] in distinction from *saguna* Brahman, which is that same reality as humanly thought and experienced as God, the Lord, Ishwara, known in many forms. In the intriguing and paradoxical words of an ancient Hindu writer, 'Thou art formless: thy only form is our knowledge of thee' (Parriskar 1978, 144).

The Mahayana Buddhist *Trikaya* doctrine of the three 'Bodies' of the Buddha distinguishes between, first, the dharmakaya, the ultimate formless reality in itself, in Conze's words 'the Buddha as the Absolute' (Conze 1975, 172) or the 'Body of Essence' (de Bary (ed.) 1972, 74); second, the sambhogakaya, the 'Body of Bliss', the realm of the heavenly Buddhas; and third, the nirmanakaya, the 'incarnate' Buddhas, the one known to us being Gautama Buddha, whose precise dates are in dispute but who lived in northern India around the middle of the first millenium BCE.

Within the Jewish tradition Maimonides (twelfth century CE), perhaps the greatest of Jewish thinkers, was himself influenced by Muslim philosophers such as al-Farabi and Ibn Rushd (Averroes), and wrote his famous *Guide for the Perplexed* in Arabic, later translated into Hebrew, and then into Latin in which it influenced Christian theologians including Thomas Aquinas. He distinguished between the essence and the manifestations of God (Maimonides 1904, I, 54). Maimonides was a strictly logical thinker. However, in general, within both Judaism and Islam it is in their mystical strands that the divine mystery, beyond human description, is most clearly recognised. Some of the Jewish Kabbalist thinkers spoke of En Soph, the Infinite, the ultimate divine reality beyond human description. David Blumenthal, having emphasised that 'Judaism has always understood God to be, in some basic way, unknowable', and after speaking of the revealed Names/attributes of God, adds, that 'to identity His Names and/or attributes with Him, with his essence, would be wrong, for they are only labels, expressions of an unknowable essence behind the word' (Blumenthal 1978, 126–7). Maimonides' distinction between the (unknown) essence and the (known) manifestations of God to humanity is basic to the view that I want to develop.

Within the mystical Sufi tradition of Islam we find the same distinction. The ultimate ineffability of God is declared by a number of writers. For example, Kwaja Abdullah Ansari says, in prayer to God, 'You are far from what we imagine you to be', and 'The mystery of your reality is not revealed to anyone' (Ansari 1978, 183 and 203). Ibn al-'Arabi distinguishes (like Maimonides) between the divine essence, which is ineffable, and God as humanly known. In *The Bezels of Wisdom* he says, 'The Essence, as being beyond all these relationships, is not a divinity . . . it is we who make Him a divinity by being that through which He knows himself as Divine. Thus he is not known [as God] until we are known' (al-'Arabi 1980, 92).

Whereas within Hinduism and Buddhism this distinction is found within their 'mainstream', within Judaism and Islam it is largely confined to their mystical strands. But within Christianity we find the divine ineffability affirmed by both the great orthodox theologians and the mystics. The fourth-century Gregory of Nyssa wrote that God is 'incapable of being grasped by any term, or any idea, or any other device of our apprehension, remaining beyond the reach not only of the human but of the angelic and all supramundane intelligence, unthinkable, unutterable, above all expression in words . . . '[5] The fourth–fifth-century Augustine said that 'God transcends even the mind'.[6] The thirteenth-century Thomas Aquinas affirmed that 'by its immensity, the divine substance surpasses every form that our intellect reaches',[7] and 'The first cause surpasses human understanding and speech'.[8] Nicholas of Cusa, writing in 1453, says that 'the names which are attributed to God are taken from creatures, since he in himself is ineffable and beyond everything that can be named or spoken'.[9] And among the mystics from the thirteenth to fourteenth centuries Meister Eckhart wrote that 'God is without name, for no one can comprehend anything about him' (Eliade 1985, 200). Eckhart also makes the important distinction between the Godhead and God. 'God and the Godhead', he says, 'are as different from each other as heaven and earth'.[10] According to the anonymous (presumed to be early fourteenth century) writer of the *Theologia Germanica*, which so profoundly influenced Martin Luther, 'God is, and yet He is neither this nor that which the creature, as creatures, can perceive, name, conceive or express' (Winkworth 1937, 113); while probably later in the same century the anonymous author of *The Cloud of Unknowing* wrote that we may come to know God but 'Not as he is in himself, of course, for that is impossible to anyone save God',[11] and the sixteenth-century St John of the Cross, that God is 'incomprehensible and transcends all things' (1958, 310). Today, when more modest theologies compete with a resurgent evangelical dogmatism and 'radical orthodoxy', it is common within the more moderate mainstream to say that God in God's inner self-existent being is ineffable.

The problem

There is a serious problem here, more acute for Christianity than for the other religions because of its heavier doctrinal superstructure. The problem is that the theologians who declare God's ultimate nature to be beyond human description or comprehension nevertheless profess to know that this same God is ultimately triune, consisting of Father, Son and Holy Spirit, three 'persons' in one and one in three, the second of whom became incarnate on earth as Jesus of Nazareth. Thus the developed system of Christian doctrine contradicts the principle of divine ineffability. It is possible to hold that God is ultimately ineffable, transcategorial, beyond the scope of our human concepts and languages. And it is possible to hold that God is ultimately a divine trinity, of which Jesus of Nazareth was the second person incarnate. But it is not possible to hold both of these within the same system of thought. And yet this is what Christian theology, embedded as it has always been in the life and liturgy of the Church, has long done, bracketing or ignoring the obvious problem.

The solution

The obvious solution is to see theological formulations, as distinguished from historical statements, as couched in symbolic or metaphorical language. This is in effect the solution proposed by the arch-ineffabilist (if there is such a word), Pseudo-Dionysius, often called Denys for short, whom I have introduced in Chapter 2.

On the one hand, Denys affirms as emphatically as he can the absolute transcategoriality (or ineffability) of God. The Supreme Cause, God, is

> not soul or mind, nor does it possess imagination, conviction, speech, or understanding ... It is not number or order, greatness or smallness, equality or inequality, similarity or dissimilarity. It is not immoveable, moving, or at rest. It has no power, it is not power, nor is it light. It does not live nor is it life. It is not a substance, nor is it eternity or time. It cannot be grasped by the understanding ... It is neither one nor oneness, divinity nor goodness. Nor is it a spirit, in the sense in which we understand that term. It is not sonship or fatherhood and it is nothing known to us or to any other being ... There is no speaking of it, nor name nor knowledge of it. Darkness and light, error and truth – it is none of these. It is beyond assertion and denial.[12]

And yet in *The Divine Names* he appears directly to contradict this when he says that the ineffable God is self-revealed in the Bible. God is 'a Source which has told us about itself in the holy words of scripture'.[13] Again, living presumably as a monk devotedly engaged in the liturgical life of the Church, Denys takes for granted such articles of faith as Incarnation and Trinity – though at the same time emphasising that they also are mysteries. Thus he says that 'The most evident idea in theology, namely, the sacred incarnation of Jesus for our sakes, is something that cannot be enclosed in words nor grasped by any mind ... That he undertook to be a man is, for us, entirely mysterious'.[14] This is not of course the orthodox way of speaking about an orthodox doctrine which had been precisely defined (in terms of two complete natures, one human and the other divine) by the Council of Chalcedon in 451. Again, he has a particular version of the doctrine of the Trinity: 'we learn from sacred scriptures that the father is the originating source of the Godhead and that the Son and the Spirit are, so to speak, divine offshoots, the flowering and transcending lights of the divinity'.[15] This is his own neo-Platonic version of the idea of the

Trinity. Nevertheless for him these dogmas were in some form simply givens, as they still are within the churches today.

However, Denys, unlike most later theologians, faced the problem directly. He asks, 'How then can we speak of the divine names [i.e. God's attributes]? How can we do this if the Transcendent surpasses all discourse and all knowledge, if it abides beyond the reach of mind and of being ... eluding their grasp and escaping from any perception, imagination, opinion, name, discourse, apprehension, or understanding?'[16]

His answer is that, while the triune nature and 'transcendent Goodness'[17] of God as Creator are revealed in the sacred scriptures, its language is necessarily symbolic: 'the Transcendent is clothed in the terms of being, with shape and form on things which have neither, and numerous symbols are employed to convey the various attributes of what is an ageless and supra-natural simplicity'.[18] And in *The Celestial Hierarchy* he insists that the scriptures speak 'by way of representative symbols' and that 'the Word of God makes use of poetic imagery'.[19] The point of this symbolic language is to affect the hearers in such a way that they are helped to turn their lives towards the Transcendent: 'It uses scriptural passages in an uplifting fashion as a way, provided for us from the first, to uplift our mind in a manner suitable to our nature'.[20]

Denys steers us away from taking the Church's theological language literally by using both negative (apothatic) and positive (cataphatic) statements to cancel one another out. We speak of God as, for example, One and as good, but we also have to say that 'It is neither one nor oneness, divinity nor goodness'.[21] He is implying that the Transcendent is beyond our distinctions between good and bad, powerful and weak, moveable and immoveable, eternal and temporal, darkness and light, mind and non-mind, intelligent and not intelligent, active and inactive, even personal and impersonal. As he says,

> we should posit and ascribe to it all the affirmations we make in regard to beings, and, more appropriately, we should negate all these affirmations, since it surpasses all being. Now we should not conclude that the negations are simply the opposites of the affirmations, but rather that the cause of all is considerably prior to this, beyond privations, beyond every denial, beyond every assertion.[22]

Today we usually call his symbols metaphors. For as Denys Turner, a contemporary Denys who is an authority on the earlier one, says, 'it is perfectly clear that he treats these affirmations and their corresponding denials in the way that is appropriate to metaphorical utterances' (Turner 1995, 35). So this is one way of reconciling ineffability with positive doctrines: the doctrines have symbolic or metaphorical meaning.

Another way of dealing with the problem of theological language is the traditional idea of analogy. It is said that God possesses such known qualities as goodness and wisdom, but not in the same sense as humans, nor in a completely different sense, but in an analogous sense. The divine goodness and wisdom are analogous to human goodness and wisdom in a way that is proportionate to the difference between the infinite and the finite. We do not know what God's goodness is, but only that it corresponds at the divine level to what we know as goodness (and wisdom, love, power, etc.) on the human level.

But formidable problems beset this venerable idea. One is that only those attributes that the theologian regards as desirable are treated in this way. But if we know that God is, in his own way, good rather than evil, wise rather than foolish, etc., we already know more than the doctrine of analogy itself offers. Another is that, according to the traditional theology, God is simple, undifferentiated, without distinguishable qualities, so that he cannot have attributes even analogous to our own. The further problem is that the concept of analogy cannot produce any knowledge of God's nature, since we have no idea what the analogues in God are of our human qualities. It *seems* to give meaning to the Church's doctrines of God without really doing so.

The outcome, then, seems to be that the categories which in theology and religious practice we apply to the objects of worship do not apply to the Transcendent either positively or negatively. To use them in that way is a 'category mistake', like asking whether a molecule is green or blue, happy or unhappy – concepts which simply do not apply to it either way. The Ultimate in itself cannot be said to be either personal or impersonal, good or bad, loving or hating, purposive or not purposive, etc.

But such attributes *do* apply to the manifestations of the ineffable transcendent reality to humanity, to the personal deities and non-personal 'absolutes' which are the definable objects of religious worship, meditation and much mystical experience. These are products of the universal presence of the Transcendent both beyond us and in the depths of our being, together with the human images and concepts that our creative imagination and conceptualising powers make possible. Thus the worshipped deities do not exist apart from the community that worships them. As Eckhart says, 'before there were creatures, God was not god, but, rather, he was what he was. When creatures came to be and took on creaturely being, then God was no longer God as he is in himself, but god as he is with his creatures'.[23] He is thinking here in purely Christian terms. But earlier, al-'Arabi had made the same point in more universal terms when he says,

> In general, most men have, perforce, an individual concept of their Lord, which they ascribe to Him and in which they seek Him. So long as the Reality is presented to them according to it they recognize Him and affirm him, whereas if presented in another form, they deny Him, flee from Him and treat Him improperly, while at the same time imagining they are acting toward Him fittingly. One who believes [in the ordinary way] believes only in the deity he has created for himself, since a deity in 'belief' is a [mental] construction.[24]

Thus, for example, the God of Israel, as imaged in the Torah and later parts of the Hebrew Bible and in the Talmud, exists within the experience of the Hebrew people, and is integral to their history, as they are to his. The later development of their image of him has been influential far beyond the Jewish people, particularly within Christianity and Islam. But nevertheless he cannot be said to have existed in China or India or Africa or the Americas for tens of centuries. Likewise, Krishna would have no existence apart from the Hindu tradition. And the Nirvana/Dharmakaya/Buddha nature of Buddhism did not exist within the experience of the Israelites. And so on round the world.

We saw in Chapter 4 the moral criterion by which the great religions distinguish between the authentic and the false, the same criterion applying not only to ancient tribal and blood-thirsty deities but also to the widespread continuing perversions and misuses of all the great religious traditions in today's world. But if someone asks how we can validate that common criterion, the love/compassion that is fellow-feeling with others, and seeing kindness as good and cruelty as bad, we can only say that it cannot be proved but that it is a basic and (apart from psychopaths) universal human insight. It is a 'properly basic belief' reflecting a fundamental human moral insight.

The question has been raised by philosophers whether the idea of a completely ineffable reality, with no attributes knowable by us, makes sense. Must it not at least have the attribute of being able to be referred to? Clearly, yes. But we have to distinguish between on the one hand purely formal attributes, like being able to be referred to, or such that it is possible to say that it is, or exists, or is real,[25] and on the other hand substantial attributes which tell us something significant about its nature, such as being personal or impersonal, purposive or not, good or evil. It is the latter that cannot be attributed either positively or negatively to transcategorial reality. But if we cannot know it in its ineffability why suppose that there is such a Reality at all? The answer is that it is *that which there must be if human religious experience globally is not purely projection* but is at the same time response to a transcendent reality. Given the moral and spiritual parity of the world faiths, that to which they are responding clearly cannot be identified with the object of any one to the exclusion of the others. In Kantian terms, then, the Real is the necessary postulate, not as he proposed of the moral life, but of the religious life of humanity.

Again in Kantian terms, the Transcendent is the noumenal reality of which the humanly thought and experienced objects of devotion are the phenomenal manifestations. This is the distinction that we saw less formally expressed by Maimonides, Ibn al-'Arabi and Meister Eckhart. It turns aside the criticism that 'not all propositions reporting experiences of the Real can be true' (Ward 1994, 315). For, according to our hypothesis, the different traditions are not reporting experiences of the Real in itself, but of its different manifestations within human consciousness.

This is of course a revisionary proposal. How then does it affect thought and practice within the different traditions? This is the subject of the next chapter.

16
Pluralism and the Religions

The problem

Religious pluralism, in my version of it, holds that all the 'great world faiths' are, so far as we can tell, equally effective contexts of the salvific transformation from natural self-centredness to a new orientation centred in the Transcendent; and that to account for this we should postulate an ultimate ineffable reality which is differently conceived, and hence differently experienced, within the different traditions. A frequent criticism is that, in believing this, 'the transformational power of [the] religious tradition would be undermined for most ordinary believers' (Clark 1997, 317). Speaking from a Christian point of view he says,

> [S]uppose that they [his children] learn that ultimate reality cannot be discovered and they just don't know whether God is really a person or not, or loving and just, or even good or evil. Perhaps he/it/whatever doesn't care about their transformation from self-centeredness into Reality-centeredness ... Whether or not he/it/nothing is really concerned about human transformation is an enigma. (Ibid., 318)

In the first sentence Clark identifies the Real with the Christian God whom he teaches his children to worship, thereby supposing that, according to the pluralist hypothesis, the Christian God is unknowable. This creates a problem which does not exist for the pluralist hypothesis, which holds that the Christian God constitutes one (but not the only) authentic, because transformative, form of human awareness of the Transcendent. This does not mean that he should cease to induct his children into his own tradition. It is appropriate for young children to be not only spiritually nourished by, but also basically indoctrinated within, their parents' tradition while innocently unaware of the wider world of religious diversity.

Religious pluralism does, however, challenge each of the traditions to develop its own self-understanding so that its people can see their neighbours of other traditions, near and far, not as enemies or rivals but as fellow people of faith. Each includes resources for such a broadening of its own thought world, though some use those resources more readily than others. For some the job is easy, and indeed has already been done, except when religious differences have been exploited for political ends in setting groups against each other – as in the bitter and violent communal conflicts that have so deeply marred the modern history of the Indian subcontinent. Left to follow their own ingrained religious outlook Hindus can readily accept Christ, Muhammad, the Buddha, the great saints of all traditions, as people to be revered along with their own many deities and gurus. They see these other faiths as 'different paths up the same mountain'. As their earliest scripture teaches, 'The Real is one, but sages name it variously.'[1]

Buddhism is more ambivalent, some Buddhists regarding theirs as the only way to attain *nirvana* or Buddhahood, others seeing the spiritual practices of other faiths as ultimately leading to the same end. In the *Dhammapada*, which is in effect the Theravada Bible, we read, 'The best of paths is the Eightfold Way. The best of truths are the Four Sayings ... This is the only Way. There is none other for the purity of vision.'[2] In contrast, the Dalai Lama says,

> All religions agree upon the necessity to control the undisciplined mind that harbours selfishness and other roots of trouble, and each teaches a path that leads to a spiritual state that is peaceful, disciplined, ethical, and wise. It is in this sense that I believe all religions have essentially the same message. Differences of dogma may be ascribed to differences of time and circumstance as well as cultural influence. (Dalai Lama, 1984, 13)

In practice, Buddhists are almost universally open and friendly to people of other faiths.

Judaism, as the covenantal religion of the Jewish people, by definition makes no claim to be the one and only true faith, and it is usually difficult, though always possible, for non-Jews to convert to Judaism. The extreme Zionist and anti-Muslim nationalism of an ultra-orthodox minority in Israel today is the ugly face of a great but tragically exploited faith.

This is mirrored by an extreme anti-Zionism among many Muslims in the Middle East and further afield. But in the past Jews and Muslims have lived side by side in many places in a peace and harmony which cannot be expected to return until some time after a just settlement has been reached in Israel/Palestine. But Islam has strong resources within itself for the acceptance of the validity of other faiths. We read in the Qur'an (as I have quoted earlier), 'If God had pleased He could surely have made you one people (professing one faith). But He wished to try and test you by that which He gave you. So try to excel in good deeds. To Him you will all return in the end, when He will tell you of what you were at variance' (5, 48. 1990, 104). Within the basic teachings of Islam, particularly as developed in its Sufi strand, a pluralistic outlook is explicit – as in Rumi's famous saying concerning the religions, 'The lamps are different, but the Light is the same: it comes from Beyond' (Rumi 1978, 166).

The problem is most acute for Christianity because of its dogmatic belief-system and its authoritative enforcement of orthodoxy. None of this goes back to the teachings, so far as we can discern them, of the historical Jesus. The central ideas of incarnation, atonement and trinity were developed later, apparently beginning with St Paul, whose influence is evident in most of the writings that became canonised as the New Testament, these doctrines only finally being officially defined at the Councils of Nicea (325 CE) and Chalcedon (451 CE).

However, there are resources within Jesus' own teaching – again, so far as we can discern them – and in the developing Christian tradition, for a wider vision. On several occasions Jesus is said to have extended his ministry of healing and help beyond the Jewish community, to whom he regarded himself as sent by God; and this can be seen as indicating a divine compassion not limited by traditional boundaries. More importantly, some of the early Fathers of the Church had a very broad view. Justin (*c*.150 CE) held that 'all who live according to reason are Christians, even though they are accounted atheists. Such were Socrates and Heraclitus among the Greeks, and those like them ...'[3] Clement of Alexandria was another of the more open-minded early theologians. An exclusive dogmatism largely took over with the fusion of Church and empire, beginning under Constantine and his successors from the fourth century, with more open thinking and questioning re-emerging with the Renaissance. Nicholas of Cusa, writing in 1453 about the relation between religions, said that 'there is only one religion in the diversity of rites'.[4] The Reformation of the sixteenth century resulted in a strict Lutheran and Calvinist dogmatism in opposition to

Roman dogmatism. Servetus was burned in Calvin's Geneva, and the Roman Inquisition tortured and burned large numbers of heretics. But with the Enlightenment of the seventeenth and eighteenth centuries the use of reason in social and religious thinking spread through such notable free-thinkers as Spinoza, Montesquieu, Voltaire, Bayle, Locke, Jefferson, Hobbes and Hume. And the nineteenth century saw major scientific discoveries about the age of the earth and biological evolution that were incompatible with a literal understanding of the biblical account of creation. This began the still-continuing decline of traditionally orthodox belief and practice. The time is now ripe for the further step, perhaps a kill-or-cure for traditional Christianity, of accepting that it is one among other equally salvific traditions. More about this later.

But is pluralism compatible with existing religious practice?

We can return to Kelly James Clark. His problem, which is shared by millions, particularly in the 'Bible belt' of the USA, sub-Saharan Africa and parts of South America, arises within a strongly evangelical and theologically dogmatic form of Christianity. Illustrating from his family story Clark says,

> [W]e put on our Sunday best and rush off to Church to celebrate the resurrection of Jesus. [Clarks' children] will hear that God loves them so much that he sent his only Son to die for them on the cross, and that he has obtained victory over sin, death and the devil, and that he has sent the Holy Spirit into their lives to secure the transactions that were settled on the cross. (Clark 1997, 318)

But the ideas that God has a son whom he sends to die on the cross, that there is a devil who was defeated by that death, which thereby 'overcame' sin and death (which, however, still continue unabated), and that God also has a Holy Spirit which he sends upon or into Church members, are theologically crude. They are, however, widespread. Among the letters printed in *The Independent* appears, 'When Jesus left the disciples to go back to heaven to be with his father, God, he gave them the instruction to go out into the world and make disciples of all people.'[5] All this is not only unwittingly unorthodox, because the doctrine of the Trinity is not that God has a son, but that Father, Son, and Holy Spirit are co-equal, together constituting God; and the passage cited in Matthew 28:19 is extremely unlikely to come from the historical

Jesus. However, this is the Christian gospel that I myself wholeheartedly believed when, around the age of eighteen, I experienced a strong evangelical conversion to a fundamentalist faith. But it is certainly not to be identified with Christianity as such and it is, fortunately, not the only form of spiritual nourishment available within the tradition. Nevertheless, the dogmatism typically associated with evangelicals leads Clark to conclude that 'if Hick's Kantian understanding of Reality is right, he should just keep it to himself' (Ibid., 319).

Granting that 'In spite of [Clark's philosophical criticisms], Hick's Kantian Explanation might nevertheless be true' (Ibid., 317), Clark is urging those who are convinced of the pluralist position to conceal what they believe to be the truth in order to preserve the simple faith of traditional, including evangelical and fundamentalist, Christians. I find this deeply anti-rational, and astonishing in an otherwise highly rational philosopher. His proposed policy is of course appropriate for small children. We have probably all talked about God to our children in the simplest terms when they were very young; and educationalists know about the various stages in which the young mind develops and is able to absorb more complex ideas. But to treat church congregations as intellectual children can only, and in fact does, produce an unthinking Christian ghetto in which theological questioning and the modern historical study of the scriptures are suppressed. (I speak here from experience of the time when, having switched from the law to prepare for the ministry of the Church, I was doing a degree in philosophy at university before going on to a theological college. As an active member of what was then called the Evangelical Union, but prompted at the same time by the study of philosophy to raise questions, I found that when I raised very obvious questions – for example, how we should understand the Old Testament story that God made the sun stand still for twenty-four hours so that the Israelites could have time to slaughter the Amorites?[6] – such questioning was regarded as a sign of backsliding. It was this that began my long slow move away from that narrow form of Christian belief.)

The existing religions

What then are the implications for existing religious practices? For the most part, little. Traditions that can accept that theirs is not the one and only valid form of faith will continue to change in the ways they always have, by gradual internal reform.

Beginning our tour in the East, Buddhist practice consists in meditation, either in solitude or communally in temples and monasteries. In the latter there is often also rhythmic chanting and the use of gongs and coloured banners and in some the presence of numerous, it could be hundreds, of Buddha figures. The two most prominent kinds of meditation are *satipatthana*, taught within the Theravada and Tibetan traditions, attending with closed eyes to one's own breathing, as something that has no distracting intellectual content. The other is *zen*, looking with open eyes at a blank wall or the floor before one. Both are well tried ways of emptying the mind of all thinking (remembering, wishing, fearing, planning, speculating, etc.) and thus opening it to the true reality within and beyond us in which we live all the time, though usually without being conscious of it. And both tend to produce a serenity and mindfulness in all the moments of life, with its moral fruit of compassion – fellow feeling and regard for all beings. As to the 'true reality' realised by the enlightened consciousness, the only way to know it is to experience it for oneself. The Buddha's message was in effect 'try it and see', spoken with the assurance of one who had attained to full enlightenment. Both methods are difficult. In the early stages the mind wanders again and again. Zen, however, is the more demanding of the two. In the stricter Japanese Rinzai (as distinguished from Soto) tradition it can take ten years to attain full enlightenment as a Zen master, and easier methods and their results are regarded as lacking full authenticity. In addition to the practice of meditation, Buddhist history contains a wealth of profound philosophical speculation expressed in the huge literature in the different schools of thought,[7] which continues to grow.[8]

But all of this takes place independently of a Buddhist's adherence to any or none of these different types of philosophy, and independently of his or her attitude to religious pluralism. Buddhist practice and its moral fruits continue unchanged in a consciously pluralistic world.

Despite the current, and in the perspective of history temporary, resurgence of a politically motivated Hindu exclusivism, Hindus in general have always been natural pluralists. Their different practices, devotion to a chosen deity, rituals, meditation, prayer and pilgrimages to sacred rivers and sites continue. These are understood as the three equally valid paths of devotion, works and insight gained through meditation. The devotees of the different gods and goddesses do not make competitive claims for theirs as the one true God, because they are all manifestations of the ultimate ineffable reality of Brahman. Such pluralistic writers as the poet Kabir, drawing upon both Hindu and Muslim imagery, have been widely influential:

> O servant, where dost thou seek Me?
> Lo! I am beside thee,
> I am neither in temple nor in mosque:
>   I am neither in Kaaba nor in Kailash
> Neither am I in rites and ceremonies,
>   Nor in Yoga and renunciation.
> If thou art a true seeker, thou shalt at once see Me: thou shalt meet me
>   in a moment of time. (Kabir 1977, 45)

Mahatma Gandhi's early upbringing typifies what I have called the natural pluralism of the Hindu mind. His family had neighbours and friends who were Jains and Muslims as well as fellow Hindus, and 'it came naturally to the young Mohan to accept the fact that the supreme could be sought in a great variety of ways' (Chatterjee 1983, 15). It was his Jain friends who introduced him to the concept of *anekantavada*, the many-sidedness of reality, leading to his pluralistic conclusion, 'I regard the great faiths of the world as so many branches of a tree, each distinct from the other though having the same source'.[9]

Here is the testimony of a Hindu-Buddhist Christian, the enormously learned and widely studied Raimon Panikkar, who is equally at home in East and West:

> I understand and can also speak more than one language as my own . . . This applies of course to religions as languages. Using a christian language I will so wholeheartedly confess that Christ is the truth that I will reverse the sentence, like Gandhi with God, and affirm that the truth is Christ . . . This is christian language, but I can speak other languages which convey liberating power and saving grace – not only for their respective believers (which is obvious) but for me as well. I am not translating from christianity, but speaking other languages, and I discover not that I am saying 'the same thing' but that it is my selfsame self who sincerely expresses his conviction . . . Reflecting on the fact that I submit religions to profound reinterpretations for which I am solely, but conscientiously, responsible, I am a christian whom Christ has led to sit at the feet of the great masters of hinduism and buddhism. It is my being as a hindu-buddhist christian. (Pannikar 1999, 44–5)

In the case of Islam, its five pillars stand firm when Muslims generally come to accept, as only a small minority do at present, the basic insight of religious pluralism. The declaration that 'There is no god but God and Muhammad is his prophet' is entirely compatible with religious pluralism when understood in its original sense as the decisive repudiation of polytheism, which was the Prophet's new revolutionary teaching in seventh-century Arabia, and when the proclamation that Muhammad is his prophet is understood in the light of the Qur'an's insistence that he was not the only prophet of God but the latest of a long line – though, orthodoxly, the final prophet. Prayers five times a day; paying *zakat*, the giving of part of one's income to the needy; fasting during the month of Ramadan; and making once in one's lifetime if one can the pilgrimage to Mecca, are all practices that harm no one, but greatly help Muslims to take their faith seriously. There is today a growing number of Islamic scholars, generally from the younger highly educated minority, who are open to religious pluralism. These are scattered around the world.[10] Originally the Prophet Muhammad thought of his revelations as providing the religion of the Arab people, as Judaism was the religion of the Jewish people. The concept of the People of the Book includes Jews and Christians, but not the Eastern faiths. But today many reforming Muslim thinkers regard the Buddha as one of the many earlier prophets of God – not in the end a viable idea, since the Buddha did not believe in a God, but nevertheless a useful interim move, like the interim move from exclusivism to inclusivism within much of modern Christianity. But the often less-educated masses in Islamic countries have yet gradually to catch up with their reforming thinkers. Lands under foreign rule, as nearly all Muslim states were in the modern period until after the Second World War, or under indirect foreign domination as several still are, do not tend to flourish culturally, and the process of assimilating new thinking is today seriously impeded by the Western allies' failure to intervene effectively to end the plight of the Palestinians, and by their invasion of Iraq and support for, and indirect control of, corrupt royal dictatorships in Muslim countries with huge oil resources. A new Islamic renaissance will come, but not yet.

Finally Christianity, which faces at least as severe a problem as Islam. If Jesus was God (or the second person of a divine trinity) incarnate, and human salvation is only possible as a result of his atoning death on the cross, then Christianity is the sole religion to have been founded directly by God in person, and is thus God's own religion, uniquely superior to all others, and designed for all humanity. But when we take account of the findings of the modern historical study of the New Testament and Christian origins we find that the incarnation doctrine was not taught by Jesus himself but is a creation of the Church, led by Paul (who did not know Jesus during his life) and reflected in the Fourth Gospel (written 90–100 CE), and finally made definitively official dogma some two centuries later. Today the idea of divine incarnation has to be re-understood as a metaphorical concept.[11] To 'incarnate' is to embody in one's life, as in 'Abraham Lincoln incarnated the will to preserve the unity of the United States' or 'Winston Churchill incarnated the British will to resist Hitler'. When incarnational language is understood metaphorically, rather than literally, its Christian use ceases to require the further doctrines of salvation by Jesus' atoning death (or in one of its more popular contemporary reworkings, the revelation in his life and death of God's co-suffering with us), and of the Trinity, both of which presuppose the deity of Jesus. Without these dogmas, the Christian message is of the reality and goodness and love of God and the consequent call to love one another.

All this is of course highly controversial, and the churches are a long way from being ready to take this step. Debate within them is intense and often bitter. I have engaged in it elsewhere (Hick 1985, 1995, 2001, 2005a, b and c), but this is not the place to continue that.

17
Spirituality for Today

We saw in Chapter 2 that 'spiritual' and 'spirituality' are today stretched in common use to the point of meaninglessness. But I want to use them now in their more limited sense as referring to the dimension of our consciousness (and probably our unconscious) together with our activity that constitutes our human responses to the universal presence of the Transcendent. And the kind of spirituality that I want to describe coheres with the wider understanding of religion that has emerged in the course of this book. It will therefore inevitably express my own personal point of view.

Our awareness of the Transcendent occurs either in some form of explicitly religious experience or often, in our secular West European and much of North American society, in the moral call of human solidarity in the face of desperate poverty, oppression and exploitation, natural disasters, and uncaring national and individual selfishness in relation to world problems, including global warming. And our response, whether we think of it in religious or secular terms, is in our lives, outer as well as inner. It is the more inner aspects that I am going to discuss now.

Cosmic optimism

I have outlined earlier (p. 150) the basic structure of the 'great world faiths'. They all recognise the sad state of human life, with each individual and group concerned for themselves at the expense of others, and the resulting oppression, violence, wars, exploitation, injustices, terror, misery and generalised unhappiness. Says the Bible, 'man is born to trouble as the sparks fly upwards' (Job 5:7). Says the Buddha, 'Birth is *dukha*, [old] age is *dukha*, disease is *dukha*, death is *dukha*, contact with the unpleasant is *dukha*, separation from the pleasant is *dukha*, every wish unfulfilled is *dukha*'.[1] And the other major faiths all say the same in their own ways. But they all also proclaim the possibility, and the real availability, of a limitlessly better state, to be realised by following the salvific path that they teach. These are all different, and yet all are paths of transformation from natural self-centredness to a new orientation centred in the Transcendent as conceived within their tradition. This begins in the individual but can come cumulatively to affect societies in varying degrees.

It is also an essential aspect of each faith that the salvific path leads beyond this life. The next and final chapter will ask what form this may take. The different traditions offer different pictures, but for all of them the present life is part of a cosmic process leading finally to a limitlessly good conclusion. In the famous words of the English mystic Lady Julian of Norwich, 'All shall be well, and all shall be well, and all manner of thing shall be well'.[2] We know that we are part of a continuous process of change through time, and in the main forms of religious experience we are aware either that this is in the presence of a loving God or is part of the life-process within a universal reality which is good, benign, friendly.

This faith is easily swamped within many human situations – the extreme poverty and starvation of millions, the brutal violence of war and the cruelty of oppression, painful illnesses, the growing limitations of old age, the prospect of death. Where is God? the victims of genocide in the Holocaust, or in Ruanda, Kosovo, the Sudan naturally ask. Although it is not a mitigation of this, it is extraordinary to see how profoundly helped by their faith and how mutually supportive many in the desperately poor world are. But the process in which we are involved, here and beyond death, is hard, challenging and demanding, as the experience and observation of all of us shows. But the power of religious experience, particularly as we see it in the rare individuals whom we regard as saints or mahatmas or enlightened persons nevertheless reveals the reality of an ultimate goodness, so that the rest of us are able to benefit profoundly from our knowledge of them.

Inspiration from the saints

I use our familiar Christian term 'saint' to cover also the equivalent within other religions – arhants, bodhisattvas and those approaching that state within Buddhism; within the Hindu tradition such identifiable individuals as Shankara and Ramanuja, and more recently Ramakrishna,

Caitanya, Maharashi and, as an activist saint, Mahatma Gandhi. The *waliy* of Islam is a 'friend of God', distinguished by special religious charisma, so that the tombs of some of the great Sufi saints and sheikhs are places of pilgrimage today. Perhaps the nearest equivalent for Jews is again mainly within its more mystical strand, where instances of a *tsaddiq*, a 'just man', have been revered. Again, the great figures of the past, especially Abraham and Moses (whether or not historical individuals), are exalted in the Jewish mind. Within the Confucian tradition the sage, of whom Confucius himself is the prime example, is highly respected, as well as later Confucian and Taoist masters.

So by saints I do not mean those officially canonised by the Catholic Church – some of these have been true saints in the sense I am using, but some were canonised for political, including ecclesiastical political, reasons, some on very inadequate information, and some are legendary figures. I mean by saints people who are/were manifestly much closer to God or living manifestly more in alignment with what Confucius called 'the will of heaven' or in other ways in response to the diversely experienced Transcendent than the rest of us, the primary criterion available to us being (see Chapter 4) the moral and spiritual fruits in their lives.

But within whatever tradition, one living saint is worth ten dead ones – not intrinsically but for us today. The saints of the past are no longer directly available to us, the stories of their lives have tended to develop and their saintliness to be magnified, and the hagiographies are notoriously unreliable. It becomes easy to forget that a saint is not a perfect human being – there are and have never been such. (The concept of a perfect human being is itself unclear and indefinable.) All saints are human and are flawed. But there are recent and living individuals, whom many today have known personally, whose lives inspire others by the 'light from beyond' that shines through them. I have myself been extremely fortunate to know four such, two Christians, a Sikh and a Buddhist, three of them activists, two of these risking their lives when their vocations required it, and one a contemplative. I have been inspired by them, and have written about them elsewhere for the interest of others.[3] None of them, of course, has for a moment thought of himself as a saint.

The emergence of the political or socially activist saint is a new, mainly twentieth- and twenty-first-century phenomenon made possible by the spread of democracy. The greatest example so far has been Mahatma Gandhi in India. Other well-known figures include Vinoba Bhave in India, Martin Luther King in the United States, archbishop Oscar Romero in San Salvador, archbishop Helder Camera in Brazil, Dag Hammarskjold of Sweden and the United Nations, Nelson Mandela and archbishop Desmond Tutu in South Africa, Thich Nat Hahn in Thailand.

But can there not also be saintly people who stand outside all organised religions? There can and are. Whereas prior, roughly, to the nineteenth century, virtually everyone lived within a religious tradition, this has now long ceased to be the case. Many are still nominally Christian, Jewish, Muslim, Hindu, Buddhist, Sikh but with only an inherited cultural relationship to their tradition, while yet others have consciously rejected the faith of their birth. A number are among those who, for example in the non-governmental organisations, but also in many other contexts of conflict and need, freely give their talents and energies to serve the desperately poor, the starving, the oppressed and exploited, the victims of war and violence, for the sake of justice and out of a compelling sense of solidarity with their fellow human beings. From a religious point of view, such secular people are responding to the universal presence of the Transcendent within and beyond them, but without using religious categories of thought or joining any of the religious organisations.

A primary function of the religions should be to produce saints, both activist and otherwise, and to nurture everyone to develop in that direction.

Prayer

If the Ultimate is not a Person but a reality beyond the personal/impersonal distinction, is there any room for prayer in the sense of intercession on behalf of other people?

Not in the form of asking God to intervene in the course of nature to cause something to happen that would not otherwise have happened – such as cure someone of a disease, make them survive a serious accident, further their career, save the victims of a flood, tidal wave, earthquake, volcanic irruption, forest fire, abolish world poverty, end war – though auto-suggestion in the form of prayer may help someone to study hard for an exam, give up harmful drugs, including excessive use of alcohol, and have various other good effects. The picture behind traditional prayer is of a God who is able at will to work miracles on earth, to whom we address our petitions and who in his infinite wisdom will respond to them or not as he sees best. But this picture creates intolerable problems. Suppose there is a car crash and three of the people involved are killed but one survives and sincerely thanks

God for this deliverance: God has protected her. This implies not only that God decided to save her but also that God decided not to save the others. It also implies that God could miraculously intervene to abolish poverty, disease, wars, injustices and disasters of every kind, but prefers not to do so. This is the ancient theological problem of evil: If God is omnipotent he must be able to abolish all evil; if he is all good he must want to abolish all evil; but evil exists; therefore he is either not omnipotent or not all good. Theodicies have been developed along both lines, and also more complex theories which avoid this dilemma.[4] But they all presuppose the personal God of traditional monotheism.

The alternative possibility, implicit in much Hindu and Buddhist thought, is that we are linked together at a deep unconscious level in a network of interdependence in which we are all the time influencing and being influenced by other's thoughts and, even more, emotions. In the East this interrelation of all things is expressed in the ancient Hindu image of the Net of Indra, also used by Buddhist writers. The Net of Indra stretches endlessly in all directions with a jewel in every knot of the net, each jewel reflecting and being reflected in all the others, so that the infinite totality is interrelated throughout. Such images symbolise the way in which the effects of our inner thoughts and emotions ramify out to affect others.

But we also of course each have a (varyingly) strong filtering mechanism which preserves our degree of individual autonomy; and, further, the multitude of different and often conflicting fragments of 'information' (in the cybernetic sense) affecting us at any given moment largely cancel out or block one another. The evidence for such a field of potential mutual influence is the evidence for ESP (telepathy), which in my opinion is very strong – not so much, however, from laboratory experiments as from impressive spontaneous cases, which are, however, from a scientific point of view merely 'anecdotal'.[5]

If such influencing exists, it is possible to take the necessary time deliberately to concentrate our thoughts on someone in need, someone whose situation we know, to identify the better state in which they could be, and concentratedly and lovingly to visualise their coming into that better state. So many different factors and influences enter into everyone's development all the time that this may or may not help them in any noticeable way. But, on this view, thought and emotion can have a genuine power both for good and for evil.

It is also possible to use this universal network without focussing on specific individuals but in the service of all life. In his Journal in January 1647 George Fox, the founder of Quakerism, wrote, 'I saw an ocean of darkness and death, but an infinite ocean of light and love, which flowed over the ocean of darkness'. In our meditation on behalf of the world we are contributing a small drop to that ocean of light and love which sustains all constructive and beneficial activity in this world.

Essentially the same end is served in a quite different idiom by Christian or other prayer for the world or for those suffering in some current disaster or destructive conflict – provided such prayer is not merely a 'shopping list' of the world's problems such as is recited in the prayers of intercession in many churches. These may serve to remind the congregation of those in need and thus have value, but real prayer for others requires a more prolonged concentration on those others than is allowed by reading out the current list. Again, in so far as the constant prayers of monks and nuns and solitary anchorites is for the world and not only for their own spiritual perfecting, it must be an important contribution to the welfare of humanity.

Whatever the method and whatever the philosophy behind it, does this kind of activity 'work'? I doubt if this can be proved either way, although no doubt some kind of organised observation, amounting to an experiment, could theoretically be devised. But the multiplicity of different factors at work in all human affairs makes it difficult to isolate any effect that prayer and meditation for others may have. From a religious point of view it is extremely likely that it does sometimes 'work'. From a 'hard' naturalistic point of view it is *a priori* certain that it cannot. Alternatively, a 'soft' naturalism need not (although it usually does) exclude such extra-sensory influence.

All this must seem religiously very dry. But it is probably as far as philosophy can take us.

Meditation

Broadly speaking, and passing over its early neo-Platonic stage, most traditional Christian forms of meditation aim to fill the mind with the imagery and beliefs of the tradition. This ranges from a constant repetition of the Jesus prayer, 'Jesus Christ, Son of God, have mercy on me', practised within Eastern Orthodoxy, to the more elaborate form in the Western Church taught by Ignatius Loyala (fifteenth–sixteenth centuries), founder of the Jesuit order. In his *Spiritual Exercises* he teaches a deliberate and vivid visualising, and even inner hearing and sometimes touching, of some specific biblical scene, say Jesus on the shore of the lake of Galilee with his disciples, or his crucifixion or ascension. Such practices embed the tradition and its doctrine ever more firmly into the believer. Having no experience of this I shall not attempt to discuss it further.

The diametrically opposite kinds of meditation, practised within the Eastern traditions, particularly Buddhism, seek to empty consciousness of all earthly content, including religious ideas and images.

One form is Zen meditation. Although this has a long history, beginning in China, it is today practised most intensively in Japan. In the monasteries in Kyoto, the world capital of Zen, in addition to sitting meditation for several, often six (not continuous) hours a day, the use of a koan, an apparently unintelligible phrase (a famous example: 'the sound of one hand clapping') given by the Rinzai master to the monk is very important. There can be no doubt that prolonged Zen practice markedly changes the configuration of the brain and the personality.[6] This has been evident in the three Japanese Rinzai Zen masters whom I have myself encountered. Paradoxically, they have transcended our ordinary ego point of view, becoming in that sense selfless, and yet at the same time they are exceptionally powerful personalities. Soto practice does not usually involve koans but consists in sitting meditation, and does not require the highly disciplined life of a Zen monastery. But although its philosophy and practice are different, it leads to essentially the same end.

On the principle that while books can give us all the 'objective' information, only experience can show us the inner reality, I shall not, having only a fascinated spectator's knowledge of Zen, discuss it further here.

The other main form within Buddhism is *sattipathana*, 'mindfulness', meditation. One does not have to be a Buddhist to practise this, as I try (I emphasise the word *try*) to do, having learned it from the famous monk Nyanaponika Thera, who lived in a forest hermitage near Kandy in Sri Lanka (where I visited him several times, and corresponded with him), and who died in 1994 at the age of 94.

The method is very simple. You sit comfortably with back straight, make a deliberate intention to become open to the reality beyond and within us, close your eyes, and concentrate on your own current breathing – in, out, in, out . . . Nyanaponika recommended focussing on the movement of the diaphragm, others on the nostrils. Take a few deep breaths first, to direct attention to it, and then hold on to the conscious breathing. The reason is not that there is anything special about our breathing, except perhaps that it is part of our life, but that it has no intellectual content or meaning; and the aim is to empty consciousness of all thinking, thus opening it to another reality. Like Zen this tends to produce a serenity and mindfulness in all the moments of life, with its moral fruit of compassion (fellow feeling and regard) for all beings. As to the 'true reality' realised by the enlightened consciousness, the only way to know it must be to experience it for oneself – which I have not yet achieved.

The practice may sound easy but is not, at least for those of us who do not live in monasteries or hermitages but in the midst of modern urban life. The first problem is to clear the necessary time, preferably (for most of us) early in the morning while we are fresh and not yet involved in the day's activities. In the first stages the mind wanders again and again. To some extent this can be pre-empted by first thinking of any problems and worries that may distract your attention and deliberately setting them aside as matters to be dealt with later. However, if you persist long enough you reach a second stage, which suddenly just happens, in which there is no more wandering, consciousness is fixed effortlessly on the breathing alone, and you feel as though you could go on indefinitely, and do go on longer than usual. It is as though you have been laboriously moving through a crowd of people speaking to you – though it is the voices of your own thoughts – to a point beyond which your mind is uninterrupted. And just once for me, so far, I have reached a third point. When after being in that second stage for some time I opened my eyes, everything was different, in two ways. Instead of I being here and the room around me and the garden seen through the window there, I was part of one indivisible whole; and, more importantly, that whole, not limited to what I could see, the totality of all reality, was 'good', 'friendly', 'benign', so that there could not possibly be anything to be anxious about or afraid of. I put the three words above in quotes because they normally refer to qualities of a personal being. And for many people that is how they will understand them – God. But in this state I was not aware of a personal God. And 'good' is also used in such phrases as 'have a good day', 'friendly' in such phrases as 'user friendly', 'benign' in such phrases as 'a benign climate'; and this is closer to what I felt. It only lasted a very short time, I should think less than a minute, but enough to leave an indelible impression. How would it affect ordinary daily life if one were all the time aware of being in a 'friendly' universe? I wish I knew, in the only way one could. This, along with its theistic equivalent, awareness of being in the presence of a loving God, would be true spirituality.

Continuing with my own practice, I try to take about half an hour (too short a time) for meditation. This includes a preliminary few minutes of reading in some classic 'mystical' text – *The Songs of Kabir*, *The Cloud of*

Unknowing, the *Bhagavavad Gita*, the *Theologica Germanica*, *The Imitation of Christ*, the *Tao Te Ching*, the poems of Rumi, parts of the Bible and of the Qur'an . . . and concluding the half hour or so with prayer in the sense that I have described above – not petition to God but what the Buddhists call loving-kindness meditation on behalf of others.

But it must be stressed that there is no spiritual practice that is *the* right or best one. What is right for one person may well not be right for another. Further, a particular approach may be useful for a given individual at one point in their life but not at another. But there can be value in sharing thoughts and experiences about this. However deeply attached anyone may be to a particular tradition or sub-tradition, they can benefit from the spiritual riches of other traditions by reading some of their writings and, if they can, getting to know some of their practitioners.

I have used before[7] an analogy which illustrates the way in which awareness of our supra-natural environment changes our awareness of our natural environment and the way in which we live in it. Imagine that I enter a large room in a strange building and find myself, to my consternation, in a meeting of a militant secret society. Many of the members are armed, and everyone takes me to be a fellow member. I judge it expedient to go along with this assumption. Subtle and ruthless plans are laid for the violent overthrow of the constitution. The whole situation is alarming in the extreme, and I am in a state of acute fear. Then I suddenly notice that behind me there is a gallery with silently whirring cameras, and I realise that I have walked by accident onto the set of a film. This realisation consists in a radical change in my interpretation of the situation, my understanding of its meaning, and hence of how to behave within it – in this case, ceasing to be afraid but joining in the pretence and not interrupting the proceedings. Until now I had automatically interpreted it as a very dangerous real-life situation; but now I am instead interested to be part, unintentionally, in the shooting of a film. But there is no corresponding change in the course of events. The meeting and the plotting and the blood-thirsty rhetoric go on as before. But the same empirical situation now has a quite different meaning for me, radically changing my attitude to it and the range of ways in which I would behave in response to the various ways it might develop.

In this scenario I have noticed new empirical data, the balcony and the whirring cameras. But now in imagination expand the room into the entire world, indeed the entire physical universe. There is no room now for any extra physical data to be discovered. This is the strange room into which we walk, unintentionally, at birth. Depending on where we enter it and the circumstances of our life, it can be a dangerous and threatening place or a delightful and beautiful place, and every mixture between these extremes. But in experiencing it as having the meaning that we find in it we are making a *total* interpretation. And the religious total interpretation is that the ultimate reality undergirding it is, in our human terms, good or loving, so that in Lady Julian's words 'All shall be well, and all shall be well, and all manner of things shall be well'.

So true spirituality means living in response to the Transcendent, whether experienced in terms of religious or secular categories of thought. And spirituality includes morality, so that its fruits are evident in life.

18
After Death?

The origin of after-life beliefs

As far back as we can trace distinctively human life there is evidence of special treatment of the dead. They are not, like other animals, eaten or left to rot. And the known burial customs have always included some symbolic indication of a belief in the continued existence of the departed spirit – often food or weapons, sometime ornaments, buried with the corpse to aid the spirit's journey to the realm of the ancestors. The late-nineteenth-century anthropologists who were able to study the then remaining primal societies in Australia, Polynesia, Africa and South America reported the widespread idea, not of an immaterial soul, but of a shade, a ghostly insubstantial double, of the bodily individual. This was assumed to continue in a dim underworld, until it gradually faded and was lost to tribal memory. And the earliest written expressions of a conception of the life to come are very similar. For the early Hebrews Sheol was a gloomy underworld deep in the earth. Job lamented, 'Let me alone, that I may find a little comfort before I go whence I shall not return, to the land of gloom and deep darkness, the land of gloom and chaos, where light is as darkness' (Job 10:20–2). And there was no hope of return from Sheol: 'He who goes down to Sheol does not come up' (Job 7:9). (The idea of the resurrection of the dead – possibly derived from Zoroastrianism – developed in the post-prophetic period of the last two or three centuries BCE.) The neighbouring ancient Sumerians, Assyrians and Babylonians shared the belief in a dark underworld. The Hades of the ancient Greeks was very similar. The shade of the great Achilles, briefly restored to consciousness by the blood of a goat, says, 'Nay, speak not comfortably of me after death, oh great Odysseus. Rather would I live upon earth as the hireling of another, with a landless man who has no great livelihood, than bear sway among all the dead that be departed' (*Odyssey*, Bk 11, 488–91). There is an old Yoruba saying, 'A corner in this world is better than a corner in the world of spirits'.[1]

The significance of this for our present purpose is that the origin of the belief in a continued life after death was not in the wish for a heavenly or paradisal state to look forward to after all the sufferings of this life. For no one would wish for what the earliest civilisations expected for the dead. They did believe in an after-life, but not a desirable one. No doubt today most people desire to live beyond death, and believe or half-believe that they will, but it is clear that historically that desire is not the origin of the belief.

That early understanding of death was correlated with the pre-axial submergence of the individual in the clan, tribe, nation, as a cell in the social organism. The first self-conscious individuals seem to have been kings and emperors and high priests, and it is they alone who were first believed to have a desirable post-mortem existence. But with the axial age and the gradual democratisation of religion, there developed both the sense of being a separate individual and also of individual moral responsibility, leading to the idea of judgement and both a heaven and a hell.[2]

Heaven and hell in the Christian tradition

Basically, Christianity affirms a future resurrected life in heaven, or hell, or heaven via purgatory, and sometimes with limbo added, and sometimes, in the modern period, annihilation instead of hell.[3] There is no need here to trace the history of hell, except to say that in the medieval world the fear of it was very real, indeed terrifying, for those who died without having received the Church's absolution for their sins. And those outside the Church were lost:

> The holy Roman Church believes, professes, and preaches that 'no one remaining outside the Catholic Church, not just pagans, but also Jews or heretics [then believed to include Muslims] or schismatics, can become partakers of eternal life; but they will go to the everlasting fire which was prepared for the devil and his angels', unless before the end of life they are joined to the Church. (Council of Florence, 1438–45)

But in the modern world, and for all but the most conservative Christians, eternal hell has faded into myth. Heaven has likewise faded.

No longer do the heavenly host sing hymns before the throne of God. Heaven is now a vague hope, and we avoid trying to describe or visualise it – although many of our hymn books still include well-loved verses from previous centuries,

> There is a land of pure delight
>   where saints immortal reign;
> infinite day excludes the night,
>   and pleasures banish pain.

or

> There all distress will be done for ever;
> there we will sing songs of Zion, and never
> never cease praising; our songs ever soaring,
> praising you, Lord, and for ever adoring.

Why have heaven and hell lost their hold on the Christian imagination – except, again, among the most conservative? The idea raises many questions. What would it be for the present self to live eternally? Would we have an ever lengthening memory going back hundreds, then thousands, then millions, and millions of millions of years? Or is the next life outside time? Are we then 'frozen' at the time of death, never to undergo further change? Or are the saved perfected in the moment of death? But would a suddenly perfected 'me' still be me? It is very rare for contemporary theologians to ask themselves these questions, although in the more liberal early and mid-twentieth century a number did. But in the nineteenth century Christian writers still provided dogmatic answers. There were numerous books of the type of C. R. Muston's *Recognition in the World to Come or Christian Friendship on Earth Perpetuated in Heaven*, of which a second edition was published in 1831. The author teaches that in the heavenly realm there will be perfection, perpetuity and progression, and draws conclusions about those with whom we should and should not makes friends in this life, including in the 'compact of marriage'. But all such thinking seems utterly unreal today. In a post-Christian age, when eternal life in the kingdom of heaven is no longer seriously believed in, we have funeral services in which the traditional words are still spoken or sung, and this often can help in the trauma of bereavement. But in face of death our secularised society is adrift. The best that is hoped for is to live on for a while in the memory of family and friends and perhaps to leave some change in the world for others, while our bodies are recycled like all other material things. The result is to make the inevitable approach of death a threat, something unacceptable which we shut out of our minds. We know that one day we will die, and we acknowledge this, and if we are wise we make legal provision for it; but nevertheless the culture hides death and forgets it so far as possible. As has often been pointed out, whereas once in Western society people did not speak openly about sex, today death is the tacitly forbidden subject. It would be considered worse than rude to raise the subject at a dinner party.

For those theologians – very numerous today – who believe in universal salvation, hell (if there is a hell) is empty. Everyone is eventually received into heaven. There is still, however, a need for purgatory in the revised sense of an intermediate state between this life and heaven. We are all capable of rehabilitation, however long and difficult, from our sinfulness, and of enormous enhancement and growth in our better qualities. Both justice and reason demand that there must be some continuation before any final heaven or hell. But this has never been spelled out in any careful way. Is the continued life embodied (in a resurrection body)? If so, where? Is it disembodied? If so, what form can it take? Does not spiritual growth require the making of moral decisions? But how is this possible without embodiment in a common environment in which people interact and in which their decisions can do good or harm?

These questions remain unanswered within orthodox Christianity, and unauthorised speculation about them leads towards the Eastern idea of reincarnation or rebirth, to which we now turn.

Reincarnation

The popular conception of this, in both East and West, is that the present conscious self, the 'me' now writing these sentences, will after death be born again as a baby; and the same for all of us. In popular Hinduism it is also sometimes believed that we may be reincarnated as an animal as the karmic result of a previous life. But staying with reincarnation in human form, it becomes in principle possible to remember one's previous lives. And in a number of countries, particularly India, Sri Lanka, but also Tibet, Brazil, Lebanon, and sporadically in many other countries, there are numerous cases of children apparently remembering their previous life. A number of these were investigated by Ian Stevenson, then head of the psychiatry department at the University of Virginia, whose reports have been published in a series of books, the first with the cautious title, *Twenty Cases Suggestive of Reincarnation.* And in the USA and Europe, under 'regression' hypnosis many people have likewise apparently experienced flashbacks of previous life.[4]

Many of these accounts are impressive. Nevertheless I am not myself confident that the reported memories are indeed of previous lives. It is possible to have false memories, apparent memories of events that never happened. A number of the cases are of children in India or Sri Lanka or elsewhere being taken to another village which they seemed to remember, recognising toys etc. that belonged to a child who had recently died there, or apparently recognising relatives of the dead child. But we have to be aware that when most of these cases were investigated it was a great benefit to a family and a rural village community to be connected with a case of reincarnation. The child and the family became famous, Western investigators arrived bringing publicity and tourists, and it is possible that to encourage all this there was conscious or unconscious coaching of the child. Again, in the cases of hypnotic regression the living individual seems so often to have been a notable figure in his or her previous life, suggesting the possibility of fantasising pseudo-memories.

These cautions do not justify a dismissal of all the claimed memories of previous lives. It may well be possible that a latent memory sometimes leaks through into consciousness. But nevertheless I doubt it we can give decisive weight to the existing reports.

Further, conscious memories are not required by the understanding of reincarnation in both Hindu and Buddhist philosophy. Here it is not the present conscious personality that is reborn, but a deeper element within us, our essential moral/spiritual nature, a basic dispositional structure which both affects and is affected by all that we do and undergo in the course of our lives. In advaitic philosophy this is called the 'subtle body' (*linga sharira*), although 'body' is misleading in Western terms in that it does not have a shape and size; it is not a ghostly image of the physical body. It is rather a psychic entity which survives the death of the body, but is later re-embodied in an embryo which grows into a new conscious personality, formed both by the basic dispositional continuant and all the innumerable genetic and environmental factors that go to create each unique new personality. This new personality will have an innate tendency to develop the basic moral/spiritual outlook of the previous bearer of the psychic continuant. Is this somehow drawn to an embryo with an appropriate genetic inheritance? If so, by what mechanism? The broad Hindu answer is karma, moral/spiritual cause and effect. But this does not amount to a detailed explanation.

The Buddhist understanding of rebirth is similar in practice, although with a different philosophical basis. Whereas Hindu advaitic thought affirms the eternal atman, soul, which is ultimately one with the ultimate reality, Brahman, the Buddhist no-self (*anatta*) teaching denies this. The empirical self, the conscious 'me', is not a continuing substance but a process, an ever-changing series of moments of consciousness. There is no enduring substantial self. Everything is transient (*anicca*). What then is the connection between one conscious moment and the next, constituting what we normally think of as ourselves? The momentary ego, seeing everything in relation to itself, is a centre of desire, hope, expectation, fear which creates the next moment of ego consciousness, and on through many lives until the end of desiring, which is the fulfilment of *nirvana* – an eternal state referred to in the Pali scriptures as 'the unfading', 'the stable', 'the peace', the 'un-decaying', 'the wonderful', the 'marvellous', 'the goal' (*Samyutta Nikaya*, IV: 369–71. Woodward 1954, 251–3). Again in the *Dhammapada*, 'there is no higher bliss than Nibbana' (the Pali equivalent of the Sanscrit *nirvana*). And again, 'Above, beyond Nibbana's bliss is naught' (*Therigatha*, 476. Davids 1964, I, 169).

From this point of view it is possible in principle, though not normally in practice, to remember previous lives, and in the story of the Buddha's enlightenment under the bo tree at Bodh Gaya, in the first part of the night he remembered all his many past lives (*Majjhima-Nikaya*, I, 247–8. Horner 1954, 302). It is this latent memory, even if it is only actualised at the end of a long journey through many lives, that constitutes the connection of this particular series of mortal lives.

As to the mechanism of the rebirth process, there is no more clarity within Buddhism than within Hinduism. There is the idea of the 'relinking consciousness' according to which the last thought of the dying person provides the connection with the immediate new birth. This last thought is not necessarily a conscious thought, and might perhaps be better described as the essential nature to which the individual's life has led. But there is also, in Tibetan Buddhism, the idea of the Bardo ('between two') period in which the self undergoes a kind of self-psychoanalytic process of coming to terms with all the good and evil thoughts and actions of the last life, thus preparing for a new incarnation.[5]

What we should take from Hinduism and Buddhism, I suggest, is the thought that in the unconscious depth of the present personality there is a deeper moral/spiritual essence which can survive bodily death and be re-embodied in a new conscious personality – or indeed in a series of new conscious personalities.

Where?

Suppose that we do live many lives, where may these lives be lived?

Not necessarily on this earth or on other planets of our solar system, or even other galaxies of our universe, but perhaps in the quite other spheres of existence of which the Hindu and Buddhist philosophies speak. Or some of our lives may be lived in this world and some elsewhere. Each successive Dalai Lama, for example, is supposed to be a reincarnation of his predecessor, not only in this world but specifically in Tibet. But Buddhism also speaks of many other spheres of existence within which life is carried on. If we ask where these realms are, meaning where in the only universe that we know, the answer is nowhere. The idea of other spaces has in the past generally seemed to be pure gratuitous imagining, but we may have to get used to the idea that there are things that are real although they don't exist in our customary sense. For the more we read those scientists who are trying to communicate with the rest of us, the more we are led to suspend many of our inherited assumptions. In his book *Our Cosmic Habitat* the cosmologist Martin Rees, who is not himself a religious believer, argues for the currently canvassed theory that this universe, beginning with its own big bang some thirteen billion years ago, is one of innumerable universes, many sustaining life, some more and some less advanced than that on our own planet. He claims that 'the multiverse concept is already part of empirical science' (Rees 2001, xvii). The physicist Paul Davies, writing about multiple space–time systems, reports the theory that 'these other universes actually exist and are every bit as real as the one we inhabit' (Davies 1980, 136), and the physicist Steven Weinberg also speaks of the possibility that 'the constants of nature may vary from region to region, so that each region of the universe is a kind of subuniverse' (Weinberg 1993, 176). Indeed the range of responsible scientific speculation is now greater and more exciting than it has ever been, and the possibilities that it opens up are much more mysterious and surprising than even a decade ago.

Many lives in many worlds

I come now to what I personally think the most likely scenario, and the reasons for it. Some will find it a welcome and others an unwelcome possibility.

The basic religious faith is, in 'Western' terms, that there is a good and loving, or gracious and merciful, personal God; or in 'Eastern' terms, that the transpersonal ultimate reality is benign, friendly, good. Given this faith, it seems evident that the moral/spiritual quality – the two go together – of our human lives must have some enduring, and not merely ephemeral, value. If the basic religious faith is well founded, it follows that all that is good in human living cannot be permanently deleted by death. This present life in which we find ourselves cannot be the totality of human existence. In other words, there must be some kind of life after death. Another consideration which points to the same conclusion is that, if this life is all, the sufferings and injustices that afflict so many so arbitrarily would mean that God is not good, or that we are not part of a friendly universe. From any religious point of view, then, there must be further life beyond this. The question is, what form may it take?

We can to some extent, by the use of reason, narrow down the options that are within the range of our present thought and imagination – though the reality could be beyond that range.

The traditional 'Western' idea of an immediate translation to an eternal heaven or hell makes little sense, because no one is fitted at the end of this life for either, not even the greatest saint or the greatest sinner. There must be an 'intermediate state', but not the purgatory of the Catholic tradition because this does not allow for continued moral and spiritual growth. The only kind of existence that we can imagine which makes this possible is a further finite life, bounded by birth and death, because it is the pressure of these boundaries that makes time precious and development possible. But one more such life will not be enough for most of us, hence the idea of many future, and probably past, lives. This option permits the cosmic optimism that through a series of lives, in which any moral/spiritual maturing achieved in one is carried forward to the next, human existence may eventually be perfected.

The idea is interestingly explored in Milan Kundera's novel *The Unbearable Lightness of Being* (1984). At one point his central character imagines,

> Somewhere out in space there was another planet where all people would be born again. They would be fully aware of the life they had spent on earth and of all the experiences they had amassed here. And perhaps there was still another planet, where we would all be born a third time with the experience of our first two lives. And perhaps there were yet more planets, where mankind would be born one degree (one life) more mature ... Of course we here on earth (planet number one, the planet of inexperience) can only fabricate vague fantasies of what will happen to man on those other planets.

Will he be wiser? Is maturity within man's power? Can he attain it through repetition? Only [Kundera says] from the perspective of such a utopia is it possible to use the concepts of pessimism and optimism with full justification: an optimist is one who thinks that on planet number five the history of mankind will be less bloody. A pessimist is one who thinks otherwise.

In Kundera's imagined scenario, on planet two we remember our life on planet one. But is conscious memory necessary to moral/spiritual progress from life to life? It seems that the 'Eastern' belief in an unconscious storing of the memory of previous lives would suffice, providing that this memory is in principle retrievable, and providing that there is an unconscious continuant which carries forward any moral/spiritual increment, or deterioration, to the next life. We might call this the soul or spirit, but these words can carry unwanted connotations, so let us, more cumbersomely, call it the dispositional continuant. This next life will not, then, be a reincarnation of the present conscious self, but a new personality formed by all the genetic and environmental circumstances which makes each of us the unique individual that we are, but embodying the dispositional continuant at the basis of this new individual.

But what is the relation between this continuant and our genetic inheritance? Our genes do not determine the use that we make of the body, including brain, that they give us. As James Mathers wrote, 'Genes are like the keys of a piano: they determine what possibilities are available, but leave pianists free to make their own music' (Mathers 2003, 274). In another analogy, nature has dealt us a set of cards, but what both affects and is affected by our basic dispositional structure is how the conscious personality plays these cards, however strong or weak the hand may be. We are all the time both expressing and forming our deeper self by our responses to the circumstances, both good and bad, in which we find ourselves. And it is this cumulative quality of response that is built into the basic moral/spiritual character that will be re-embodied in another conscious personality.

The cosmic optimism of the religions anticipates a final end state that has a value in itself so great as to make worthwhile the many lives that have led to it, with all their mixture of happiness and misery, justice and injustice, good fortune and bad fortune, goodness, wickedness and horrendous evil, prosperity and dire poverty – all the varied light and shade and darkness and joy and sorrow of the human condition as we know it, and with some of our many temporary selves much more fortunate than others.

Such cosmic optimism depends on the principle that the significance of our present actions and reactions is created by the larger pattern of our lives to which they contribute as this develops over the years. On the personal level we can all recall personal relationship decisions, career decisions, commitments of many kinds, deliberate and accidental actions and inactions, whose significance both positive and negative has only revealed itself retrospectively. And it is true of us collectively, as societies and nations, that the meaning or significance of what we do now is largely determined by what comes out of it in the future. We can project this principle onto a much larger scale in which a present human life receives its ultimate meaning from the future lives to which it leads, and the ultimate future to which they all lead. There are, to use visual imagery, widening circles of meaning, from the often intense immediate meaning inherent in each present moment of experience, to that same moment as it takes its place in the larger context of a further, say, fifteen years of living, to the further, sometimes different, meaning that it takes on after another period of years, and so on as our life develops, to its meaning far beyond this life in the light of the all-encompassing ultimate future.

And because of the interlinked nature of all life, there is what in Eastern terms is collective as well as individual karma. We are contributing not only to our own future finite selves but also to the future of humanity in and beyond this life.

My proposal, then, is to see our present life as contributing something to a cumulative process which continues through many more impermanent selves. In an analogy used before, we are like runners in a relay race, carrying the torch for a short time during which we bear a unique responsibility. Our present lives thus have profound meaning, contributing something positive or negative, by advancing or retarding the succession of future selves who will continue the same spiritual project, eventually to its completion.

But the hard lesson of the religions is that we have to learn to transcend our deeply ingrained self-concern. So long as we are dominated by the importance of our present self, anxious for its existence to be prolonged as long as possible, regardless of its quality, death will remain the ultimate threat, from which we can only avert our thoughts. And yet the present self is mortal. If I can cease to cling to my fragmentary and very imperfect ego, seeing it as only the present moment in a long creative process, then hopefully I can accept my mortality without fear or resentment and live freely in the present.

Concluding Summary

This is partly a summary of what has gone before and partly an expansion of some key points.

Religion as institutions and as spirituality

In the first group of chapters (1–4) I distinguished between, on the one hand, religion as embodied in institutions interacting with all the other forces that go to make up human history and, on the other hand, what for lack of a better word I am calling spirituality. I noted the stretching of the word in popular use to the point of near meaninglessness, but by spirituality I mean each individual's response to the universal presence of the Reality beyond and within us, whether experienced in religious or non-religious terms. This is largely independent of the power structures and the ambiguously balanced social and psychological benefits and harm of the religious organisations.

Our customary Western term for that transcendent reality of overarching importance is 'God'. But in most people's minds this is too firmly linked for my purpose with the idea of an infinite all-powerful Person who created and presides over the universe, intervening to guide cosmic evolution and sometimes, miraculously, in human history – above all, for orthodox Christians, in the miracles of incarnation and bodily resurrection of Jesus. But the concept of a personal God does not cover the range of human religious experience. It excludes Buddhism, Taoism, Confucianism, some forms of Hinduism. Alternative terms include Ultimate Reality, the Ultimate, the Real, the Transcendent – and I have used them all, for the sake of variety, but usually in this book the last.

In order to keep the discussion within manageable compass I drew my examples mainly, though not exclusively, from Christianity and

Buddhism, because these are at the same time the most alike (in their moral teaching) and yet most strikingly unlike (in their metaphysical teaching).

I briefly surveyed the different kinds of religious experience, focussing mainly on such 'ordinary' forms as the sense, perhaps in a place of worship but often in some moment of daily life, of being in the presence of God; the momentary or prolonged seeing of the natural world in a new light in which it is suffused with a profoundly uplifting and empowering meaning; the experience in non-discursive meditation of being part of the total flow of a universe that is benign, liberating the individual from fears or anxieties, and releasing a natural fellow-feeling for others. I added that if there is indeed a transcendent reality of which we can be aware in such ways, its universal presence is also felt in our present secular age in the West in the use of such concepts as the claim of human solidarity to serve the suffering or to work for global justice and peace and a viable future,.

The often highly dramatic experiences of visions and voices of many of the great mystics also entered into the discussion but were not the main focus. Nor were such paranormal experiences as extra-sensory perception and near-death experience, important though these are.

The criterion that operates within all the great world faiths to distinguish delusion from an authentic awareness of the Transcendent is the long-term fruits of the experience in the individual's life; and these are essentially the same within all the world faiths.

The primacy of religious experience

If religion is not ultimately based on religious experience, what is it based on? The standard answer within the religions, particularly the 'religions of the book', is revelation. God, it is said, has revealed the saving truth to us in the Torah or in the Bible or in the Qur'an. But, as John Locke pointed out, 'Whatever God hath revealed is certainly true; no doubt can be made of it . . . but whether it be a divine revelation or no, reason must judge' (Locke 1924, 357. Bk IV, ch. 18). For no one could possibly accept as authentic everything that is claimed to be an infallible divine revelation. In practice, the great majority of religious believers have accepted their own particular holy book as a result of being born into a family and/or community which reveres it, and have been brought up to revere it themselves. But behind any wholehearted participation in a tradition, an implicit criterion has operated. This is that the 'revelation' evokes some sense of the holy, of final authority, of contact with the Transcendent. Those who do not share that sense remain purely formal members of their tradition – and this includes many within the priestly class as well as laypeople. But given that spiritual response, any elements within our sacred book which uncomfortably stretch our credulity today, in the light of modern historical and scientific knowledge, are 'hermeneutisized' by the scholars as symbolic or mythological, although still swallowed uncritically by the unthinking. Thus within the Torah the story, for example, of the six-hundred-year-old Noah and his ark, and the flood which covered the entire earth, including its mountains, is not insisted upon as literal history by many modern Jews. It is thought that there may lie behind it a historical memory of some major flood, but the story's enduring religious value does not depend upon its historicity.

The New Testament pictures of Jesus are modernised and domesticated within modern non-fundamentalist Christianity. Jesus' indifference to family commitments, his numerous threats of hell, his restriction of his message (with a few exceptions) to the children of Israel, his expectations of an imminent end to history through a dramatic divine intervention – which did not happen – are brushed out of the picture. And such ideas as unredeemed sinners being finally cast into a lake of fire are likewise generally tactfully ignored by many Christians today. We focus on the moral teaching of the Sermon on the Mount, the (undefined) idea of the Kingdom of God, the parables of the love of God, and the Lord's Prayer – which last does not refer to any of the later doctrines of incarnation, atonement and trinity.

Again, within Islam, the 'night journey' of Muhammad from Mecca to the al-Aqsa mosque in Jerusalem, for example, has been developed within the Muslim tradition far beyond the brief Qur'anic passage (17:1). The story is understood in a variety of ways – as a literal physical flight through the air, as a dream, as a spiritual experience. And many other Qur'anic verses are likewise interpreted in different ways by different schools of Islamic thought, taking account of the situations in the Prophet's life to which they were revelatory responses.

Buddhism, which I have been using in comparison with Christianity, lacks the monotheistic concept of revelation. Its approach is: this is the Way, try it. The Buddha taught a path, the Noble Eightfold Path outlined in Chapter 3, which he said leads eventually to *nirvana*. But the only way to test this is for each individual to begin to live it for him or herself.

Many religions point to a revered or worshipped individual revealer. But a prior, often unnoticed, moral criterion is at work when, in the case of Christianity, Jesus is regarded as God (or God the Son) incarnate. If we had reason – which we do not – to believe that Jesus was secretly amassing wealth at his followers' expense, was selfishly deceitful and immoral, we would not regard him as 'Son of God' or as our 'window onto God'. We bring an already existing basic moral judgement to the figure of Jesus, which is then deepened and extended by his teachings.

Revelation, then, whether written or in the person of a revealer, does not stand unsupported by moral and spiritual criteria. It is not an alternative to religious experience as the basis of living religion. Ordinary religious experience is central to the normal practice of religion in worship, prayer, meditation. It is of course possible, and indeed common, to go through the motions of worship in synagogue, church, mosque, gurudwara, or temple as routine behaviour without this evoking within us any sense of divine presence or transcendent meaning. But when worship is 'genuine', it makes some degree of difference within the worshipper's life by orienting him/her a little more towards the Ultimate, reinforcing or developing an existing faith. Without that inner experience, the religious organisations would be purely cultural or political or welfare organisations. And of course to a too great extent this is what they are. The distinction I drew in Chapter 1 between religion as human institution and as spirituality remains valid and important.

Religion and neuroscience

In the second group of chapters (5–10) I faced the challenges from the neurosciences to religious experience considered as awareness of the Transcendent. The neuroscientists nearly all share the naturalistic, or materialist, assumption of our culture, which sees religious experience as a delusional, even if sometimes beneficial, phenomenon caused by some neural malfunction. However, they generally mean by religious experience any experience structured in terms of religious concepts, and on this basis there are indeed innumerable instances of the delusional, often with their explanation in brain malfunction. But the all-inclusive diagnosis of all forms of religious experience in neuro-physiological terms involves the fallacy of equating correlation with identity. All events in consciousness are correlated with neural events. But I argue that mind/brain identity, at one time widely favoured by philosophers of mind and still defended by some, is untenable; and also that the more sophisticated naturalistic alternatives now available, in terms of emergent properties, functionalism, etc., are also entirely inadequate. They are forms of epiphenomenalism, according to which the qualia (the direct contents) of consciousness are other than brain-function but have in themselves no executive power. But if consciousness cannot affect behaviour, why has it evolved? There are no convincing answers to this question. I conclude that the relationship between brain and consciousness is like that between two dancers who always move together, but sometimes with one and sometimes the other taking the lead. This involves a defence of non-compatibilist free will, which hinges finally upon the performative contradiction involved in claiming, as a fully determined mind/brain, to know or rationally believe that one is a fully determined mind/brain. Not only all personal relationships but all creative work in literature, painting, music, architecture, and equally in all the great scientific advances, presupposes a significant degree of intellectual and physical freedom.

The upshot of all this is that the nature of consciousness (as many leading neurophysiologists now accept) is a sheer mystery. This means that the possibility lies open that as well as physical reality there is non-physical reality, including the kinds of reality referred to by the religions.

Epistemology and religious experience

And then in the final group of chapters (11–18) I have argued that it is entirely sane, rational and epistemically justified for those who participate in the wide field of religious experience to proceed in thought and action on the basis that this is an awareness of transcendent reality[1] – always subject to the 'fruits' criterion. However, we then met the fact that there are many different forms of religious experience, not only within a given tradition but even more so between the great traditions.[2]

Are the religions responses to different deities and transpersonal foci of spiritual practice? I argued that this does not make sense, because it would be impossible to reconcile the conflicting jurisdictions of the different gods – there can be only one sole creator and ruler of the universe. However, when the theist experiences the ultimate as a divine Thou, whereas the non-theist does not, some suggest that we have a good analogy for this in ourselves, in that we are both personal minds and impersonal bodies. Thus the apparent contradiction between the theistic and non-theistic faiths may be only apparent, the theisms experiencing the personal and the non-theistic religions the impersonal aspect of the Ultimate. However, this is not a persuasive, or even a plausible, suggestion. In the non-theistic faiths the ultimate reality is not thought of as a 'thing' in any way comparable to a person's body in distinction from their mind. To take just one example, Brahman is thought of as ineffable, 'formless', 'beyond the sphere of predication...It cannot be truly designated. Any description makes It into something' (Radhakrishnan 1968, 67–8). It is not in any way analogous to a physical body in distinction from a non-physical mind.

Nor does it make sense, given the apparent parity in value of the fruits in life of the different forms of religious experience, to maintain our customary elevation of one religion alone (namely, our own) as the one and only Truth. And so I have offered a pluralist religious interpretation of religion globally. In briefest summary, the religions are different culturally formed human responses, employing different conceptual systems, and hence different forms of religious experience, to an ultimate ineffable transcendent Real. The Real, or the Transcendent – whose nature is transcategorial, beyond the scope of our human concepts – is that which there must be if human religious experience globally is not delusion. We cannot know it as it is in itself, but we do know it as it affects us. And that there is one Real, rather than many, is the simplest hypothesis.

And then, finally, I have discussed the shape of a viable spirituality in today's world, and my speculation about an after-life, amounting to a form of multiple reincarnations.

So this is the series of suggestions and proposals developed in the earlier chapters, that I must now leave with the reader.

Notes

1 Religion as human institutions

1. BCE (before the Common Era) and CE (Common Era) are used today instead of BC (before Christ) and AD (anno domini, the year of the Lord) to avoid the latter's religiously imperialist connotation. There is, however, no ideal way of replacing BC and AD. The Common Era is common only to the limited extent that three major religious movements began around the same time – Christianity, rabbinic Judaism and Mahayana Buddhism. But nevertheless we use BCE and CE for want of anything better.
2. The most comprehensive and up-to-date treatment of the axial age is in Armstrong 2006.
3. See Smith 1978, 1991 and his many other writings.
4. See particularly Smith, 1991.

2 Spirituality and mysticism

1. E.g., Katz (ed.) 1978 and 1983; Pike 1992.
2. Hay and Hunt 2000.
3. Combining Finney 1992 and Handley 1992.
4. *The Independent*, 11 June 2004.
5. *The Independent*, 12 March 2005.
6. See Harris Interactive on the internet.
7. Julian of Norwich 1978 (Short Text), ch. 3, 129.
8. Julian of Norwich 1978 (Long Text), ch. 86 (142).
9. For a discussion of Julian's contribution to Christian thought see Hick 1999, chs 13–14.
10. Julian of Norwich 1978 (Long Text), chs 47, 45, 49 (260, 257, 263).
11. Julian of Norwich 1978 (Long Text), chs 59 and 60 (295 and 298).
12. Julian of Norwich 1978 (Long Text), ch. 32.

3 What is religious experience?

1. Many of them drawn from an unpublished collection made available to James by the psychologist E. D. Starbuck.
2. This centre, now housed at the University of Wales, Lampeter, continues the work of the Alister Hardy Research Centre, founded at Oxford in 1969 by the late Sir Alister Hardy, formerly Linacre Professor of Zoology at Oxford University. Several books (from some of which I shall be quoting) have been published containing some of the centre's several thousand reports.

3. However, a similar research programme in China, conducted by Professor Xinzhong Yao, is expected to publish its findings in 2006. See also Boulter 1998, Braybrooke 1999, Yaran 2004 and Greaves 2001 (all published as Occasional Papers by the Religious Experience Research Unit in the University of Wales, Lampeter). These are all interesting but do not provide reports by individuals.
4. For a fuller account see Hick 2002, 74–5.
5. On these topics see, for example, Wolman (ed.) 1977; Badham 1997; Montefiore 2002.
6. *Sat* is usually translated as 'being', but in some contexts it is better translated as reality or the real, as for example in the famous prayer, 'From the unreal (asat) lead me to the real (sat)' (Brhad-aranayaka Upanishad , I.3.28). Likewise in 'The Real (*sat*) is one, but sages name it differently' (Rig-Veda, I, 164, 46). Again, in the Bhagavad Gita, 17, 23, *sat* is translated by Kees Bolle as Real (Bolle 1979, 193).
7. The usage here is that of some of the Sufis, as for example Jami, for whom God, 'the unique Substance, viewed as absolute and void of all phenomena, all limitations and all multiplicity, is the Real (al Haqq)' (Nicholson 1979, 81).

4   'By their fruits you will know them'

1. *Metro* (Birmingham), 2 November 2005.
2. *The Independent*, 3 April 2004.
3. *The Guardian*, 7 October 2005.
4. In one of the major sutras an occasion is described when the Buddha addressed 1250 monks and 500 nuns, laymen and laywomen, all of whom had attained to *nirvana* (Conze 1975, 38). The figures are not necessarily accurate, but attest to the tradition that large numbers of people became enlightened and attained liberation during the Buddha's ministry.
5. As I write there is much discussion in the English media about a well-known football commentator who, at the end of a recent radio interview and when he thought the microphone had been switched off, called one of the black players 'a fucking lazy thick nigger'. Was it the speech-act itself that was reprehensible, so that, if the microphone had been turned off and the millions of listeners had not heard the remark, it would not have mattered, or was the worst element the racist attitude of mind which his words revealed? Surely the latter. For without a racist frame of mind there would be no racist speech or, going beyond this particular incident, none of the racist taunts of black players that are still too often heard from elements in the crowds at English football matches.
6. These brief remarks barely hint at the significant differences between the New Testament writers, or to the wide range of conflicting points of view today among the scholars. For an up-to-date survey of this vast field see the comprehensive two-volume encyclopedia, *Jesus in History, Thought, and Culture*, ed. Houlden 2003.

5   The neurosciences' challenge to religious experience

1. I use 'faith' here in its customary sense of firm belief exceeding its evidence or grounds, not in the sense that I have developed elsewhere (Hick 1967) of the subjective element within all conscious, including religious, experience.
2. Rita Carter describes the Tibetan monks with whom Newberg was experimenting as practising Zen meditation. In fact the Zen form of meditation is different, though both are ways to the same end.

6   Caveats and questions

1. For the international statistics for the 1970s and 80s see Hay 1990, Appendix on pp. 79–84.
2. Austin's massive (over 800 pages) book is one of the most important, because most comprehensive, in the literature. His philosophical background is naturalistic: 'The only assumption this book makes about mind is that it originates in the brain . . . most neuroscientists, including myself, are monists' (1999, 293–4).
3. See, e.g., Hick 2004, ch. 24.
4. Since the 1960s Thich Nhat Hanh, who has been 'one of the leading spokesmen of the Vietnamese Buddhist peace movement, has taken himself into the market place, into the twentieth-century hell of war-ravaged Vietnam, and has brought an "engaged" Buddhism into the mainstream of life of the Vietnamese masses. In face of threats of persecution, imprisonment, and even death, he has repeatedly spoken out, urging his countrymen to avoid hatred and acrimony, and insisting that the real enemy is not man but the grenades of greed, anger, and delusion in the human heart' (Kapleau 1974, 1).
5. See Tutu 1999.
6. For the statistical evidence, see Hay 1982.
7. Citing Koenig, 1999 and Worthington, Kuruso, McCullough and Sandage 1996.
8. Citing D. Tucker, R. Novelly and P. Walker, 'Hyperreligiosity in Temporal Lobe Epilepsy: Redefining the Relationship', *Journal of Nervous and Mental Disease*, no. 175 (1987), 181–4.
9. For a full account of the prophet Muhammad's revelatory experiences see Wensinck and Rippin 2002.
10. 'Symptoms of a Seizure', Epilepsy.com (internet), 2005.
11. For an accessible account of the relation between the Prophet's revelations and particular events and problems arising in his leadership of the early Muslim community, see Armstrong 2001.
12. See, for example, Blue 2000 and Armstrong 2005.
13. See Huxley 1977. I should add at this point that, without the use of drugs, some negative 'spiritual experiences' are reported. See Jakobsen 1999.
14. In the Society's first experiment in the 1880s their collection was closed, for the sake of manageability, after recording 17,000 reports. This was then refined down to 702 cases by imposing rigorous standards of evidence. Since then several other collections have been made. In 1942 there was a careful examination of 61 'collected, checked, and validated' cases; another study of another collection was made in 1942, with yet others in 1955 and 1970, with analysis continuing since. For an account of all this see Rhine 1977.

7   Mind/brain identity?

1. Someone has argued, as an attempt at possible falsification, that it could conceivably be discovered that the skull is full of air and that there are no brains, in which case would not the consciousness/brain identity theory be thereby falsified? But that is not a sense of falsification that counts for scientific purposes. It would be on a par with saying that the theory that cancer is caused by a malicious invading evil spirit is a scientific hypothesis because although it cannot be verified it would nevertheless be falsified by discovering that there is no such thing as cancer! But that is an irrelevance. Hypotheses concerning the cause of cancer proceed within the parameters of the fact that cancer does observably exist. And hypotheses in neuroscience proceed within the parameters of the fact that there observably are brains.
2. For the implications of ESP (telepathy) for materialism see Price 1995, ch. 3.

8   Current naturalistic theories

1. Austin cites S. Hillyard, 'Electrophysiology of Human Selective Attention', *Trends in Neurosciences*, vol. 8 (1985), 400–5.
2. See, e.g., Bonebeau and Theraulaz March 2000, 73f.

9   The alternative possibility

1. *Neurone News*, 20 March 2000.
2. *New Scientist*, vol. 178, no. 2396, 24 May 2003, 44.

10   Free will?

1. Dennett himself advocates compatibilist freedom.
2. Like each of the books by major thinkers to which I have referred in these chapters, Dennett's would justify an almost equally long response – in which case my own present book would be many volumes in length. But this is not its purpose.
3. Aphorism 40 in the Vatican Collection.
4. Alan Torrance (Torrance 2004) makes essentially the same point, in the context of the truth-seeking freedom presupposed in the research work of the academic world.

11   The epistemological problem

1. The term 'the critical trust approach' has been introduced by Kai-man Kwan (2003, 152–69), and I use it in preference to the earlier 'principle of credulity', first used by Thomas Reid in 1764, and recently by Richard Swinburne (Swinburne 1979, 254–71), and my own 'principle of rational credulity' (Hick 2001, 20). Swinburne's use has been criticised in Martin 1986, but Swinburne uses the principle as part of his probability argument for Christianity as the

uniquely true religion, which makes him vulnerable, in a way in which my own use of it is not, to the problem that the same principle applies to religious experience within other faiths.
2. This medieval situation is described more fully in Nineham 1993.

12 The epistemological solution

1. See, e.g., Anderson 1975, Dember 1960, Fiske 1984, Harvey, Hunt and Schroder 1961, Berger and Luckmann 1967, Holzner 1968, Arbib and Hesse 1986.
2. For another angle on this see Schellenberg 1993.

13 Any particular religion?

1. For a list see Hick 1989, ch. 17, section 5.
2. One historian of religion, Robert Ellwood, has traced the life cycle of religions in a fascinating and thought-provoking book (Ellwood 1988).
3. One philosopher, Kelly James Clark (1997, 316), argues that we can never know whether the visible 'fruits' of faith come from genuinely good motives, or are a deception, because we can never see into the inner self and so 'cannot judge whether their... actions are of genuinely moral worth or not'. This seems to be the kind of absurdity of which only (some) philosophers are capable! If it is never possible to discern moral goodness, and spiritual trans-formation, when we meet it, the terms cease to have any meaning. Apart from psychopaths, who are fortunately very few, humans are ethical beings, able to distinguish between good and evil people, and between saints and grossly selfish individuals.
4. *International Bulletin of Missionary Research* (January 2005).
5. *International Bulletin of Missionary Research* (July 2004).

14 Responses to religious diversity

1. The term 'polycentric pluralism' comes from Schmidt-Leukel 2005.
2. For the multiverse theory see, e.g., Rees 2001.

15 A philosophy of religious pluralism

1. Primarily in Hick 1998, with responses to philosophical objections in the 2nd edn (Hick 2005c).
2. 'In quantum physics, observational conditions and results are such that we cannot presume a categorical distinction between the observer and the observing apparatus, or between the mind of the physicist and the results of physical experiments. The measuring apparatus and the existence of an observer are essential aspects of the act of observation.' (Nadeau and Kaftos 1999, 41).
3. *Summa Theologica*, II/II, Q.1, art 2. Pegis 1945, 1057. The Latin is 'cognita sunt', plural, but this is often translated as singular, meaning 'anything'.

4. Brhadaranayka Upanishad, IV.5.15. Radhakrishnan 1968, 286. Cf . Meister Eckhart's 'He is neither this nor that' (Sermon 26. Eckhart 1941, 219).
5. *Against Eunomius*. Gregory of Nyssa 1954, 99.
6. *De Vera Religione* 36:67. Burleigh 1953, 259.
7. *Summa contra Gentiles* I:14:3. Pegis 1955, 96–7.
8. *In Librum de Causis*, 6. Copleston 1955, 131.
9. Nicholas of Cusa, 1990, 20.
10. Sermon 27. Eckhart 1941, 225.
11. Ch. 14. Wolters 1978, 79.
12. *The Mystical Theology*, ch. 5. Lubheid 1987, 141.
13. *The Divine Names* 1, 2. Lubheid, 1987, 51.
14. *The Divine Names* 2, 9. Lubheid 1987, 65.
15. *The Divine Names* 2, 7. Lubheid 1987, 64.
16. *The Divine Names*, 1, 5. Lubheid 1987, 53.
17. *The Divine Names*, 1, 5. Lubheid, 1987, 54.
18. *The Divine Names*, 1, 5. Lubheid, 1987, 52.
19. *The Celestial Hierarchy* 1 and 2. Lubheid 1987, 146 and 148.
20. *The Celestial Hierarchy* 2. Leubheid 1987, 148.
21. *The Mystical Theology* 5. Lubheid, 1987, 141.
22. *The Mystical Theology*, 1. Lubheid, 1987, 136.
23. Sermon 28. Eckhart 1941, 228.
24. al-'Arabi 1980, 137.
25. The world faiths are totally eviscerated if deprived of their belief in a transcendent reality, of limitless importance to us, which is not identical with the physical universe, although immanent within as well as transcending it. We thus have to reject non-realist or anti-realist understandings of religion according to which such ideas as God, Brahman, the Dharmakaya, etc. do not refer, in however inadequately human terms, to any reality beyond the physical universe (including the human brain) but are ways of expressing our own ideals or hopes or fears. Non-realist theories of religion are popular today, going back to Ludwig Feuerbach in the early nineteenth century and eloquently advocated today by such writers as Don Cupitt, particularly in some of his earlier books, such as Cupitt 1980.

16   Pluralism and the religions

1. *Rig-Veda*, I, 164, 46.
2. *Dhammapada*, 20. 1972, 220–1.
3. Justin's *Apology* I, 46.
4. Nicholas of Cusa, *De Pace Fidei*, para 6 (Nicholas of Cusa, 1990, 7).
5. *The Independent*, 14 September 2005.
6. Joshua 10:7–14.
7. For a general introduction, see Kalupahana 1976.
8. Its most accessible form in the West is in the work of the Kyoto school in Japan, e.g., Hajime 1986; Nishitani (whom I met in Kyoto in his old age) 1982; Nishida 1990; and the many works of Masao Abe (a colleague at one time at the Claremont Graduate University), such as Abe 1985.
9. *Harijan*, 28 January 1939.

10. For the nineteenth- and early twentieth-century Islamic reformers, see Moadel and Talatoff 2000, plus a major figure whom they do not include, Mohamed Taha in the Sudan. Contemporary reforming thinkers include Abdolkarim Soroush (Iran), Mohamed Arkoun (Algeria/France), Ali Ashgar Engineer (India), Riffat Hasan (Pakistan/USA), Shabar Akhtar (Pakistan/England), Abdullah Ahmed An-Na'im (Sudan/USA), Mohamed Talbi (Tunisia), Mahmut Aydin (Turkey), Nasr Hamed Abu-zayd (Egypt/Netherlands), Fatima Mermissa (Morocco), Amina Wahdud-Muhsin (USA), Leila Ahmed (Egypt/USA), Farid Esack (South Africa) and Omid Safi (USA). Several of these are among the new feminist voices within Islam.
11. For the argument for this, see, e.g. Hick 2005a.

17 Spirituality for today

1. *Dukha* is variously translated as unsatisfactoriness, undesirable, sorrow, its universality being the first of the four basic truths, quoted here from the *Samyutta Nikaya* 5.
2. Nine times at different points in her *Showings* (the Long Text).
3. See Hick 2002.
4. Such as I proposed in *Evil and the God of Love* (1977).
5. For a good introduction to this area of research and reports see, e.g., Wolman (ed.) 1977.
6. For clinical evidence see the neuro-physiologist Austin 1999.
7. In *Faith and Knowledge* (1967), 113–14, and *The Fifth Dimension* (2004), 56–7.

18 After death?

1. Quoted by Tyler 1871, vol. 2, 80.
2. There are exceptions both in ancient Egypt, as early as the third millennium BCE, when inscriptions show that both the pharaohs and high noblemen were believed to face a divine judgement after death, and in some of the early Vedic texts of India. For a much fuller account of all these developments, see Hick 1976, ch. 3.
3. For a full account of the biblical material see Simon 1958.
4. For a sympathetic survey of the whole subject see Cranston and Williams, 1984.
5. This is described in *The Tibetan Book of the Dead* (Freemantle 1975). For a much fuller discussion of both Hindu and Buddhist understandings of reincarnation/rebirth see Hick 1976, chs 17–18.

Concluding summary

1. Within contemporary analytic philosophy this was first argued by myself in Hick 1967 and 2001, but much more fully by William Alston in Alston 1991, and earlier articles.
2. In response to this problem of religious diversity, Alston and I part company. See our discussion, reprinted in Hick 2001.

Reference Bibliography

Aleksander, Igor
  1999: 'A Neurocomputational View of Consciousness', in Steven Rose (ed.)
  1999.
Alston, William
  1991: *Perceiving God* (Ithaca and London: Cornell University Press).
Anderson, Barry
  1975: *Cognitive Psychology* (New York and London: Academic Press).
Ansari, Kwaija Abdullah
  1978: *Intimate Conversations*, trans. Wheeler Thackston (New York: Paulist Press;
  and London: SPCK).
Aquinas, Thomas
  1945: *The Basic Writings of Saint Thomas Aquinas*, trans. Anton Pegis, vol. 2
  (New York: Random House).
  1955: *Summa contra Gentiles*, trans. Anton Pegis, vol. 1 (New York: Doubleday).
Arbib, Michael, and Mary Hesse
  1986: *The Construction of Reality* (Cambridge and New York: Cambridge University Press).
Armstrong, Karen
  2001: *Muhammad: a Biography of the Prophet* (London: Phoenix).
  2006: *The Great Transformation: the World in the Time of Buddha, Socrates,*
  Confucius and Jeremiah (London: Atlantic Books, and New York: Alfred
  A. Knopf).
Augustine
  1953: *Augustine: Earlier Writings*, trans. John Burleigh (London: SCM Press, and
  Philadelphia: Westminster Press).
Austin, James H.
  1998: *Zen and the Brain* (Cambridge, Massachusetts: MIT Press).
Badham, Paul
  1997: *Religious and Near-Death Experiences in Relation to Belief in a Future Life*
  (Lampeter: Religious Experience Research Unit).
Baillie, John
  1962: *The Sense of the Presence of God* (London: Oxford University Press).
Basham, A. L.
  1987: 'Asoka', in Mircea Eliade, ed., *The Encyclopedia of Religion*, vol. 1 (New
  York: Macmillan).
Berger, Peter, and Thomas Luckmann
  1967: *The Social Construction of Reality* (New York: Doubleday Anchor).
Blue, Lionel
  2004: *Hitchhiking to Heaven: an Autobiography* (London: Hodder & Stoughton).

Blumenthal, David
  1978: *Understanding Jewish Mysticism: a Source Reader* (New York: Ktav Publishing House).
Bolle, Kees
  1979: *The Bhagavadgita* (Berkeley and London: University of California Press).
Bonebeau, E., and G. Theraulaz
  2000: 'Swarm Smarts', *Scientfic American*, March.
Boulter, Hugh
  1998: *Religious Experience in the Inter-Faith Context*, 2nd series Occasional Paper 15 (Lampeter: Religious Experience Research Centre).
Braybrooke, Marcus
  1999: *Spiritual Experience That Crosses Religious Divisions*, 2nd series Occasional Paper 20 (Lampeter: Religious Experience Research Centre).
Butler, Cuthbert
  1967: *Western Mysticism* (London: Constable).
Byrne, Peter
  1995: *Prolegomena to Religious Pluralism* (London: Macmillan, and New York: St. Martin's Press).
Carrasco, David
  1987: 'Aztec Religion', in Mircea Eliade, ed., *The Encyclopedia of Religion*, vol. 2 (New York: Macmillan, and London: Collier Macmillan).
Carter, Rita
  1998: *Mapping the Mind* (London: Weidenfeld & Nicholson).
  2002: *Consciousness* (London: Weidenfeld & Nicholson).
Charlesworth, James (ed.)
  1991: *Jesus' Jewishness* (New York: Crossroad).
Chatterjee, Margaret
  2005: *Gandhi and the Challenge of Religious Diversity* (New Delhi and Chicago: Promilla & Bibliophile South Asia).
Chittick, William
  1983: *The Sufi Path of Love* (Albany: State University of New York Press).
Churchland, Patricia
  1986: *Neurophilosophy* (Cambridge, Massachusetts: MIT Press).
Churchland, Paul
  1988: *Matter and Consciousness*, revised edition (Cambridge, Massachusetts: MIT Press).
Clark, Kelly James
  1997: 'Perils of Pluralism', in *Faith and Philosophy*, vol. 14, no. 3 (July).
Conze, Edward
  1975: *Buddhism: Its Essence and Development* (New York and London: Harper & Row).
Copleston, F. C.
  1955: *Aquinas* (Harmondsworth: Penguin).
Cupitt, Don
  1980: *Taking Leave of God* (London: SCM Press).
Dalai Lama
  1984: *A Human Approach to World Peace* (Boston: Wisdom Publications).
  1990: *A Policy of Kindness* (Ithaca, New York: Snow Lion Publications).

Damasio, Antonio
  1994: *Descartes' Error* (New York: HarperCollins).
  1999: *The Feeling of What Happens* (New York and London: Harcourt).
D'Aquili, Eugene, and Andrew Newberg
  1999: *The Mystical Mind* (Minneapolis: Fortress Press).
Davids, C. A. F. Rhys (trans.)
  1964: *Psalms of the Early Buddhists (Therigatha)* (London: Luzacs).
Davies, Paul
  1980: *Other Worlds: Space, Superspace and the Quantum Universe* (London:
  J. M. Dent).
De Bary, Theodore (ed.)
  1972: *The Buddhist Tradition* (New York: Random House).
Dember, William
  1960: *The Psychology of Perception* (New York: Henry Holt).
Dennett, Daniel
  1991: *Consciousness Explained* (Boston, New York, London: Little, Brown
  & Co.).
  1996: *Kinds of Mind: Towards an Understanding of Consciousness* (London:
  Weidenfeld & Nicholson).
  2003: *Freedom Evolves* (London: Allen Lane).
Dhammapada
  1972: *The Dhammapada*, trans. Narada Thera, 2nd edn (Colombo: Vajirarama).
Dhammika, S. (trans.)
  1993: *The Edicts of King Asoka* (Kandy: Buddhist Publication Society).
Dumoulin, Heinrich
  1963: *A History of Zen Buddhism* [1959], trans. Paul Peachey (Boston: Beacon
  Press).
Duprés, Louis
  1987: 'Mysticism', in *The Encyclopedia of Religion*, ed. Mircea Eliade, vol. 10
  (New York: Macmillan).
Durkheim, Emile
  1963: *The Elementary Forms of the Religious Life* [1912], trans. Joseph Ward Swain
  (London: Allen & Unwin).
Eckhart, Meister
  1941: *Meister Eckhart: a Modern Translation*, trans. Raymond Blakeley (New York
  and London: Harper Torchbook).
Eliade, Mircea
  1985: *A History of Religious Ideas*, vol. 3 (Chicago and London: University of
  Chicago Press).
Ellwood, Robert
  1988: *The History and Future of Faith* (New York: Crossroad).
Finney, John
  1992: *Finding Faith Today: How Does It Happen?* (Swindon: British and Foreign
  Bible Society).
Fiske, S. T.
  1984: *Social Cognition* (Reading, Maryland: Addison-Wesley).
Freemantle, Francesca, and Chogyam Trungpa (trans.)
  1975: *The Tibetan Book of the Dead (The Bardo Thodol)* (Berkeley and London:
  Shambhala).
Fried, Itzak
  1988: 'Electrical Current Stimulates Laughter', *Nature*, vol. 391.

Freud, Sigmund
  1955: *Totem and Taboo* [1913] (London: Hogarth Press).
  1961: *The Future of an Illusion* [1927] (London: Hogarth Press).
Greaves, Ron
  2001: *Religious Experience in Islam*, 2nd series Occasional Paper 29 (Lampeter: Religious Experience Research Centre).
Greenfield, Susan
  1999: 'How Might the Brain Generate Consciousness?', in Rose, ed., 1999.
Gregory of Nyssa
  1954: *Against Eunomius*, I, 42, in Schaff and Wace, series 2, vol. 5.
Haight, Roger, SJ
  1999: *Jesus Symbol of God* (Maryknoll, New York: Orbis).
Haldane, J. B. S.
  1927: *Possible Worlds* (London: Chatto & Windus).
Handley, P.
  1992: *Finding Faith Today: the Technical Report* (Swindon: British and Foreign Bible Society).
Harvey, O. J., David Hunt and Harold Schroder
  1961: *Conceptual Systems and Personality* (New York and London: John Wiley).
Hay, David
  1982: *Exploring Inner Space* (Harmondsworth: Penguin).
  1990: *Religious Experience Today* (London: Mowbray).
Hay, David, and Kate Hunt
  2000: *Understanding the Spirituality of People Who Don't Go to Church* (Nottingham: University of Nottingham).
Heelas, Paul, and Linda Woodhead
  2005: *The Spiritual Revolution* (Oxford: Blackwell).
Heim, Mark
  1995: *Salvations: Truth and Difference in Religion* (Maryknoll, New York: Orbis).
  2001: *The Depth of the Riches: a Trinitarian Theology of Religious Ends* (Grand Rapids, Michigan: William B. Eerdmans).
Hick, John
  1967: *Faith and Knowledge*, 2nd edn (London: Macmillan, and Ithaca, New York: Cornell University Press).
  1976: *Death and Eternal Life* (London: Collins, and New York: Harper & Row).
  1977: *Evil and the God of Love*, 2nd edn (London: Macmillan, and San Francisco: Harper & Row).
  1985: *Problems of Religious Pluralism* (London: Macmillan, and New York: St. Martin's Press).
  1989: *An Interpretation of Religion* (London, now Basingstoke: Palgrave Macmillan).
  1995: *The Rainbow of Faiths* (London: SCM Press = *A Christian Theology of Religions*, Louisville: Westminster/John Knox).
  1999: *The Fifth Dimension: an Exploration of the Spiritual Realm* (Oxford: One World).
  2001: *Dialogues in the Philosophy of Religion* (London, now Basingstoke: Palgrave Macmillan).
  2002: *An Autobiography* (Oxford: One World).

2004: *The Fifth Dimension: an Exploration of the Spiritual Realm*, 2nd edn (Oxford: One World).

2005a: *The Metaphor of God Incarnate*, 2nd edn (London: SCM Press, and Louisville: Westminster/John Knox).

2005b: 'The Next Step beyond Dialogue', in *The Myth of Religious Superiority*, ed. Paul Knitter (New York: Orbis).

2005c: 'Introduction to Second Edition', *An Interpretation of Religion* (London, now Basingstoke: Palgrave Macmillan).

Holzner, Burkhart

1968: *Reality Construction in Society* (Cambridge, Massachusetts: Schenkman).

Horner, I. B. (trans.)

1954: *The Middle Length Sayings (Majjhima-Nikaya)*, vol. 1 (London: Luzac, The Pali Text Society).

1957: *The Middle Length Sayings (Majjhima-Nikaya)*, vol. 2 (London: Luzac, The Pali Text Society).

Houlden, Leslie (ed.)

2003: *Jesus in History, Thought, and Culture: an Encyclopedia*, 2 vols (Santa Barbara, California, and Oxford: ABC Clio).

Hugh of St Victor

1951: *On the Sacraments of the Christian Faith*, trans. Roy Deferrari (Cambridge, Massachusetts: Harvard University Press).

Hume, David

1935: *Dialogues concerning Natural Religion*, ed. Norman Kemp Smith (Oxford: Clarendon Press).

Huxley, Aldous

1977: *The Doors of Perception* and *Heaven and Earth* (London: Grafton).

Ibn al-'Arabi

1980: *The Bezels of Wisdom*, trans. John Farina (London: SPCK).

Ibn 'Ata' Illah

1978: *The Book of Wisdom*, trans. Victor Danner (New York: Paulist Press, and London: SPCK).

Idel, Moshe

1988: *Kabbalah: New Perspectives* (New Haven and London: Yale University Press).

Inge, W. R.

1899: *Christian Mysticism* (London: Methuen).

Isherwood, Christopher

1965: *Ramakrishna and His Disciples* (London: Methuen).

Ives, Christopher

1992: *Zen Awakening and Society* (London: Macmillan).

Jacobs, Louis

1973: *A Jewish Theology* (London: Darton, Longman & Todd).

Jakobsen, Merete

1999: *Negative Spiritual Experiences: Encounters with Evil* (Lampeter: Religious Experience Research Centre).

James, William

1979: *The Varieties of Religious Experience* [1902] (London: Collins Fount).

1981: *The Principles of Psychology* [1890], 3 vols (Cambridge, Massachusetts: Harvard University Press), vol. 2.

Jaspers, Karl
    1953: *The Origin and Goal of History* [1949], trans. Michael Bullock (New Haven, Connecticutt: Yale University Press).
Jeeves, Malcolm
    2003: 'The Mystery of the Mind', *Research News in Science and Theology*, vol. 3, nos 11/12.
Jessop, T. E. (ed.)
    1945: Berkeley's *The Principles of Human Knowledge* (London: Thomas Nelson & Sons).
John of the Cross, St
    1958: *Ascent of Mount Carmel*, trans. Allison Peers (Garden City, New York: Doubleday Image Books).
Johnson, Steven
    2002: *Emergence: the Connected Lives of Ants, Brains, Cities, and Software* (New York: Touchstone).
Jordan, Ray
    1972: 'LSD and Mystical Experiences', in John White, ed., *The Highest State of Consciousness* (New York: Doubleday).
Julian of Norwich
    1978: *Julian of Norwich: Showings*, trans. into modern English by Edmund Colledge and James Walsh (New York: Paulist Press, 1978).
Kabir
    1977: *Songs of Kabir*, trans. Rabindranath Tagore (New York: Samuel Weiser).
Kant, Immanuel
    1947: *The Moral Law: Kant's Groundwork of the Metaphysic of Morals*, trans. H. J. Paton (London: Hutchinson).
Kaplan, Stephen
    2002: *Different Paths, Different Summits* (New York and Oxford: Rowman & Littlefield).
Kapleau, Philip
    1974: Introduction to *Zen Keys* by Thich Nhat Hanh (New York: Anchor Books).
Katz, Steven (ed).
    1978: *Mysticism and Philosophical Analysis* (New York: Oxford University Press).
    1983: *Mysticism and Religious Traditions* (Oxford and New York: Oxford University Press).
Klostermeier, Klaus
    1969: *Hindu and Christian in Vrindaban*, trans. Antonia Fonesca (London: SCM Press).
Koenig, H. G.
    1999: *The Healing Power of Faith* (New York: Simon & Schuster).
Küng, Hans
    2003: *My Struggle for Freedom* (Grand Rapids, Michigan: Eerdmans).
Kuschel, Karl-Josef
    1995: *Abraham: Sign of Hope for Jews, Christians and Muslims* (New York: Continuum).
Kwan, Kai-man
    2003: 'Is the Critical Trust Approach to Religious Experience Incompatible with Religious Particularism?', *Faith and Philosophy*, vol. 20, no. 2.

Lanier, Jaron
　1999: 'And Now a Brief Word from Now', *Journal of Consciousness Studies*, vol. 6, nos 8–9, reprinted in Libet, Freeman and Sutherland (eds), 1999.
Libet, Benjamin
　1999: 'Do We Have Freewill?', *Journal of Consciousness Studies*, vol. 6, nos 8–9, reprinted in Libet, Freeman and Sutherland (eds) 1999.
Libet, Benjamin, Anthony Freeman and Keith Sutherland (eds)
　1999: *The Volitional Brain: Towards a Neuroscience of Freewill* (Thorverton, UK and USA: Imprint Academic).
Libet, Benjamin, E. W. Wright, B. Feinstein and D. K. Pear
　1979: 'Subjective Referral of the Timing for a Conscious Sensory Experience', *Brain*, vol. 102.
Ling, Trevor
　1979: *Buddhism and Imperialism in War* (London and Boston: George Allen & Unwin).
Locke, John
　1924: *Essay concerning Human Understanding*, ed. A. S. Pringle-Pattison (Oxford: Clarendon Press).
Lowe, Jonathan
　1999: 'Self, Agency and Mental Causation', *Journal of Consciousness Studies*, vol. 6, nos 8–9, reprinted in Libet, Freeman and Sutherland (eds) 1999.
Lubheid, Colm (trans.)
　1987: *Pseudo-Dionysius: the Complete Works* (New York: Paulist Press).
Ludwig, Kirk
　1995: 'Why the Difference between Quantum and Classical Physics Is Irrelevant to the Mind/Body Problem', *Psyche: an Interdisciplinary Journal of Research on Consciousness*, vol. 2, no. 16.
Magee, Bryan
　1997: *Confessions of a Philosopher* (London: Weidenfeld & Nicholson).
Maimonides, Moses
　1904: *Guide for the Perplexed*, trans. M. Friedlander, 2nd edn (London: Routledge & Kegan Paul).
Martin, Michael
　1986: 'The Principle of Credulity and Religious Experience', *Religious Studies*, vol. 22, no. 1.
Marx, Karl
　1970: *The German Ideology* (London: Lawrence & Wishart).
Masters, R., and J. Houston
　1966: *The Varieties of Psychedelic Experience* (New York: Holt, Rinehart & Winston).
Mathers, James
　2003: *Kaleidoscope: an Anthology of the Papers of James Mathers* (Cheltenham: Reardon Publishing).
Maxwell, Meg, and Verena Tschudin
　1990: *Seeing the Invisible* (London: Penguin Arkana).
McGinn, Bernard
　1994: *The Growth of Mysticism* (London: SCM Press).
Moaddel, Mansoor, and Kamran Talattof (eds)
　2002: *Modernist and Fundamentalist Debates in Islam* (New York and London, now Basingstoke: Palgrave Macmillan).

Montefiore, Hugh
  1995: *Oh God, What Next? An Autobiography* (London: Hodder & Stoughton).
  2002: *The Paranormal* (Leicestershire: Upfront Publishing).
Moore, G. E.
  1925: 'In Defence of Common Sense', in J. H. Muirhead, ed., *Contemporary British Philosophy*, Series 2 (London: George Allen and Unwin).
Morris, James
  1973: *Heaven's Command* (London: Faber & Faber).
Nadeau, Robert, and Menas Kaftos
  1999: *The Non-Local Universe* (Oxford and New York: Oxford University Press).
Nagel, T .
  1974: 'What Is It Like to Be a Bat?', *Philosophical Review*, vol. 83.
Newberg, Andrew, and Eugene D'Aquili
  2001: *Why God Won't Go Away* (New York: Ballantine Books).
Nicholas of Cusa
  1990: *Nicholas of Cusa on Interreligious Harmony (De Pace Fidei)*, trans. James Biechler and Lawrence Bond (Lewiston and Lampeter: The Edwin Mellon Press).
Nicholson, Reynold
  1979: *The Mystics of Islam* [1914] (London and Boston: Routledge & Kegan Paul).
Nineham, Dennis
  1993: *Christianity Mediaeval and Modern* (London: SCM Press).
Nishitani, Keiji
  1982: *Religion and Nothingness*, trans. Jan Van Bragt (Berkeley and London: University of California Press).
Oman, John
  1931: *The Natural and the Supernatural* (Cambridge: Cambridge University Press).
Pahnke, Walter
  1972: 'Drugs and Mysticism', in John White, ed., *The Highest State of Consciousness* (New York: Doubleday).
Panikkar, Raimon
  1999: 'Religious Identity and Pluralism', in Arvind Sharma and Kathleen Dugan, eds, *A Dome of Many Colors* (Harrisburgh, Pennsylvania: Trinity Press International).
Parriskar, Vasudeva Laksmana (ed.)
  1978: *Srimad – Valmiki – Maharsi – Panitah Yogava'sistha*, 2nd edn (Bombay: Tukaram Javaji).
Pascal, Blaise
  1947: *Pensées*, trans. W. F. Trotter (London: J. M. Dent, and New York: E. P. Dutton).
Paul, Gregor
  2004: 'War and Peace in Classical Chinese Thought', in Schmidt-Leukel (ed.) 2004.
Penrose, Roger
  1995: *Shadows of the Mind* (London: Vintage).
  1999: 'Can a Computer Understand?', in Rose (ed.) 1999.
Persinger, Michael
  1995: 'Dr. Persinger's God Machine', by Ian Cotton, *Independent on Sunday*, 2 July.

Pike, Nelson
1992: *Mystic Union* (Ithaca and London: Cornell University Press).
Popper, Karl, and John Eccles
1977: *The Self and Its Brain* (Berlin, London and New York: Springer International).
Price, H. H.
1995: *Philosophical Interactions with Parapsychology*, ed. Frank Dilley (London: Macmillan, and New York: St. Martin's Press).
Qur'an
1990: *Al-Qur'an*, trans. Ahmed Ali (Princeton, New Jersey: Princeton University Press).
Radhakrishnan, S.
1953: *The Principal Upanishads* (London: George Allen & Unwin).
Ramachandran, V. S.
1998: *Phantoms in the Brain* (New York: William Morrow).
Rees, Martin
2001: *Our Cosmic Habitat* (Princeton, New Jersey: Princeton University Press).
Rhine, Louisa
1977: 'Research Methods with Spontaneous Cases', in Wolman (ed.) 1977.
Rose, Steven
1973: *The Conscious Brain* (Harmondsworth: Penguin).
1999: 'Brains, Minds and the World', in Rose (ed.) 1999.
2005: *The 21st Century Brain* (London: Jonathan Cape).
Rose, Steven (ed.)
1999: *From Brains to Consciousness* (London: Penguin).
Rumi
1978: *Rumi: Poet and Mystic*, trans. Reynold Nicholson (London and Boston: Unwin Paperbacks).
Russell, Bertrand
1948: *Human Knowledge: Its Scope and Limits* (London: Allen & Unwin).
Ruusbroec, John
1985: *John Ruusbroec: the Spiritual Espousals and Other Works*, trans. James Wiseman (New York: Paulist Press).
Ryle, Gilbert
1949: *The Concept of Mind* (London: Hutchison).
Sanders, E. P.
1985: *Jesus and Judaism* (London: SCM Press).
Schaff, Philip, and Henry Wace
1956: *Nicene and Post-Nicene Fathers*, Series 2 [1892] (Grand Rapids, Michigan: Wm B. Eerdman).
Schellenberg, J. L.
1993: *Divine Hiddenness and Human Reason* (Ithaca, New York: Cornell University Press).
Schimmel, Annemarie
1987: 'Hallaj, Al', in Mircea Eliade, ed., *The Encyclopedia of Religion*, vol. 6 (New York: Macmillan).
Schmidt-Leukel, Perry
2004: 'War and Peace in Buddhism', in Schmidt-Leukel (ed.) 2004.
2005: *Gott ohner Grenzen: eine christliche und pluristische Theologie der Religionen* (Gutersloh: Güttersloher Verlaghaus GmbH).

Schmidt-Leukel, Perry (ed.)
  2004: *War and Peace in World Religions* (London: SCM Press).
Scholem, G. G.
  1955: *Major Trends in Jewish Mysticism* (London: Thames & Hudson).
Searle, John
  1984: *Minds, Brains and Science* (London: British Broadcasting Corporation).
  2004: *Mind* (Oxford and New York: Oxford University Press).
Selby-Bigge, L. A. (ed.)
  1896: Hume's *Treatise of Human Nature* (Oxford: Clarendon Press).
Shankara
  1978: *Crest Jewell of Discrimination*, trans. Swami Prabhavananda and
  Christopher Isherwood, 3rd edn (Hollywood, California: Vedanta Press).
Shore, David, C. Spence and R. M. Klein
  2001: 'Visual Prior Entry', *Psychological Science*, vol. 12, no. 3.
Simon, Ulrich
  1958: *Heaven in the Christian Tradition* (New York: Harper & Brothers).
Singer, Wolf
  1998: 'Consciousness from a Neurobiological Perspective' in Rose (ed.)
  1999.
Smith, Wilfred Cantwell
  1978: *The Meaning and End of Religion* [1962] (Minneapolis: Fortress Press).
Stace, Walter
  1960: *Mysticism and Philosophy* (Philadelphia: Lippincott).
Stanner, W. E. H.
  1979: 'The Dreaming' [1956], in William Lesser and Evon Vogt, eds, *Reader in
  Comparative Religion: an Anthropological Approach*, 4th edn (New York and
  London: Harper & Row).
Stapp, Henry P.
  1995: 'Why Classical Mechanics Cannot Naturally Accommodate Conscious-
  ness but Quantum Mechanics Can', *Psyche: an Interdisciplinary Journal of
  Research on Consciousness*, vol. 2, no. 5.
Stevenson, Ian
  1966: *Twenty Cases Suggestive of Reincarnation* (New York: American Society for
  Psychical Research).
Suzuki, D. T.
  1956: *Zen Buddhism*, ed. William Barrett (Garden City, New York: Doubleday
  Anchor Books).
  1982: 'The Buddhist Conception of Reality', in Frederick Franck, ed., *The Buddha
  Eye* (New York: Crossroad).
Swinburne, Richard
  1979: *The Existence of God* (Oxford: Clarendon Press).
Tallis, Raymond
  1992: *The Explicit Animal: a Defence of Human Consciousness* (London, now
  Basingstoke, and New York: Palgrave).
Tart, Charles
  1975: *States of Consciousness* (New York: E. P. Dutton).
Taylor, Charles
  1991: *The Ethics of Authenticity* (Cambridge, Massachusetts: Harvard University
  Press).

Teresa of Avila
  1960: *The Life of Teresa of Jesus: the Autobiography of St. Teresa of Avila*, trans. Allison Peers (Garden City, New York: Doubleday Image Books).
Torrance, Alan
  2004: 'Theism, Naturalism and Cognitive Science', in David Lorimer, ed., *Science, Consciousness and Ultimate Reality* (Exeter: Imprint Academic).
Turner, Denys
  1995: *The Darkness of God* (Cambridge: Cambridge University Press).
Tutu, Desmond
  1999: *No Future without Forgiveness* (New York: Doubleday).
Tyler, E. B.
  1871: *Primitive Culture*, 2 vols (London: John Murray, 1903).
Underhill, Evelyn
  1999: *Mysticism* [1910] (Oxford: Oneworld Publications).
Vermes, Geza
  1973: *Jesus the Jew* (London: Collins).
  1993: *The Religion of Jesus the Jew* (London: SCM Press).
Vygotysky, Lev
  1986: *Thought and Language* (London: MIT Press).
Ward, Keith
  1994: *Religion and Revelation* (Oxford: Clarendon Press).
Weinberg, Steven
  1993: *Dreams of a Final Theory* (London: Hutchinson).
Wensink, A. J., and A. Rippin
  2002: 'Wahy' (Revelation), in *Encyclopaedia of Islam*, vol. 11 (Leiden: Brill).
Winkworth, Susanna (trans.)
  1937: *Theologia Germanica* (London: Macmillan).
Wittgenstein, Ludwig
  1953: *Philosophical Investigations*, trans. Elizabeth Anscombe (Oxford: Blackwell).
Wolman, Benjamin (ed.)
  1977: *Handbook of Parapsychology* (New York and London: Van Nostrand Reinhold).
Wolters, Clifton
  1978: *The Cloud of Unknowing* (London: Penguin).
Woods, Richard (ed.)
  1980: *Understanding Mysticism* (New York: Image Books).
Woodward, Frank (trans.)
  1956: *The Book of the Kindred Sayings (Samyutta Nikaya)*, Part 4 (London: Pali Text Society, Luzac).
Worthington, E. L., T. A. Kuruso, M. E. McCullough and S. J. Sandage
  1996: 'Empiricial Research on Religion and Psychotherapeutic Processes and Outcomes: a Ten-Year Review and Research Prospectus', *Psychological Bulletin*, no. 119.
Yaran, Cafer S.
  2003: *Muslim Religious Experience*, 2nd series Occasional Papers 31 (Lampeter: Religious Experience Research Centre).

Index